Void and Fullness

1. His Holiness the Dalai Lama, Tenzin Gyatso (Photo: Angus McDonald).

Void and Fullness

in the Buddhist, Hindu and Christian Traditions

Śūnya — Pūrṇa — Plerôma

edited by

Bettina Bäumer

John R. Dupuche

with a Concluding Speech by

His Holiness the Dalai Lama

D.K. Printworld (P) Ltd.
New Delhi

Cataloging in Publication Data — DK
[Courtesy: D.K. Agencies (P) Ltd. <docinfo@dkagencies.com>]

Void and fullness : in the Buddhist, Hindu and
Christian traditions : śūnya, pūrṇa, plerôma / edited by
Bettina Bäumer, John R. Dupuche; with a concluding
speech by His Holiness the Dalai Lama.
p. 23 cm.
Papers presented at an inter-religious retreat seminar organized by the Abhishiktananda Society, Delhi.
Includes bibliographical references.
Includes index.
ISBN 8124603405

1. Sunyata — Congresses. 2. Philosophy, Buddhist — Congresses. 3. Philosophy, Hindu — Congresses. 4. Christianity — Philosophy — Congresses. 5. Philosophy, Indic — Congresses. I. Bäumer, Bettina, 1940- II. Dupuche, John R., 1940-

DDC 181.043 21

ISBN 81-246-0340-5
First published in India in 2005

Published and printed by:
D.K. Printworld (P) Ltd.
Regd. Office: 'Sri Kunj', F-52, Bali Nagar
Ramesh Nagar Metro Station
New Delhi-110 015
Phones: (011) 2545-3975; 2546-6019; *Fax*: (011) 2546-5926
E-mail: dkprintworld@vsnl.net
Website: www.dkprintworld.com

Preface

THE present volume is the outcome of a seminar on the same theme which was held in Sarnath, Varanasi, from December 11 to 16, 1999, at the Central Institute of Higher Tibetan Studies, organized and financed by the Abhishiktananda Society (registered in Delhi). Most of the papers contained in this volume were presented at the seminar, others have been added later by participants (A. Kalliath, J. Figl). Apart from the papers read, the discussions were important since they bridged the different traditions. But it was not possible to include these, with the exception of the final session comprising statements of the panelists. Another important aspect of this "interreligious retreat seminar" were the common meditations, and the chanting of hymns and sacred scriptures from the three traditions at the beginning and end, and every day at noon time. Thus, the papers and discussions were complemented by a practical experience of listening to sacred chants and silent meditation.

The highlight of the seminar was the presence of His Holiness the Dalai Lama on the last day, and his sharing with us his concern for interreligious understanding and peace, as well as concrete suggestions, as to how such a dialogue can be carried out in practice.

There is a vast literature on the themes of *śūnyatā, pūrṇatā* and *plerôma*, but the special contribution of this volume is the interaction between these themes in the different traditions, because they are in no way exclusive, but contained in different ways in different traditions. Ultimately, as was repeatedly stated, each tradition has to go beyond its concepts to reach that which they ultimately intend.

Shimla, Himalaya **Editors**
Buddha Purnima, May 2005

Contents

Concluding Session

Acknowledgements

FIRST of all we wish to thank the Central Institute of Higher Studies, Sarnath, Varanasi, for offering us the space for holding the seminar and for providing all kinds of assistance. Especially its then Director, Prof. Ven. Samdhong Rinpoche, at present Prime Minister of the Tibetan Government in Exile, Dharmasala, has given us all encouragement and support.

Without the guidance of Professor Raimon Panikkar, the seminar could not have taken place. In spite of his delicate health he shared his rich experience in interreligious dialogue and guided the discussions.

Lama Rameshvar Negi of CIHTS, an experienced Vipassana teacher, sat with us in the meditation sessions. His silence was as important as the words recorded in this volume.

The Abhishiktananda Society (registered in Delhi) has entirely financed both, the seminar and the preparation of this volume.

We thank the Alice Boner Institute, Varanasi, for using their infrastructure.

Thanks is due to the contributors of this volume, but also to the participants who have taken part in the deliberations and enriched the dialogue.

In the organization of the seminar, some have been particularly helpful: we thank especially Dr. Pema Tenzin of CIHTS, Dr. Christiane Handl and Dr. Sadananda Das. Dr.

Anjan Chakraverty has helped in designing the logo. Mrs Manju Sundaram has contributed her beautiful voice in musical expression of the theme, in the *maṅgalācaraṇa* and in reciting Kabīr's *bhajans*.

The computer work of preparing the volume has been done partly in Varanasi and partly in Shimla, and we thank Mr. Basant Lal and Mr. Brahmchand Rana for the preparation of the press copy.

Finally, Mr. Susheel K. Mittal of D.K. Printworld deserves thanks for his patient reminders, and for looking after the publication with much care.

Editors

Prologue

Bettina Bäumer

IN his famous dialogue with Daisetz Suzuki, published under the title *Wisdom in Emptiness,* Thomas Merton relates the Buddhist concept of emptiness, *śūnyatā,* to innocence. In his introductory note he says:

> As Dr. Suzuki makes clear in his analysis of 'innocence,' this is really something beyond the level of problem-and-solution. When the monk acts in the primitive emptiness and innocence, which the Zen practitioner calls 'suchness,' and the Christian calls 'purity of heart' or 'perfect charity,' then the problem does not even arise.[1]

I think that speaking of void and fullness, or *śūnya-pūrṇa-plerôma,* we should not limit our discussion to metaphysical concepts, which may or may not be contradictory, complementary, neither contradictory nor complementary: contradictory as well as complementary — to speak in terms of Nāgārjuna — we should bring these fundamental terms of three major religious traditions down to the level of experience. Daisetz Suzuki writes in the same dialogue with Thomas Merton: "As spiritual beings we strive after innocence,

---

1. D.T. Suzuki and Thomas Merton, "Wisdom in Emptiness: A Dialogue," in Thomas Merton, *Zen and the Birds of Appetite* (Part Two), New York: New Directions Publishing Corporation, 1968, p. 100.

emptiness, enlightenment and a prayerful life."[2] He relates the Buddhist emptiness to the spiritual poverty of the Beatitudes: "Blessed are the poor in spirit," with its mystical interpretation by Meister Eckhart:[3]

> The metaphysical concept of emptiness is convertible in economic terms into poverty, being poor, having nothing. 'Blessed are those who are poor in spirit.' Eckhart defines:
>
> "He is a poor man who wants nothing, knows nothing and has nothing." This is possible when a man is empty of 'self and all things,' when the mind is thoroughly purified of Knowledge or Ignorance, which we have after the loss of Innocence. In other words, to gain Innocence again is to be poor. What strikes one as somewhat strange is Eckhart presenting the poor man as 'knowing nothing.' This is a very significant statement. The beginning of Knowledge is when the mind is filled with all kinds of defiled thought, among which the worst is 'self.' For all evils and defilements start from our attachment to it. As Buddhists would say, the realization of emptiness is no more, no less than seeing into the nonexistence of a finite ego-substance. This is the greatest stumbling-block in our spiritual discipline, which, in actuality, consists not in getting rid of the self, but in realizing the fact that there is no such existence from the first. The realization means, being 'poor' in spirit. . . . Nothing to gain, nothing to lose, nothing to give, nothing to take; to be just so, and yet be rich in inexhaustible possibilities — this is to be poor in its most proper and characteristic sense of the word. This is what all religious experiences tell us. To be absolutely nothing is to be everything. When one is in possession of something, that something will keep all other somethings from coming in.[4]

---

2. *Ibid.*, p. 108.
3. In his Sermon 32 *Beati pauperes spiritu.*
4. *Ibid.*, pp. 108-09.

One way of experiencing this innocence is when we enter into a dialogue with people of other religious traditions. Those who participate in an interreligious seminar are all very familiar with their own tradition, and very knowledgeable about their own philosophy or theology. But a real meeting with another religious or secular person creates a kind of void. We do not share the same presuppositions, the same concepts, the same attitudes, the same faith, myths, or whatever. Facing this void within ourselves and between us may itself be an important spiritual experience, an emptying of concepts, which is the goal of many spiritual ways. In Kashmir Śaivism this void is precisely found in all the in-between states — the most important and yet not easy to catch being the void between breathing in and breathing out. And in this in-between is found the pure consciousness, the thought-free state: *nirvikalpa,* which in other terms could be called "innocence."

If we are ready for this kind of exercise, we are ready for dialogue. The confrontational, highly politicized discussions between religions which we have witnessed in the last months and years, in India and elsewhere, show precisely that no real dialogue is possible when concepts are understood in a frozen, fixed framework, when there is no attempt to understand what is lying behind, below or beyond these concepts. Then positions become hardened, and out of solidarity religious groups become closed, and clashes in words and in actions seem to be unavoidable. I mention this by way of contrast, to show that our dialogue is not a spiritual luxury, but if we can really break the artificial boundaries of our respective concepts and reach a deeper level of understanding, we are contributing in a small, but no less effective way to a greater harmony among the various religious groups and traditions.

The dialogue between Thomas Merton and Daisetz Suzuki was focused on the concept of emptiness. In this volume we are focusing on two more concepts: *pūrṇa*, fullness, plenitude, perfection, which in its various meanings has moulded a great part of the Hindu traditions; and *plerôma* (Greek), fullness in a theological and eschatological sense, in the Christian tradition. For the Vedic-Upaniṣadic and Āgamic traditions, *pūrṇa* is both, the starting point from which everything comes, and the goal of every search, that which is always present but only clouded by our individual limitations. It is a theological concept, as Utpaladeva (at the end of ninth century CE) sings:

> Praise be to Śambhu, the root, the middle and the top of everything, who assumes the form of the root, the middle and the top, but who is neither the root nor the middle nor the top, because he is always full.[5]

In commentating on this passage, Kṣemarāja, explains that fullness is that which has no sequence, but which is simultaneous, since the Divine is present to everything, because it is nothing but pure Consciousness. Fullness, for the Advaita Śaiva tradition of Kashmir, is, then, the fullness of absolute I-consciousness or *pūrṇahantā,* which remains complete even when there is a differentiation between subject and object, time and space.[6] The articles in this volume will throw light on the different aspects of *pūrṇa* and its spiritual implications.

The Christian concept of *plerôma* is not outside history, it is its goal and fulfilment. It is the fullness of the Divinity which is dwelling in the person of Jesus Christ, from whom all fullness and fulfilment comes for the believer. As the supreme Divine Word, all things proceed from him. In this way he holds within him all fullness, *pūrṇa*, which is at the same time

---

5. *Śivastotravali*, 2.9.

6. Cf. *The Īśvarapratyabhijñakārikā of Utpaladeva*, ed. and tr. R. Torella, New Delhi: Motilal Banarsidass, 2002. II.1.8, p. 156, and III.2.4, p. 198.

śūnya because it is without limitation of any sort. The Word is made flesh which has the double meaning of taking to himself all created reality and therefore taking on the fullness of things; and of self-emptying, even to the pint of being rejected and crucified, and therefore entering into the void of death and desolation. By being both "fullness" and "emptiness," both eternally and in time, he is the fullness, *plerôma,* in a total way. He stands at the completion of time, as he does at its beginning.

This would be of little value to humanity if it applied only to Jesus of Nazareth. However, what is true of him is to be true of all who also experience, by divine grace, the fullness and the emptiness: the identity with Divine love and the self-emptying of compassion and who, as a consequence likewise hold all reality, created and uncreated, in their embrace. The term *plerôma* therefore adds a significant contribution to the discussion.

At the beginning of every traditional religious or philosophical treatise in India, every Śāstra, the statement of purpose (*prayojana*), has to be made. The social dimension of dialogue was certainly one of the main purposes of this seminar, but it was balanced by an equally strong purely spiritual purpose. And if we call it "spiritual," it has to be purposeless, because we do not meditate "in order to . . .," we just meditate.

More and more people are no longer satisfied with the practice of their own religion, either because they have experienced its limitations, or because they have discovered spiritual treasures outside their own tradition. Whatever may be the dangers of syncretism, of changing ideas and practices, of mixing up different elements, every religion has to face this phenomenon and deal with it in a positive, and not exclusivistic way. After all, whatever may be the personal motivation, all these phenomena reveal a great spiritual thirst. The reasons are clear: the increasing materialization of the world, which does not stop before anything sacred; the technological impoverishment; the desacralization and exploitation of Nature and Man . . . , to mention only some of the great issues troubling us today.

Is it not preposterous to think that a small gathering of people from different traditions could bring a change or give a spiritual direction to the fundamental problems humanity is facing? But what if there were no such meetings? Certainly, the pretence would be *hybris, abhimāna,* were it not for the translation of emptiness by Daisetz Suzuki and Thomas Merton as "innocence." Spiritual motivation cannot be based on an egocentric desire to change the world; it just has its value in itself. It is like a moment of wonder before nature, like a moment of deep meditation, like a moment of compassion. By stressing these aspects I do not want to minimize the importance of philosophical and theological discussions. The intellectual discourse should neither be neglected nor be of a less academic level, but should be conducted in an atmosphere of shared silence, so that the words we speak and hear are coming out of silence.

Dialogue is not comparative religion. If we cannot help but compare, this comparison should come out of a listening to each other, and out of a spiritual experience. Thomas Merton has given a beautiful example of this approach in his comparison of Zen and Christianity:

> We begin to divine that Zen is not only beyond the formulations of Buddhism, but it is also in a certain way 'beyond' (and even pointed to by) the revealed message of Christianity. That is to say that when one breaks through the limits of cultural and structural religion — or irreligion — one is liable to end up by 'birth in the Spirit,' or just by

> intellectual awakening in a simple void where all is liberty, because all is the actionless action, called by the Chinese *Wu-wei,* and by the New Testament the 'freedom of the Sons of God.' Not that they are theologically one and the same, but they have at any rate the same kind of limitlessness, the same lack of inhibition, the same psychic fullness of creativity which mark the full and creative activity of the 'enlightened self.' The 'mind of Christ' as described by St. Paul in Philippians 2, may be theologically worlds apart from the 'mind of Buddha' — this I am not prepared to discuss. But the utter 'self-emptying' of Christ — and the self-emptying which makes the disciple one with Christ in his *kenosis* — can be understood and has been understood in a very Zen-like sense as far as psychology and experience are concerned.
>
> Thus with all due deference to the vast doctrinal differences between Buddhism and Christianity, and preserving intact all respect for the claims of the different religions, in no way mixing up the Christian 'vision of God' with Buddhist 'enlightenment,' we can nevertheless say that the two have this psychic 'limitlessness' in common. And they tend to describe it in much the same language. It is now 'emptiness,' now 'dark night,' now 'perfect freedom,' now 'no-mind,' now 'poverty' in the sense used by Eckhart and Suzuki.[7]

As Thomas Merton led a dialogue with Zen Buddhism, Swami Abhishiktananda lived an inner as well as outer, spiritual as well as intellectual, dialogue with Hinduism, or rather, with Advaita as present in the Upaniṣads and re-lived in the twentieth century by Śrī Ramana Maharṣi. It is his experience which inspired the dialogue-seminar contained in this volume. He found the fullness of his Christian faith in the fullness of the Upaniṣads. An expression of the experience resulting from this double experience, which ultimately became one, is found in his spiritual Diary:

---

7. *Ibid.,* p. 8.

> A being lost in my source, a being lost in my fulfillment. And in this very loss, I am.
>
> Jesus is this mystery of Advaita in which I can no longer recognize myself separately. Lost as much in the space (*ākāśa*) of the heart as in that of the span of the universe, as much in the Source as in the shining, the radiance that empties me.
>
> And I am Fullness, *pūrṇam*, precisely in this letting-go of myself everywhere. . . .
>
> And my *pūrṇam* is precisely this emptiness of all self. The *kenosis* (self-emptying) of Christ![8]
>
> — Diary, dated 24 December, 1971

In such a condensed experience, Swami Abhishiktananda merges the mutual complementary aspects of self-emptying as the condition for spiritual fulfilment, for the plenitude of the "I" (in terms of Kashmir Śaivism). The seminar was inspired by Abhishiktananda and his openness to a dialogue among spiritual traditions which goes beyond concepts and theologies.

The greatest inspiration for this dialogue seminar was received from His Holiness the Dalai Lama who accepted to address us on the last day in the concluding session. This positive response and his participation were a sign of his deep commitment to interreligious dialogue. In his Foreword to the *Gethsemani Encounter Volume*, His Holiness writes:

> Gatherings of spiritual practitioners from different backgrounds are of immense value. I believe it is extremely important that we extend our understanding of each other's spiritual practices and traditions. This is not necessarily

---

8. Abhishiktananda, *Ascent to the Depth of the Heart*, New Delhi: ISPCK, 1998, pp. 336-37.

> done in order to adopt them ourselves, but to increase our opportunities for mutual respect. Sometime, too, we encounter something in another tradition that helps us to better appreciate something in our own.[9]

The papers contained in this volume, coming from within the respective traditions and in an openness to other traditions, are not in the form of conclusions on such a vast topic, but they are an invitation to further reflection, exchange and mutual enrichment.

---

9. *The Gethsemani Encounter*, ed. Donald W. Mitchell and James Wiseman, New York: Continuum, 1997, pp. x-xi. Cf. also "Kenosis and Sunyata: A Buddhist Contribution," in Monastic Interreligious Dialogue, Bulletin 48, October 1993.

1

Opening Address

Raimon Panikkar

I AM expected to give a philosophical introduction. An introduction it will be, because it will not enter into the profundities of these three words. It is philosophical — in the real sense of the word: philosophy is as much the love of wisdom as the wisdom of love. Perhaps one of the signs of the crisis of modern times is that philosophy has become a matter of the brain, *opus rationis*, and left subordinated another part which is as essential, as fundamental and as indispensable: love. Anything human includes the heart, what we may call awareness, intellect, *sat*, *cit*, and *bhakti*, *ānanda* as well.

I would like to comment very briefly on the meaning of the three words — the *Mahābhārata* says that every three things are perfect.

Three words have called us here together. Three words have allured us to come here to share our experiences and our respective insights. Three words, not three concepts. There are dozens of concepts of *śūnyatā*, *plerôma* and all the rest. What attracted us is the power hidden in these three words, not barren discussions with concepts. A concept is only valid there where it has been conceived, and not outside that particular field. And we are precisely here transgressing the different fields of the different human traditions of the world. A concept is a construct, it is our creation. A concept is not an object of experience, is an object of rational abstraction. I cannot experience the concept of horse, I can experience *my* horse or a particular horse. We want to stress the experiential level.

Not three concepts are the objects of our discussions, but three symbols. The word is not only a sign, it is not only a concept, it entails a concept and we can draw from the word many concepts. The word is a symbol, and therefore polysemic. A symbol is not an objectifiable reality. A symbol is not an object. A symbol includes the subject for whom the symbol is symbol as much as the object which we may somewhat point out as a part of the symbol. The symbol and the symbolic awareness is a hidden chapter which I cannot unfold here. Such symbolic awareness is needed precisely in our times which for too long has been simply enthused by modern science which is the colossal and genial production of concepts, not of symbols. The symbol reveals, besides, that the symbol (gr. *symballein*, "together") is what brought us together, that is precisely the power of the symbol, which in itself should be *svayaṃprakāśa* (self-effulgent). A symbol does not need a hermeneutic, for that by means of which I explain and interpret the symbol that would be the real symbol. And the crisis of our times is that we have almost lost this symbolic awareness, something which for an ancestor of ours put him or her into an interrelationship with reality has lost its power of attraction and needs to be explained. Now, to explain a symbol is to explain it away. The symbol reveals the symbolized in the symbol itself, not outside, transcending thus the dichotomy between subjectivism and objectivism. The symbol is a matter of experience. And the three words have the power to symbolize precisely the most profound experience of the three great religious traditions. These three symbols are used predominantly, not exclusively.

Three symbols — *śūnya, pūrṇa, plerôma* — symbolize what? There are many symbols, but the three symbols which, to me and I think to most of us, are characteristic of the three great human traditions living in our times, and in crisis also in our times, are symbols of the Ultimate: *aprapañca, nirvikalpa, acintya* and *avivādya* — ineffable, beyond verbal designation, beyond thought-construct, inconceivable, what cannot be known otherwise. I could have also quoted words from Mādhyamika texts.

Then how is it that we speak of that which is unconceivable, ineffable? Surely, we cannot have a concept of that. But the symbol approaches us, lets us touch reality in a very personal and I would say even unique way, because it is fruit of an experience. Three symbols of the Ultimate. And here is the challenge, and that is why the atmosphere we want to create is essential to our discussions; better, to our being together. Knowledge, even in the sense of *jñāna*, will not lead us to the deep symbolic awareness, *avidyā* — ignorance, much less, obviously. I would put it into words, in philosophical jargon: *the awareness of an absence is the knowledge of a presence, which is not what it appears to be.* But if I take away that absence, if I take the appearance, the whole thing disappears. What is this absence? To put it in poor and simple words, this absence is emptiness, is fullness, is completeness. But the way of approaching can only be an experiential way. we are looking for that ultimate — and here the cross-cultural reflection is essential: why am I looking for *śūnyatā*? Why am I interested in *pūrṇatā*? Or why do I think that *plerôma* is the symbol of the Ultimate, of what it is all about? Because we start our search, our pilgrimage within a field — that is the *mythos* — which makes us believe that here is meaning in this direction, not in another direction. In that field is where we hope to find "it," "that thing," not outside. So, there are different ways. If I were to make a caricature out of this cross-cultural reflection,

I would say: We are looking for happiness of all sentient beings, for the elimination of *duḥkha*. Nothing satisfies us. All is full with insatisfaction. Thus, I am looking for eliminating all the obstacles and therefore, the higher obstacle is *tañha, tṛṣṇā,* thirst, desire, ambition, or whatever we want to call it. I am looking in the direction towards emptiness, because all the other things do not satisfy. Or we are suffering from the fragmentation of our knowledge. The Upaniṣad asks: "What is that, knowing which everything is known?" This is the contrary of present-day science: which knows more and more particular things and less and less about the whole. The obstacle is ignorance. So we are looking for wholeness, for *pūrṇatā*, because being full of this *vidyā*, full of this desire to know *Brahman* — *brahmajijñāsā* — which is so full that even when we take out the full, the full remains.

Is there another way to look? We discover ourselves imperfect, inachieved, longing for per-fection, sinful, aware of our imperfections. Here sin, fragmentation, is the obstacle. We look for fullness. We ask: Do the three symbols symbolize the same? Or are we looking for different things? These three human pilgrimages are meaningful and can be explained if we understand the three different fields in which centuries of reflection have taken place.

Today's hermeneutics says that no text is understandable without a context. We should today learn precisely from the experience of others and perhaps also from the misinterpretations and failures of the others. I introduce a third element in the knowledge of a text: I know well the text. I have studied enough the context. But if I am not immersed, plunged in the experience from where the text has emerged, in spite of all my indological knowledge, philosophical acumen, I have to know the "pretext" of the author. And here it is where experience is important. And touching one another is important, something which is more subtle. Beyond and besides knowing the text I have to know the context and the pre-text which has led the author to write that text which has a meaning in that context. And the pre-text is the socio-historical-economic concrete situation of a particular author which is in one place or another. Without knowing this pre-text which I can only know if I know the person directly or the representative of that tradition at first hand, I will not be able to decipher the text.

But the question remains: Do they symbolize the same? The question is unavoidable. Allow me to say "yes," to say "no," to say "neither." The modern crypto-Kantianism, that has invaded also the Eastern minds, makes us believe that yes, we speak of the same thing, as if the *noumenon*, the "thing in itself" were existing. We say, we are speaking about the same thing, forgetting that my speech about that thing, like the ways which lead to the mountain belong also to the mountain. If I take all the ways to the peak, the peak will collapse. There is an a *priori* that this *noumenon,* this "thing in itself" exists. And we speak then about the Ultimate. Now, this Ultimate by its very nature, cannot have a further point of reference which will allow me to say "it is the same" or "it is not the same." How can I say "it is the same" or "it is not the same" if I do not have a canvass behind the Ultimate which allows me to say "they are the same" or "they are not the same?" Thus the paradoxical language of the mystics. That is the whole difficulty which, if one is not in the context and does not know the pre-text, one is not able to understand the text. Do they speak of the same? I am not sure that this "same" exists. If we say that the "same" is not a concept, and the experience is the personal re-enactment of something integral in a psycho-historical reality, perhaps this Kantian thinking itself is a way of approach, but in these ultimate problems it does not help.

If we say "no," we are in chaos, sheer plurality, total relativism, impossibility of contact. You have your thing, I have my thing, and if you are powerful I will have to tolerate you, and if you are not powerful, I will try to eliminate you. So "neither-nor." Are we coming together to speak about the same thing? Harmony does not mean that we all say the same thing. Are we then saying something totally different, and we respect each other, because you have your language and I don't understand what you say?

Here I betray my bias if I say that the Advaita approach may offer us a key — not to understand, because Advaita is not totally understandable with the intellect which just points to say "this" or "that" — but it overcomes the dialectical dilemma that either we speak about the same or we do not speak about the same: neither-nor. I have introduced the notion of homeomorphic equivalents or analogy of third degree in order to facilitate bridges of mutual understanding and entering into a certain type of communion and communication.

But let me continue the same type of argument trying to show that I cannot know whether I say the same or I say a different thing. How can we know if the Ultimate has no further point of reference? Here is the place of pluralism as different from plurality. Here is the place in which the human intercourse on this highest level belongs essentially to the human condition. And in this kind of "dialogical dialogue," as I call it, the rules of the game are created in the very moment of the encounter and not postulated *a priori*, e.g., that you have to know English, or that you have to accept the principle of non-contradiction, or the *catuṣkoṭi* is absolutely irrelevant, etc. It is in the very encounter in which we find the ways in which we may dialogue, encounter or find differences.

Here lies the weakness of comparative philosophy. My submission is that comparative philosophy is not possible, because in order to compare I have to be outside the *comparanda* in order to be fair and compare two different things. From which point of view do we compare? We are already one of them — we cannot dispense with philosophy as a kind of human reflection of what we are and what we do and what we say in the meaning of our words. Comparative philosophy there is — playing with words — an "imparative philosophy," because in Medieval Latin *imparare* means learning from one another. Learning from one another, learning from and in the "Auseinandersetzung," the discussion itself. Generally speaking we know only one language. I know the *śūnyatā*-language, and I am totally at home with the *pūrṇatva*-language or the other one. And in that language we are trying to express, to formulate the fundamental intuition or one of the most basic intuitions of that particular tradition. Here we come together, people who speak at least one language, and all together the three languages.

That is the challenge and the possibility, that we listen to one another, and in order to listen we have to make a little void in ourselves. And that's why this symposium is existential. Meditation or silence, or being together, or even eating a meal together — these are not accidental to that communication, if we are somewhat responsible and aware of our responsibility. If we really speak two different languages — then I answer my first question — "Are we saying the same or are we not saying the same?": Yes and no. A universal language will chop off every kind of *dhvani*, nuances, resonances. And it is a symphony that emerges. I cannot speak all the languages, but I can learn from the language of the other and enrich my intuition, not — as the Dalai Lama says and Samdhong Rinpoche has also told — as mixture, syncretism, and all saying that it is the same. But we have to attune our intellectual ears to the music — and each language is a music — of the other person's language. And then fecundate, deepen and criticize the shortcomings of what we thought was almost ultimate and definitive. And then we discover that the so-called Ultimate is relatively ultimate, and in a relatively delimited field of experience and historical religion. If we really speak two languages, we discover immediately that a language is more than just meaning. In German there is a difference between "Sinn" ("sense") and "Bedeutung" ("meaning"). It is more than "Sinn," it is more than "Bedeutung" — it is the music of the language.

Well, this I think is our task: to listen to the music, to sing the meaning, the intuitions and allusions and symbolism of the other language. If we succeed in deepening these intuitions which are symbolized in these three rich, polysemic and difficult words, then our seminar will have fulfilled not only our expectations, but also perhaps contributed a little bit to what we are all seeking: to peace in the world.

2

Śūnya and Pūrṇa

Ven. Samdhong Rinpoche

WE deeply appreciate the theme of this seminar, chosen by Dr. Bettina Bäumer and her assistants with the intention of having a deeper dialogue among different religions. This type of sincere in-depth dialogue is one of the greatest achievements of the twentieth century. Another way of looking at it is that, at the end of the twentieth century humanity has been so hard-pressed, that if we do not have a deeper understanding and dialogue among different religious traditions, we may not be able to have a better future, or any hope for the future. Thus, from whichever viewpoint this type of dialogue may be perceived, it is a great achievement. In ancient times, a truly spiritual religious harmony did exist in the various Nikāya or Buddhist traditions, but religious dialogue and interaction was quite rare.

In 1960 I began to attend international religious conferences. The first large conference I attended was the eighth general conference of the World Fellowship of Buddhists around 1964-65. In that conference it was almost impossible to have dialogues between Theravāda and Mahāyāna Buddhists. The Theravāda monks refused to sit with Mahāyāna monks even for meals and prayers, not to mention for dialogue and discussion. These types of barriers have gradually disappeared, and today dialogues can take place not only within the same religious tradition, but also among religions. These inter-religious dialogues or understandings have improved the world socially and spiritually. They have brought closer together many spiritually enlightened and elevated individuals, as a result of which we can look forward to a harmonious co-existence of various religious traditions. In this way, the so-called conflicts of civilizations looming large over the horizon may be postponed or eliminated, and we can hope for a better future for humanity. My esteemed friend Prof. Raimon Panikkar has played a very effective role along these lines in many places. He is respected both for his academic achievements and for his way of life, which has been an embodiment of inter-religious harmony and dialogue, and has promoted understanding among various faiths. Some years ago in Barcelona, as the key speaker of a UNESCO seminar on the contribution of religion to culture and peace, he said: "I am a Hindu by birth, a Catholic priest by training, a Buddhist by initiation, and a staunch secular person." This is an extraordinary declaration that sheds great light on how it is possible for a staunch secular person to embody various religious traditions. It also reflects Mahatma Gandhi's utterance that "because I am a good Hindu, I am also a good Christian, and a good Muslim," and so forth. Both statements carry the same message. Anyone who is really evolved in his or her own religion must surely be in harmony with all other religious traditions. And those who are intolerant of any religious tradition cannot be truly religious or mature in their own faith. An effective measure of the evolution of a person's religious mind is the degree to which that person respects lineages or religions, different from his or her own tradition or belief. This experience of sharing, meditating, striving and living together with sincere religiosity is very valuable. Thus, I appreciate the efforts of the Abhishiktananda Society for arranging this seminar and making it possible for all of us to have the opportunity to share our experiences.

The *śūnya/pūrṇa* — emptiness/fullness combination, duality, or non-duality, what we are trying to discuss is indeed a difficult task because we are trying to verbalize a theme that is beyond verbalization, thought and words. Human language is the manifestation of thought, and thought is limited and conditioned. Whatever we think, say and comprehend is only fragmented. All three processes are possible only partially, and it is impossible to convey the wholeness that one tries to express through the word *śūnya*, or nothingness, because whatever meaning may be suggested or conceived by that word necessarily goes to only its parts and alternatives. Realizing this limitation, the Buddha spoke about two truths: relative and absolute, *saṁvṛtti* and *paramārtha*. When we discuss these, it appears that they are two levels or two different groups of truth. Or we may conceive them as two sides of one coin because we are talking about two. Yet, they are really not different. And we cannot say that one level of truth is higher or superior and the other is lower or inferior. Truth means truth. One may be relative and the other absolute, but yet they are both to be considered as truth. Why did the Buddha speak about these two different kinds of truth? We may infer that because that is the only way we can discuss and begin to understand truth. *Saṁvṛtti*, or relative truth, implies a conditioned mind; and how can a conditioned mind approach the truth? That is an important question, faced by Nāgārjuna or by anyone in search of truth. Yet the conditioned mind has to perceive something, which means perceiving the theme. The theme that is facing the conditioned mind also represents the whole, the truth. And when the mind is de-conditioned and becomes free from limitations, it perceives the totality of the whole. It does not perceive something different or superior, but it perceives in a different way what was perceived by the conditioned mind.

It is necessary to discuss how to inculcate the conditioned mind to proceed to de-condition itself about the search for truth, the process of the path, *mārga*s and meditation, because there is no other alternative. In spite of the limitations involved in talking about these things, speech is the only instrument human beings have at their disposal. That is why the Buddha spoke about the middle path in order to avoid both extremes: (1) negating too pervasively and (2) not negating sufficiently. To understand either *śūnya* or *pūrṇa* one needs to pinpoint what is to be negated. This is a very sensitive and delicate point at which the human mind finds it difficult to operate. If it negates too much, it falls into the extreme of nihilism, *ucchedavāda*. If it does not negate enough, it remains in the extreme of eternalism, *śāśvatavāda*, or the wrong perception of things as existing conventionally or independently, not depending on other things, having their own root substance, *svabhāvataḥ*. Staying away from these two extremes, understanding the suchness between them is the middle path, Mādhyamika, and that is also *śūnya* and *pūrṇa* according to the Nāgārjuna tradition, or whatever else it may be called.

The Buddha, Nāgārjuna, and more recent teachers in the lineage of this tradition have spoken precisely about the two truths I have been talking about: relative and absolute, as not being different in their nature, but different by their distinctiveness. The two truths, the *satyadvaya*, are one in their nature or root substance. They are really one entity with two identities in their different aspects, *vyāvṛtti*. The conditioned mind is only capable of approaching two truths in a fragmented way, which only touches on relative truth, not the totality, or absolute truth. But, as mentioned earlier, once the mind is de-conditioned through meditation practice and rationalization, the limitations cease. Once the intelligent mind, or wisdom, *prajñā*, is able to see the truth as it is, then it can see the absolute truth. However, when it comes to verbalizing and communicating with others, we have to again revert to the limited nature of the mind, and then whatever we try to say is an alternative of something else. When we speak about *śūnya* our mind automatically thinks: "that is not *pūrṇa*, it is the alternative of *pūrṇa*." When we speak about *pūrṇa*, a similar mental process takes place. They are alternatives, not the whole, and we are not able to go beyond both alternatives. Whenever we talk about truth, we think it is the opposite of falsehood; and when talking about falsehood, we think it is the alternative of truth. The problem is that we cannot verbalize beyond all the alternatives and fragmentations. An unfragmented thing cannot be expressed with words or conceived through thought. In this case, how can we engage in a dialogue or discussion with a limit placed on the Absolute, or truth, as such? After attaining enlightenment, the Buddha did not teach for seven weeks. As he was wondering whether he should teach or not, he said to himself: "This truth I have realized is so subtle and profound, it cannot be put into words or understood by thought. So what is the use of preaching when almost no one will be able to understand it?" In one of the Mahāyāna Sūtras there is a story about Prajāpati Brahmā himself imploring the Buddha not to withhold the sublime truth, *amṛta*, and telling him that there are ways to teach people as clearly and simply as possible, trusting that the truth will impress itself on their minds according to their own *karma*. He also told the Buddha that this truth was the only way of salvation, and every individual had an equal right to have it pointed out to him or her. Brahmā suggested that one simple method of preaching to inquisitive laypeople would be through appropriate metaphors. Another method would be by negating each of the things that do not lead to the realization of truth. Through these methods, people who apply themselves, are fully mature, and capable of understanding, can be led to the realization of truth.

The *Prajñā-Pāramitā-Sūtras* are full of repetition. Different aspects of the same thing are reiterated because that is the way human thought process functions. However, Nāgārjuna's dialectical method of explaining interdependent origination, *pratītyasamutpāda*, is able to establish and convey some of the Buddha's teachings more effectively than any other treatise. Interdependent origination can be explained in two ways — one is based on causality. When some causes are accumulated, the effects originate automatically. The accumulation and ripeness of the causes themselves generate or manifest the effects. So the effects do not have an independent nature, they are outcomes of the activity of the causes. The accumulation of causes further depends on other causes, so there is no beginning and no end to them. Another way of explaining interdependent origination is through dependency, or relativity. Smallness exists only in relation to bigness, and vice versa. In the absence of one, the other cannot exist. Through this dependency, all things originate or are manifest, become real or facts, not allowing the extreme of nihilism. Also, because of this process of dependency or relativity, nothing is permanent or can exist independently, saving us from the extreme of eternalism. So this method of explaining interdependent origination leads the mind to realization of the middle path, the real way in which things exist. One of Nāgārjuna's statements is very powerful and pervasive: "All existence is possible because *śūnya* is there. If *śūnya* is not there, nothing can exist." *Śūnya* is what provides the space, the room, that facilitates or makes it possible for things to exist, to happen, grow, decay and change. *Śūnya* is unmanifested nature, and things are manifested. The manifest is possible because there is un-manifested space. The theory of interdependent origination is one of the most significant and sacred teachings of the Buddha. This theory explains the nature of phenomena, of *dharma*, how things exist. Due to ignorance of this nature of *dharma*, people begin to retreat into ignorance and kārmic forces in an unending vicious cycle.

The Buddhist concept of the three *kāya*s (embodiments): nothingness, no manifestation, and the process of manifestation, is very much in consonance with the meaning of *śūnya* and *pūrṇa*. If *śūnya* is properly understood, then *pūrṇa* automatically comes into existence. Without understanding *śūnya*, the concept of *pūrṇa* may not be a reality, or not a perfect one. In Buddhist terminology, *śūnyatā* and interdependent origination, as mentioned before, are really two aspects of one nature. With this understanding, the theme of this seminar might be very easily explained and understood!

Response to Questions

In the *Prajñāpāramitā Hṛdaya-Sūtra* it is said: "*rūpa* is *śūnya*, *śūnya* is *rūpa*." That is exactly what I was trying to submit, that *śūnya* is *pūrṇa* and *pūrṇa* is *śūnya*. *Rūpa* (the realm of forms) comes through the person's sensory mind that perceives the form. In relative truth, the form or object being perceived is true. It cannot be denied. But when one penetrates or searches the truth of that object, it cannot be pinpointed or found. One cannot establish "this is *rūpa*" through analytical searching, since there is a *śūnya*. Because there is a *śūnya*, one is able to designate something as a form. If *śūnya* is not there, the designation of *rūpa* is impossible. The possibility of designation of *rūpa* is facilitated because of *śūnya*. This cannot be established through an analytical search. This is also applicable to the question about the knower, knowing and the known. All these three exist in dualism and are true to the relative mind. This mind is able to prove them or to establish them as truth and as not less than absolute truth. But when you search through the analytical mind, all three categories will automatically disappear. It will all be negated by itself. An analytical search shows that negation by itself exists only in nothingness, not in something. Thus nothingness and everything are in a sense equal. They are neither opposite nor alternative. When you perceive the non-existence of things in absolute terms, that perception in itself is the existence of things. Negation does not mean that things are non-existent. Negation is the establishment of things. This is why Nāgārjuna said: the theory of interdependent origination saves you from both extremes simultaneously. It establishes appearance, which negates inherent existence, which in turn establishes apparent existence. This is how interdependent origination works when there is a dual existence of a self and the other. When the nature of the "self" and "other" is understood through interdependence, then *karuṇā,* or compassion, naturally flows from the realization of that fact. This is because in this state the feeling of separation, superiority and inferiority, or "self" and "other" as opposites, alternatives or different, does not exist.

The self exists because of the others, and others exist because of the self. Thus interdependent origination negates or avoids the source of both hatred and attachment, because these two emotions arise only due to ignorance, or the imposition of a different, independent existence of "one" and "other." When the illusion of this independent existence is negated and disappears, there cannot be a different feeling or emotion for one and the other. That equality of all beings is compassion, and it cannot create any form of hatred or attachment. This is because the ground of both hatred and attachment is not based on perceiving things as they are. It is based on things that are imposed and do not really exist.

The following *śloka* is attributed to Nāgārjuna from the *Mādhyamika-Kārikā* (22.11):

> *śūnyamiti na vaktavyam, aśūnyamiti vā bhavet* ।
> *ubhayaṁ nobhayaṁ ceti, prajñāptyarthaṁ tu kathyate* ॥

This refers to what I was saying, about there being no difference between *śūnya* and *pūrṇa*. These are all verbalizations of the same thing. The conventional interpretation of this *śloka* is: If *śūnyatā* exists by its own nature, then that is not *śūnyatā*; if no *śūnyatā* exists by its own nature, then that is also not *śūnyatā*; if neither *śūnyatā* nor the absence of *śūnyatā* exists by its own nature, again it is not *śūnyatā*. All these four categories are the possible hiding places of our concentration on the soul (*ātmadhāraṇā*) and on the root substance of things (*svabhāvadhāraṇā*). The mind that is always fixed on the independent nature of things falls into these categories. If it negates one category, immediately it goes to the next category. Then it negates the next category and finds itself in between, and it also negates the in between. None of them exist. So all these possible categories have to be negated, and then what will remain? If anything is left that has not been negated, it will be neither *śūnya* nor *pūrṇa*. Since there is no *śūnya*, there can be no *pūrṇa*. For this reason Nāgārjuna said that in the process of dialectical search, whatever position you take is wrong. Therefore Nāgārjuna stated: "I have no position." So all accusations or allegations could not defeat him because he had not taken any position. He took *śūnya* because it is not a position, since it cannot exist by its own nature. He did not take the position of non-*śūnya* or that of both *śūnya* and non-*śūnya*. In this way, his position could not be pinpointed. In the lower schools of Buddhist philosophy, they negate something, and with negation will establish something else: "This does not exist, but this exists." A little higher they simply say: "This does not exist; this exists." The Vaibhāṣikas and Sautrāntikas say there is something that really exists by its inherent nature, and the only thing to be negated is the unchangeable *nitya* (permanent) and the everlasting *ātmā* (soul). This is to be negated; otherwise the *pudgala,* or person, does exist coherently. The Vijñānavādins say everything is a reflection of the mind. Only mind exists by its own nature and nothing else does. The *svātrāntrika* Mādhyamikas say that nothing exists by its own independent nature, but there is the root substance. A person does exist by its root substance. And still there is another position. When we reach the *prāsaṅgika* Mādhyamikas, all the positions are denied. They do not accept *ālayavijñāna* (basic consciousness). Only the interdependently originated person is sufficient to carry the *vāsanā*s (impressions), and so on. So they are not talking about *ālayavijñāna* either.

In reference to the suggestion made by Dr. Bettina Bäumer about the relation between the Buddhist concept of interdependence and the Christian concept of communion, we can say that they are similar in a sense. But the interdependent origination theory is more philosophical (*darśana*), and communion is more practical (*caryā*). Communion has to do with how to live interdependently, and the interdependent origination theory deals with how to see the interdependence of all things philosophically. To answer the next question, in the tāntric or *yoga* practice, three *nāḍī* (veins) are mentioned, and the middle one is sometimes designated as *śūnya mārga* or *śūnya nāḍī* because at the entrance stage, when the middle *nāḍī* is submerged with *prāṇa*, the realization of *śūnyatā* almost emanates naturally. Therefore, it is called *śūnya mārga*.

In response to how the concepts of mindfulness and *śūnyatā* can be related, mindfulness is training of the mind — how to train the mind to be concentrated and, at the same time always to retain its *prajñā* (wisdom) and alertness, knowing what kind of mental activity or process is taking place. A great deal of thought process goes on without awareness of it. So the training of mindfulness is to create awareness within the mind. It is common to all the different schools of Buddhist tradition: Theravādin, Vijñānavādin, Mādhyamika and the rest. The various processes of meditation — *śamatha* (one-pointed concentration), *vipaśyanā* (true insight), and the four *smṛtyupasthānas*, or training in mindfulness in four different ways — are all the same. They all definitely relate with the concept or philosophy of *śūnyatā*, because mindfulness will ultimately create awareness. The ultimate goal of training in mindfulness is to reach the awareness of *śūnyatā*. Then, at some stage, this awareness will become direct perception of *śūnyatā*. When in mindfulness one becomes directly aware of *śūnyatā*, one has attained *prajñā* (wisdom), and that eliminates all negative emotions. The permanent emergence of one's mindful state into *śūnyatā* is Buddhahood. Thus mindfulness and *śūnyatā* always go together.

Finally, the recognition and respect of the differences in various religious traditions is a basic requirement for the existence of religious co-operation and harmony among all traditions. Trying to find only similarities will not work. The Buddha had an approach to this diversity of religions. He clearly said that each sentient being has an individual nature, always unique, and also always common. Therefore, only one type of religious teaching, philosophy, or practice will not be suitable to all humanity. According to different people's needs, likes and dislikes, attitudes and capacity there need to be different religious traditions and teachings. This is why the Buddha was never consistent, and why within Buddhism there have been a great number of different traditions, viewpoints and philosophies, sometimes in complete opposition to each other. There are four schools with different philosophical viewpoints, each school having subsets, and each subset its subdivisions, none of which are consistent with each other.

All this inconsistency and variety is for the benefit of the disciples.

If only Buddhism existed in this world, the majority of humanity would not be benefited by it. Thus, we need Christianity, Islam, and other religious traditions better suited for the many different types of people who will follow them. So religious differences are to be recognized and respected. We should leave it there, and not try to interpret them as similarities. Then there will be a distortion of religious traditions, as they cannot all be standardized or interpreted as one truth. Truth is beyond categorization. Therefore, we cannot say truth is one, or truth is two. There is no duality. We are talking about the opposite of duality, and that is also partial.

Many say, *Īśvara* is one, truth is one. How can we say that when one can exist only in relation to two? So we are talking about something in relation to something else. And if we say that truth is one, how will you number the truth? If we say that this implies that truth is one, not two, it is less than two, then truth becomes fragmented. It is an alternative or the opposite of something. When we talk about the truth, *Īśvara*, and no-*Īśvara* — all these are within the realm of thought, and we can talk a great deal about it. The differences are there. So it is very correct to say that the basic foundation of religious harmony and co-operation is to recognize and respect the differences, and to accept one's own faith, as it exists. If one would like to take something good from other religious traditions, there should not be any objection from either side. Only then can real coexistence, harmony and co-operation among religious traditions take place. Concerning the different and similar points of various religions, to understand and respect the different positions of various religions is one of the ways to create harmony among religious traditions. But, at the same time, the concern is that the method through which today's students of religion try to study or understand various religions is not satisfactory, because all of us are greatly influenced by modern study methods. Comparative study is only possible in material sciences, where there is use for comparisons. Perhaps making comparisons is also possible and useful in secular philosophical studies. But religions cannot be compared with each other. The comparative study of religions is not one of the desirable methods for studying a religion. Another unadvisable way to understand religions is to try to interpret their similarities. While studying a religion, one needs to follow the religious tradition in its original methodology. If one wants to understand Buddhism, one has to do it in a Buddhist way. The same applies to Hinduism or any other religion. Only then will one be able to study and understand a religion, otherwise it will be neither study nor research. It will lead nowhere.

3

Concept of Fullness or Pūrṇatva in Indian Philosophy

Deba Brata Sen Sharma

THE Sanskrit word *pūrṇa* is used in the ancient Sanskrit texts either as adjective or adverb, or as noun. Wherever it is seen used as adjective or adverb, it signifies the meaning "perfection," "completion," "abundance," etc. In philosophical texts however, the word *pūrṇa* assumes the form of a philosophical term connotative of the Supreme Reality which is full-in-itself, the Absolute. Since we are here primarily concerned with the use of this expression, *pūrṇa* as a philosophical term used mainly to describe the nature of the ultimate Reality as an ontological entity, we propose to confine our study of this concept as it developed in the philosophical texts of different schools of Indian philosophical thought. We would however begin our study by surveying briefly its usage in the Vedic literature, the chief source of inspiration for the development of Indian philosophical thought where this word is used mostly in the form of adjective or adverb.

Surprisingly enough the Vedic lexicon *Nighaṇṭu* lists this word as noun as a synonym of Water.[1] It is not known why this meaning has been suggested by Yāska as its usage in different Vedic Saṁhitās and Brāhmaṇas belie this connotation.

---

1. *Nighaṇṭu*, I.12, under *udaka-nāmāni*.

It is possible that the allusion here has been made to the *Nāsadīya Sūkta*[2] where the seer, while describing the state prior to the manifestation of the multiplicity of the world, says that the universe was submerged under the all-pervasive water. There was water everywhere, the multiplicity of creation remained hidden underneath the water. The world of multiplicity gradually emerged from the under sheath of water-cover at the time of creation. Here probably the expression "water" symbolizes the all-pervasive Reality which holds within its bosom the multiplicity of the world, it does not refer to the physical element of water.

When we take up the Vedic Saṁhitā texts like the *Ṛgveda,*[3] *Taittirīya Saṁhitā,*[4] *Kāṭhaka Saṁhitā,*[5] *Atharvaveda Saṁhitā,* to look for the use of the word *pūrṇa,* we find that this word is used in these texts either as adverb or adjective. For instance, in the *Viṣṇu Sūkta* of the *Ṛgveda* the word *pūrṇa* is used as adjective, qualifying the steps of Viṣṇu which are described as full of "honey," i.e., celestial bliss (*yasyatrī pūrṇā madhunā padāni*).[6] God Viṣṇu is said to cover the entire creation in three steps, and it is for this exploit, that he is praised by all in the world (*urugāya*). The symbolic meaning of this feat on the part of Viṣṇu is that he, while providing sustenance to the creation, also fills it up with the bliss flowing out perennially from his highest step lying in the heaven (*viṣṇoḥ parame pade madhva utsaḥ*).[7] This *mantra* is repeated verbatim in the *Taittirīya*

---

2. *Ṛgveda,* X. 190 (*Nāsadīya Sūkta*).
3. *Ibid., I. 154. 1.*
4. *Op. cit.,* II. 3.11.2.
5. *Op. cit.,* III.2.1.
6. *Ṛgveda* I.154.4.
7. *Ibid.*

Saṁhitā.[8] The word *pūrṇa*, used as an adjective in the *Kāṭhaka Saṁhitā* (III.2.1), denotes the "fullness of wealth" in quantitative sense. Prajāpati, the lord of creation, is described as full of wealth which diminished with his creating the world.[9]

The word *pūrṇa* occurs in the *Atharvaveda* in several hymns as adjective and noun in different contexts, viz., the description of moon on full moon night, ritual and the nature of the Supreme Being. The fullness of the moon on full moon night is comprised of sixteen digits (*kalā*) which is revealed on both sides — the visible front side and the invisible back side. This description of the full moon in the hymn (*pūrṇā paścāddhuta pūrṇā parastādunmadhyate pūrṇamāsī jigāha*) suggests the fullness of the Supreme Being who too has two faces, one turned downwards representing his immanent side, and the other looking upward beyond the creation, symbolizing his transcendent nature. The reference in the hymn to the victory of full moon in the battle for dispelling the veil of darkness on the full moon night suggests the victory of the self-effulgent illumination of the Supreme Being in dispelling the veil of ignorance from the minds of the individual beings. The seer prays to the supreme Being to grant him the opportunity to stay in heaven to enjoy the company of gods. In another hymn the idea of fullness is expressed symbolically in ritualistic language to describe the fullness of the Supreme Being. "Forth from the Full he lifts the Full, the Full he sprinkles with Full. Now also we may know the source from which it is sprinkled around" (*pūrṇātpūrṇamudyati pūrṇaṁ pūrṇena sicyate* । *uto tadya vidyāma yatastat pariṣicyate* ॥)[10] The *Atharvaveda* thus marks a turning point in the development of philosophical thought in

---

8. *Op. cit.*, II. 3. 11. 2.

9. *pūrṇo vai prajāpatiḥ samṛddhi ūno vyaddhibhiḥ*, *op. cit.*, III. 2. 1.

10. *Atharvaveda*, X.8.29.

general and in the use of the word *pūrṇa* expressing philosophical meaning in particular.

It may be mentioned here that the same idea is echoed almost in similar words in the *Bṛhadāraṇyaka Upaniṣad*[11] as well as the introductory verse of the *Īśa Upaniṣad* which we propose to examine in detail in the following paragraphs. The invocation verse in the *Īśopaniṣad* reads thus:

> *oṁ pūrṇamadaḥ pūrṇamidaṁ pūrṇāt pūrṇamudacyate* ।
> *pūrṇasya pūrṇamādāya pūrṇamevāvaśiṣyate* ॥

This verse may be freely rendered into English in this manner:

> *Oṁ* that or the Reality is the embodiment of fullness. *This* (visible) world is also of the nature of fullness. From the Reality, the embodiment of fullness, the world which is infinite, emanates. (Thereafter) the fullness of the nature of the Reality remains as it was before even after the emergence of the world which is fullness embodied.

Here in the Upaniṣads the word *pūrṇa* appears to develop into a full-fledged, philosophical term for the first time, connoting the real nature of the Ultimate Reality.

R.D. Ranade in his well-known book entitled *Constructive Survey of the Philosophy of the Upaniṣads* has beautifully summed up the spiritual import of the above mentioned verse in these words:

> The identification of the *Ātman* with the *Brahman* or individual spirit with the universal spirit, of the self and the Absolute is also proclaimed by epistolary stanza of the *Īśa* and the cognate *Upaniṣad* where, we are told, that the *Ātman* must be regarded as verily the *Brahman*, that the *Ātman* is infinite in nature as also the *Brahman*; that the *Ātman*

---

11. *Op. cit.*, V. 1.1.

> derives its being from the *Brahman;* that substracting the infinity of *Ātman* from the infinity of *Brahman,* the residuum is infinite. Thus does the epistolary stanza pile infinities over infinities, and taking the mathematical lead, speak as if when the infinity of the *Ātman* is deducted from the infinity of the *Brahman,* the reminder itself is infinite.[12]

Gopinath Kaviraj in his essay in Bengali while explaining the meaning of the word *pūrṇa* occurring in this Upaniṣad as a synonym of the Supreme Being, has shed light on the spiritual import of this verse which may be reproduced here in a nutshell. He says that this verse describes the integral nature of the Supreme Reality in terms of fullness which is beyond the grasp of the finite mind of man. The Supreme Reality is always full-in-itself, the one without a second; therefore it is self-subsistent and always independent. It does not suffer from any want or deficiency. It is present everywhere when we look at it from the world point of view, at all times as the embodiment of fullness. It is the locus of both creation and dissolution of the world which is going on eternally due to its innate power, without affecting in the least its integral nature. It is always "one whole" (*paripūrṇa*). Looking from the level of creation, it has two aspects: one which underlies the entire manifestation of the world, as the immanent reality, therefore capable of being apprehended by the finite mind. This aspect is denoted by the word *idam* in the *mantra;* and the other aspect which is beyond the reach of the mind, therefore indicated by the word *adaḥ* in the *mantra.* As a matter of fact, there is no difference between these two aspects of the nature of the Supreme Reality because what once appears as within the reach of the mind due to its becoming perfect instrument of cognition and the consequent expansion of its capacity may well go out of the individual grasp when the power of the mind contracts.

---

12. *Op. cit.,* chapt. V, Metaphysics, p. 277.

The Supreme Reality, however, remains the integral whole at all times. It is immutable and formless, yet appears to be ever changing and having a form, attributeless yet with all attributes, far yet near, all-pervasive yet transcendent. All contradictions dissolve in its being and all that emerges from it. It is also of the nature of all inclusive fullness. It can be compared to the *śūnya* (zero) which symbolizes infinity in the field of mathematics. Any addition does not make any change as it remains the immutable infinity. Thus the Supreme Reality, *Brahman*, is the integral Fullness which follows from its self-subsistent independent nature.[13]

The *Chāndogya Upaniṣad*, while describing the nature of the *Brahman*, uses the word *pūrṇa* to signify the Supreme Being as the embodiment of fullness. The Upaniṣadic sage notices the similarity between the space (*ākāśa*) existing within the "heart" of an individual and the space outside the individual being. Both these spaces existing within and outside the individual being are one and identical and these symbolize his fullness nature and lack of any movement.

> *yad vai tad brahmeti idaṁ vāva tad yo'yaṁ bahirhā puruṣādākāśaḥ . . . ayaṁ vāva sa yo'yaṁ antaḥ puruṣaḥ . . . ākāśaḥ ayaṁ vāva sayo'yamantarhṛdaya ākāśaḥ tadetat pūrṇam pravarti . . . .* ||[14]

As the embodiment of "fullness," the *Brahman* always remains immersed in its integral being. This implies total absence of movement or action. For every action or movement involves change which means deviation from its self-resting state, which is denied in the immutable *Brahman* on account of its "fullness." Also movement presupposes the existence of space

---

13. *Paramārthaprasaṅga* (in Bengali), ed. J. Pal, vol. IV. See the chapter: Gopinath Kaviraj on Pūrṇa, pp. 229-232.

14. *Chāndogya Up.*, III. 12.7-9.

surrounding the *Brahman*. This is also denied because the immutable *Brahman is* beyond space and time.

The *Taittirīya Upaniṣad* mentions the five sheaths covering the self, all appearing as all-pervading and complete by themselves as they hide the all-pervading real self. These layers or sheaths are enveloping the *Ātman*. But of the essence five elements, namely food, vital breath, mind and intellect exist one over the other on the mundane plane.[15] These sheaths or layers must be peeled away, one by one, in order to discover the real self, self-shining embodiment of fullness.

Let us now turn our attention from the Upaniṣads to the different schools of Indian philosophical thought which developed from the realization of the Vedic seers and the metaphysical thought of the Upaniṣadic sages. But, before discussing the concept of fullness or *pūrṇatva* seen in the metaphysical formulations of the different schools of Indian philosophical thought, let us attempt to identify the conditions or factors conducive to the concept taking roots in the metaphysical thought of these schools. The first and foremost condition favouring the development of the idea of fullness in the conceptualization of the nature of Reality by a particular school is its belief in non-dualism as the guiding principle in the formulation of its metaphysical thought. The concept of "fullness" or *pūrṇatva* is consistant with the philosophy of non-dualism, hence, it is found in the metaphysical thought of the schools that subscribe to non-dualistic philosophy. The fullness or *pūrṇatva* as a philosophical concept is incompatible with the dualistic or pluralistic thought, hence it has no place in the metaphysical thought of the dualistic Sāṁkhya-Yoga or the pluralistic Nyāya-Vaiśeṣika school. Every non-dualistic school postulates one Reality that serves as the locus for the

15. *Op. cit.*, II. 2-5.

manifestation of the multiplicity of the world. At the same time, the same non-dual Reality is said to be not confined to the manifestation of the world as the substratum, it also transcends the world-manifestation. The fullness nature of such Reality, one without a second, is only a logical corollary to such conceptualization.

The second precondition that contributes to the development of the concept of fullness consisting of the nature of Reality is the particular type of non-dualism accepted by a particular school. Non-dualism advocated by the different non-dualist schools broadly speaking, are of two distinct kinds, one which is based on negation, *neti, neti,* the other based on affirmation or integration. To illustrate, the Śāṅkara Vedāntins follow the path of negation. They deny the existence of everything else other than the *Brahman,* the sole Reality on the transcendent plane. The fullness of the *Brahman* in their view is based on negation of all in the one Supreme Reality. Other non-dualistic schools like the Vedānta propagated by Rāmānuja, some Śaiva and Śākta schools base their non-dualistic outlook on affirmation or integration. These schools appear to enlarge their concept of non-dualism by extending as it were, the scope of non-dualism to encompass the multiplicity of the world and then integrate it in the unity of the Ultimate Reality. They regard the Ultimate Reality as expressing itself simultaneously in two forms — as the all-pervasive Cosmic Reality and the transcendent Reality, all at once. Their stress on the integration as the core principle in their philosophical thinking is reflected in their concept of "fullness" or *pūrṇatva* constituting the nature of the Ultimate Reality.

The third factor contributing to the development of this concept is the realistic outlook that some non-dualistic schools are found to propagate. These schools look upon the multiplicity of the world as real as the unity of transcendent

Reality. In other words they try to integrate the transcendence of ultimate Reality with its all-pervasive and all-inclusive cosmic nature, regarding these two aspects of its nature as real and co-existent. These schools further hold that the transcendent and immanent nature of the Ultimate Reality are not mutually exclusive aspects but these represent the two faces of the same Reality, one looking upward and beyond, and the other, visible from the level of the world.

When we apply these determinants or conditions constituting the parameters for the development of the concept of fullness in the conceptualizing of the nature of Reality in the non-dualistic schools, we find the non-dualistic schools of Śāṅkara Vedānta, Viśiṣṭādvaita School of Rāmānuja, Śākta School and the Advaita Śaiva School of Kashmir also called Trika School, satisfy these conditions to some extent. The Advaita Vedāntins of Śaṅkara's School postulate three levels of existence of Reality, technically called the *prātibhāsika* level (illusory level), the *vyāvahārika* level (the phenomenal or the empirical level) and the *pāramārthika* level (the transcendent level) which exist in hierarchical order as it were with the non-dual *Brahman* serving as the locus (*adhiṣṭhāna*). These levels are mutually opposite in nature, one cancelling the other as one elevates himself through them to reach the final goal, the realization of oneness with the *Brahman*. The *prātibhāsika* level is likened to the dream state in which one experiences objects that are fanciful or imaginary, having no existence in concrete form. The substratum, *Brahman* then is not experienced as it lies hidden under the thick veil of ignorance. The *vyāvahārika* or phenomenal level is characterized by the experience of multiplicity of the world. There is then no possibility of the experience of *Brahman* as the veil of ignorance continues to hide the substratum, *Brahman*. When one succeeds in elevating oneself to the trans-empirical or transcendental level of *Brahman* through intense personal efforts in the form of spiritual discipline, the veil of ignorance is removed resulting in the gradual fading of one's vision of the world of multiplicity. The true self-effulgent *Brahman*, the ultimate Reality, shines forth. The spiritual seeker has then direct experience of *Brahman* in its true form. The *Brahman*, who is always full, is realized as such by the spiritual seeker, according to the Advaita Vedānta. The fullness nature of the *Brahman* is thus based on negation of all that is not *Brahman*, i.e., the multiplicity of the world.

Taking a realistic view of the world of multiplicity, the Non-Dualist School of Vedānta propagated by Rāmānuja admits three realities, namely the *cit* or the conscious selves, the *acit* or the principle of matter and the *Īśvara*, the God held together in the unity of the all-embracing Reality or *Brahman* by a relation of identity. The *Īśvara* or God is nothing but the *Brahman* in qualified form and he permeates, in the *cit* and the *acit*, constituting the core of their being. Rāmānuja thus takes a broader view of Reality, attempting to assimilate and incorporate as it were its different components in the Being of God, called the *saguṇa Brahman* (the qualified *Brahman*). Rāmānuja's projection about the nature of *saguṇa Brahman* appears to be an extension of Upaniṣadic philosophy of non-dualism. God, being the highest Reality, alone is Full, because nothing exists outside him, the *saguṇa Brahman*. If we compare Rāmānuja's concept of fullness with that of Advaita Vedānta of Śaṅkara, we find the latter view about fullness nature of the *Brahman* to be narrow and truncated as it is guided by negation or denial of everything else other than the *Brahman*.

Let us now turn our attention on the concept of fullness of the ultimate Reality as conceived by the Advaita Śaivites of Kashmir. Being advocates of an integral non-dualism, they believe in the existence of one Reality which they call by various names as Parama Śiva (Supreme Śiva), Parameśvara

(Supreme Lord), Parāsamvit (Supreme Experiencing Principle), Caitanya (Universal Consciousness), *ātman* (Universal Self), etc. Parama Śiva is said to be endowed with Śakti which being associated with him, is technically called divine freedom (*svātantrya śakti*). The divine freedom is not held to be an adjunct (*upādhi*) or attribute (*guṇa*) of the Supreme Lord, but it is said to constitute the essence of his being inalienable from him as the Lord. Exercising his divine Śakti, the Supreme Lord is said to manifest himself out of his free will as the Universe comprised of 36 *tattva*s or levels of creation during the creative phase. When he voluntarily manifests himself as the Universe, he does not remain aloof as a spectator (*sākṣī*), he participates actively in the display of his glory as the Universe, assuming different roles of limited subjects, objects, and the means for their enjoyment on the different levels of creation. At the same time, he does not forsake his form as the Supreme Lord. He remains beyond his self-manifestation as the Universe as the transcendent Being, the Absolute. Being the Sole Reality he is endowed with infinite or unrestricted power: *svātantrya śakti*. He manifests himself to himself in two forms, namely as the Universal Being in which form he pervades and permeates the entire universe as the immanent Reality, at the same time, he transcends all and remains beyond all in which form he manifests himself as the transcendent being, the Absolute. According to the Advaita Śaivites of Kashmir his self-manifestation in these two forms — the Universal Being and the transcendent Being are not mutually exclusive, one denying the other, but are held to be simultaneous or concurrent. His fullness-nature logically flows from this depiction of his nature.

The Advaita Śaivites stress the point that there is nothing in the world that is not Śiva. He exists everywhere in different forms when we look at him from the point of view of the world at all times as embodiment of fullness; when we look at him as the transcendent Being, he remains the integral whole, as embodiment of fullness. He is immutable yet appears as everchanging in the world, attributeless yet with all attributes, all-pervasive yet transcendent. All contradictions dissolve in his being. He always exists immersed in his being that is of the nature of all inclusive fullness.

Utpaladeva (ninth-tenth century) in his *Īśvara-Pratyabhijñā Kārikā* (II. 1.7) says:

> *svātmaiva svātmanā pūrṇā bhāvā bhāntyamitasya tu.*[16]
>
> To the Universal subject, i.e., Parama Śiva, the objects shine as identical with himself, therefore as fullness-nature like the self itself.

The author seeks to convey the idea that the Supreme Being is full (*pūrṇa*), so is he when he shines as the object. Abhinavagupta in his *Vimarśinī* commentary explains the metaphysical implication of the above passage in this way:

> *apūrvāparaṁ hi idaṁ mūrtitaḥ kriyāyaśca sarvaṁ sarvataḥ pūrṇam*[17]
>
> This, i.e., the eternal subject is changeless. He is always perfect, i.e., full in all respects in form and action.

At another place, Abhinavagupta in his commentary further elucidates the concept of fullness, first by identifying the concept of fullness with the Supreme Śiva, then extending it to all his self-manifestations as the infinite multiplicity. He is one when he has the self-experience as "Pure I." He is then self-contained (*pūrṇa*), resting in himself (*svātmaviśrānta*) and beyond all manifestation (*nirābhāsa*). Subsequently in order to manifest himself as many he divides himself into the two — the Pure "I" (*aham*) and the pure "This" (*idam*), both of fullness-

---

16. *Op. cit.*, II. 1.7.

17. *Vimarśinī* comm. on the above verse, p. 23 (Bhāskarī edn.).

nature, and also identical in essence. The pure "I" symbolizes his form as the subject which, in that stage, is universal and full in nature. The pure "This" (*idam*) also represents him in the form of the object which too is universal and full in nature in that stage. Later, when the Supreme Śiva, exercizing his power of divine freedom, voluntarily manifests himself externally in diverse forms of limited subjects, objects, etc. He remains the embodiment of fullness, self-contained and self-resting (*svātmaviśrānta*) as before.

Abhinavagupta in his *magnum opus*, the *Tantrāloka* describes the Supreme Lord this way:

tathā hi svasvatantratvaparipūrṇatayā vibhuḥ ।
niḥsaṁkhyairbahubhiḥ rūpairbhātyavacchedavarjanāt ॥[18]

The Supreme Lord, because of his innate freedom of Will and Fullness, shines in myriad forms without undergoing any limitation whatsoever in his form.

He remains as the Supreme illumination, free from all limitations as ever.

At another place, Abhinavagupta gives a reason for naming the Supreme Reality as Parama Śiva.

tāvānpūrṇasvabhāvo'sau paramaḥ śiva ucyate ।[19]

The Supreme Lord is called Parama Śiva on account of all Śaktis (numbering twelve) existing as identified with him in him, therefore he is perfect in nature.

Jayaratha explains this saying:

pūrṇe sarvamasti sarvatra pūrṇamasti anyathāsya pūrṇataiva na syāt ॥[20]

---

18. *Tantrāloka*, IX. 52-53.
19. *Tantrāloka*, I. 108.
20. *Vivṛtti* comm. on the above verse, p. 164.

> In the Full (i.e., the Supreme Lord) everything exists, fullness exists everywhere, otherwise it would be impossible to call him as the Fullness incarnate.

Elucidating the implication of the expression — *susampūrṇam* occurring in the *Parātrīśikā*,[21] Abhinavagupta in his commentary says:

> *sarvatattvaiḥ suṣṭhu abhedena samyaganapāyitayā pūrṇatvam* ।
> *sarvatra ca paramāṇāvapi yadā samantāt bharaṇaṁ sarvāttmīkaraṇam* ॥[22]

> The Supreme Being exists fully and invariably identified with all the *tattvas*. There the fullness nature of the Supreme Being shines when he makes everything in all directions, even in atoms wholly His own.

The Advaita Śaivites hold that the attainment of *śivatva* is the ultimate goal in the spiritual journey of every individual seeker. They name the highest state of spiritual realization as the attainment of *bhairavībhāva* (oneness with Bhairava or Śiva nature) when the spiritual seeker experiences himself as Śiva, the world does not disappear from his view. He finds himself engaged in worldly activity as embodied being, and also, at the same time, watchful of the cosmic drama going on from time immemorial as the spectator. This experience is in conformity with their philosophy of integration which is the cardinal point in their metaphysical position.

When the spiritual seeker reaches this state, he experiences divine bliss. Siddha Somānanda, the founder of the philosophical school of Pratyabhijñā (ninth century), had shed light on the source of the divine delight which, flowing from

---

21. *Vivaraṇa* on *Parātrīśikā*, V. 31 (Jaideva Singh edition, p. 77).
22. *Vivaraṇa* on v. 31, p. 97.

the fullness-nature of the Supreme Being resting in himself (*svātma viśrānta*), permeates the entire creation. He says:

> *sa yadā'ste cidāhlādamāmtrānubhavatallayaḥ* ।
> *tadicchā tāvatī tāvajjñānaṁ tāvatkriyā hi sā* ॥
>
> *susūkṣmaśaktitritaya sāmarasyena vartate* ।
> *cidrūpa-āhlādaparamo nirvibhāgaḥ parastadā* ॥[23]

> When Śiva (the Supreme Being) exists immersed in his conscious bliss nature, then his powers of will, knowledge and action remain dissolved in his being. When his extremely subtle powers (mentioned above) exist in him held in perfect equilibrium, then his form as conscious-bliss is the highest state of his existence, it is the state when there is no emanation.

This is the state when the Supreme Being rests in his fullness nature, his self-experience remains confined to himself only, this is the state in which he exists identified with his bliss-nature. This is also called the state of *nivṛttacit*, in which the consciousness nature rests in itself, it is the state of blissful existence. He is then full, because he does not feel any want or deficiency. His fullness nature follows from his lacking the experience of any deficiency to fulfil which he needs to move out.

To sum up, the concept of fullness which made its first appearance in the Vedic texts as adjective or adverb developed in the Upaniṣads as connotative of the ultimate Reality, later reached the climax of its evolution in the metaphysical thought of the Advaita Śaiva Philosophy of Kashmir, passing through the philosophical thoughts of other nondualistic schools of Vedānta.

---

23. *Śivadṛṣṭi* by Somānanda I, V.3-4.

References

Nighaṇṭu and Nirukta, ed. and tr. into English by L. Svarupa, New Delhi: Motilal Banarsidass, 1984 (Reprint).

Ṛgveda Saṁhitā, ed. Sripad Damodar Satvalekar, Paradi: Svadhyaya Mandala, 1984.

Atharvaveda Saṁhitā, ed. Sripad Damodar Satvalekar, Paradi: Svadhyaya Mandala, 1985

R.D. Ranade, *A Constructive Survey of the Philosophy of the Upaniṣads*, Poona: Oriental Book Agency, 1926.

Īśvarapratyabhijñā Kārikā with Vimarśinī by Abhinavagupta, and *Bhāskarī*, ed. K.A. Subramanya Aiyer & K.C. Pandey, New Delhi: Motilal Banarsidass, 1986, Reprint.

The Tantrāloka of Abhinavagupta with the Commentary of Jayaratha, ed. R.C. Dvivedi and N. Rastogi, New Delhi: Motilal Banarsidass, 8 vols., 1987 (First edition: Srinagar 1918-38).

Abhinavagupta, *Parātrīśikā Vivaraṇa*, The Secret of Tantric Mysticism, tr. Jaideva Singh, ed. Bettina Bäumer, New Delhi: Motilal Banarsidass, 1988.

Śivadṛṣṭi by Somānanda, ed. M.S. Kaul, Srinagar: KSTS 1934.

4

The Plerôma of God, Jesus Christ and the Christian

Paddy Meagher

I SHALL develop in this paper some ideas around the paradox of Void and Fullness from the perspective of Christian sacred writings. We shall preface the study of *Plerôma* with some remarks on religious discourse. These remarks overlap and mutually complete each other.

Religious Language

All language about transcendence, be it the transcendence of the divine or of the human, is *symbolic* or *analogical* in character. What is said is not what is meant. We need to respect the nature of the language to grasp what is signified. This implies that each affirmation must be followed by and bound to a parallel denial. The truth or the meaning is to be found in the tension created by the paradox and this meaning emerges from the permanent tension between the two aspects of the statement.

When I state "God exists" I must immediately state "God does not exit" and the reality of God is beyond both of these statements. A grasp of the reality about which I am attempting to speak will emerge beyond both statements. When I say God is Mother, Father, creator, provident. . . . I am not using normal language. I am attempting to point to a reality, which has some relationship to the meaning of the terms within human experience and yet so radically surpasses this experience that I must add a full denial.

Implied in this is that all genuine language about God is *paradoxical*. Religious discourse is both symbolic and paradoxical. Reality is actually paradoxical. However, our normal human tendency is to imagine and speak of reality in terms of contradiction in which we separate what needs to be distinguished and held in the tension of paradox. We play over against each other being and non-being, good and evil, life and death, God's love and God's anger, soul and body in the human, divine and human, secular/profane and sacred/religious, pure and impure, freedom and obedience, eating and fasting, activity and passivity. . . .

All religious language is also conditioned profoundly by culture, tradition and world-views. The challenge is to be faithful to the culturally conditioned discourse and yet to transcend it and search for the reality about which various religious traditions speak and which is rooted in the commonality of the human. The polarities uncovered and used by forms of structuralism in hermeneutics remind us of this possibility.

When we turn to Christian sacred writings we must take account of the nature of communication through letter, exhortations and narrative or story. The accounts of Jesus of Nazareth, Christ and Lord in the four texts called *Gospels* are essentially narrative in character. This is true of most of the sacred writings of the Jewish people. The great narratives of the Jewish people to be found in the *Torah* in a special way and the former prophets also form the background to the Christian narrative. This also implies that the narrative of God and Jesus Christ is not intelligible unless the narrative as told by the Jewish people is kept in mind. There are continual references and allusions to this much larger story.

What I am emphasizing in the above paragraph is the importance of literary genre and forms used in sacred writings. The interpretation of a writing cannot be adequate without close attention to the patterns of communication used by the author. We must also remind ourselves that the same reality can be described in very many different ways, drawing on different symbols, in different figurative ways and images and symbolic narratives or conceptual forms.

The Study of Plerôma — Fullness

The explicit topic given to me is the study of *Plerôma* in some Christian scriptures.[1] The particular term comes from the Greek language in which it has the most mundane meanings and can carry rich significance.[2] In Christian scriptures the term occurs

---

1. There are not many monographs or long entries in Dictionaries on this term. A classical study would be G. Delling *Plerôma* in *Theological Dictionary of the New Testament*, ed. G. Friedrich (tr. and ed. G.W. Bromiley), Grand Rapids, Wm. E. Eerdmans, 1971, vol. VI, pp. 298-305. We could also mention R. Schippers, Plérôma in *Dictionary of New Testament Theology*, ed. C. Brown, vol. I, Exeter, Paternoster Press, 1975, pp. 733-41 where there are some comments on *Plerôma*. A major monograph on this term which was not available to the writer is J. Ernst, *Plerôma und Plerôma Christi*. Geschichte und Deutung eines Begriffs der paulinischen Antilegomena, Regensburg, Pustet, 1970.

2. It has three major areas of meaning: 1. "that which has been filled," rare in classical Greek; ship manned with its crew/ body of believers filled with the presence, power, agency and riches of God and of Christ; 2. "that which fills" or "with which a thing is filled," common in classical Greek and our writings; 3. Fullness, abundance. *A Greek-English Lexicon of the New Testament*, by J.H. Thayer, 4th edn., Edinburgh, T.T. Clark 1896. In the classic lexicon of the Greek language we find the following meanings: (a) →

in a number of texts with various traditional meanings.[3] In the Greek translation of the Jewish Scriptures the term does not occur very often.[4] The term becomes a technical term in some Gnostic writings like the Corpus Hermeticum, Christian Gnostic texts and in Iamblichus' *De Mysteriis*.[5] It is not a technical term in any of the normative writings of the Christian community, namely the New Testament nor has any form of Gnostic thought influenced its use.[6]

→ complement/that which fills; (b) satiety (food); (c) full number (ships . . . .); (d) sum/total (of years . . . .); (e) patch; (f) fullness/full and perfect nature/complete nature [some of our texts]; (g) reserves; (h) mass/complex; (i) duties of office; (j) cargo/freight. *A Greek English Lexicon*, by H.G. Liddel, R. Scott, H. Stuart Jones, vol. II, Oxford: Clarendon Press, 1940, pp. 1420-21.

3. We shall list the texts: Mk 2: 21 and Mt 9: 16 (patch); Mk 6: 43 and 8: 20 (pieces which make full baskets); Jn 1: 16 (fullness/totality); Rom 11: 12 and 25 (full inclusion/full complement); 13: 10 (love as sum total of the law); 15: 29 (sum total of Christ's blessings); 1 Cor 10: 26 (everything that fills the earth); Gal 4: 4 (fullness of God's time/God's time in a state of fullness); Eph 1: 10 (time in a state of fullness); 1: 23 (Church as Christ's body fully filled by the one who fills all in all ways); 3:19 (filled to all the fullness of God); 4: 13 (the fullness which belongs to Christ); Col 1: 19 and 2: 9 (all the fullness of God/deity in Christ).

4. G. Delling *TDNT*, p. 299. It occurs about 12 times with some other occurrences in other versions of the LXX with the meaning of the sea/land and its fullness.

5. Delling, *TDNT*, pp. 300-01 who provides a good summary of usages. We also have a precise summary of some Gnostic uses and their meaning in, *A Commentary on the Epistles to the Colossians and to Philemon*, E. Lohse, Philadelphia: Fortress Press, 1971, pp. 57-58.

6. Schnackenburg says of the use of *Plerôma* in Jn 1: 16 ". . . and has certainly nothing to do with Gnostic speculation on the *Plerôma*. The term has no cosmological connotations here." *The Gospel According to John*, R. Schnackenburg, London: Burns & Oates, →

The consequence is that in the normative writings of the Christian community *Plerôma* does not have the same importance or significance as *śūnya-pūrṇa* in Buddhist and some Hindu writings.

In the writings of the early great commentators on the Christian scriptures and beliefs the term is used in the sense of plenitude/fullness/divine perfection of God, of the Son and of the Trinity. In responding to Gnostic thinkers and writings, the Fathers of the Church (the term used to refer to these writers) often use this term in its technical senses. Nearly half the references under "theological use" are concerned with Gnostic usage.[7]

The texts, which are significant for our study are texts found in a body of writings penned not by Paul himself but probably by a disciple in the 60s of the Christian Era. There is also the single text from the writing attributed to "John," (John 1: 16) a narrative interpretation of the ministry and life of Jesus Christ. The first group of texts are found in the letter to the Ephesians [Eph 1: 23; 3: 19; 4: 13] and the letter to the Colossians [Col 1: 19 and 2: 9]. These are found in occasional letters to specific groups (though the audience of Ephesians is uncertain) in which the writer takes up specific issues and relates them to an exposition of core aspects of the experience of the Christian community. We also looked at the use of the verb and adjective to see if there were any significant texts for our consideration. Though the word fields of fullness,

---

→ vol. I, 1968, p. 275. Dunn argues to the same conclusion in his study, *The Epistles to the Colossians and to Philemon*, J.D.G. Dunn Grand Rapids, Wm. E. Eerdmans, 1996, p. 100-01. He sees how later Gnostic writers could develop their thought from a seed which can be found in the use in these texts.

7. G.W.H. Lampe, *A Patristic Greek Lexicon*, Oxford: Clarendon Press, 1961-69, pp. 1094-95.

abundance, totality . . . are very significant since they are used to convey the sense of ultimacy in God's actions in history and in the life and teaching of Jesus of Nazareth, Lord and Son, yet we found no text which deserves special attention. We shall now study significant texts.

John 1: 16

There are three texts which use *Plerôma* and which describe Jesus Christ in his human existence in relationship to God. We shall quote each text within its immediate context and comment upon the text. The first text is from John:

> And the Word became flesh and lived among us and we have seen his glory, the glory as of a father's only Son [the Father's only Son], full of grace and truth. . . . From his fullness [from his *Plerôma*] we have all received, grace upon grace. The Law indeed was given through Moses; grace and truth came through Jesus Christ. No one has ever seen God. It is God, the only Son [It is an only Son/ It is the only Son] who is close to the Father's heart [bosom], who has made him known.
>
> — Jn 1: 14.16-18

Without going into all aspects of the text, one major point being made is that the enfleshed Word, Jesus Christ, sharing in our history and being able to be seen and known by us, has revealed the invisible God. Earlier in this hymn the writer has emphasized the profound intimacy between God as Origin and God as Word, "In the beginning was the Word, and the Word was totally turned towards God and the Word was divine (God)." He has also highlighted his primary role in creation, and that life and light reside in and come from him. He underlined that he has entered into the essential conflict of all human history, the conflict between darkness and light and is responsible for the victory of the light (1: 1-5). He has summarized his story, the story of rejection and acceptance with emphasis on the gift which he gives from God to all who surrender to him as the gift and revealer of God, namely "to be children of God" (1: 14).

Our text underlines the fact that the incarnate Word, namely Jesus, does not lose his unique relationship with God, but shares in God's glory. He is the total expression of God's graciousness and fidelity ("full of grace and truth") and has the unique role of revealing the invisible God with whom he shares unparalleled intimacy. For these reasons he is the source of endless gifts or unparalleled gifts to the world, to all who believe.

The Cost involved in Sharing Fullness

What we need to examine is the price he must pay, if I may use this term, namely the demanding journey to fullness, if he is to be the source of life to others. We need to examine the journey he must make to be the one who reveals the mystery of the invisible God and be the source of his life. I will work from a particular core text. The text is:

> Now my soul is troubled. And what should I say — "Father, save me from this hour?" No, it is for this reason that I have come to this hour. Father, glorify your name. Then a voice came from heaven, "I have glorified it, and will glorify it again." . . . Jesus answered, "This voice has come for your sake, not for mine. Now is the judgement of this world; now the ruler of this world will be driven out. And I when I am lifted up from the earth, will draw all people to myself." He said this to indicate the kind of death he was to die.

Within the story line of the Gospel narrative this text occurs after the leaders of the Jesus' nation have decided that he must die (11: 45-53). They are at a loss because of his popularity and Greeks also have come seeking to meet him. Jesus comments at this juncture:

> The hour has come for the Son of Man to be glorified. Very truly I tell you, unless a grain of wheat falls into the ground and dies, it remains a single grain, but if it dies, it bears much fruit. Those who love their life lose it, and those who hate their life in this world will keep it for eternal life.
>
> — 12: 23-25

Jesus faces his death. He is caught within that paradox of choice and duty, of freedom and obedience, of his self and the Self and surrenders himself to the Self. This takes us to a thread, which has run through John's interpretation of Jesus' known life. In various ways he returns to the basic choice of his life, the emptying of his self and the total adherence to the Self. He spoke of his life in terms of "My food is to do the will of him who sent me and to complete his work" (4: 34; cf. 5: 19-20.36; 6: 38; 9: 4; 15: 10). Turning to his Father, Jesus sums up his life in these words: "I glorified you on earth by finishing the work that you gave me to do" (17: 4) and dies with this most pregnant phrase on his lips: "It is finished" (19: 30). This death is described in a paradoxical way, namely "being lifted up" (3: 14; 8: 28; 12: 32-34) and to his being glorified and departing from this world to the Father (12: 23; 13: 1; 17: 1.5). These phrases refer to Jesus' crucifixion and glorification. One cannot be without the other and both remain forever in tension. Thus Jesus has been gifted with *The Fullness of God* and is the source of life for all who believe.

Service as an Image of Self-Sacrifice

There are two other scenes, which explain the origin of that fullness which enables Jesus to be the source of divine life. In the first incident the writer solemnly introduces the scene. He summarizes the story of Jesus up to this point, underlining the presence of the source of all evil, the devil in the heart of Judas, a disciple. He notes:

> Jesus knowing that the Father had given all things into his hands, and that he had come from God and was going to God. — 13: 3

At this point Jesus washes the feet of his disciples. This act is framed by the explicit mention of his betrayal (13: 2), the longer discussion of this betrayal (13: 21- 30) and the writer's comment on Jesus' awareness of the betrayal (13: 11). The washing of the feet is the ritual and figurative expression of Jesus' death, that self-emptying at the service of others and its fruitfulness.

The Death of the Shepherd as Symbol

The second text uses the traditional image of the shepherd (Jeremiah 23: 1-6; Ezekiel 34: 1-16.23-24; Is 40: 10-11). Jesus describes his inner journey. There are two aspects to this journey, his relationship with his Father and with the human family. At stake is his "laying down his life" for the sheep (10: 16). This action is in response to his Father, "I have received this command from my Father" (10: 18) who "loves me because I lay down my life in order to take it up again" (10: 17). Rising from sovereign freedom (10: 18), the action is also the expression of his committed dedication to his sheep as the "good shepherd" in contrast to the hired hand and thieves and bandits who either prey upon the sheep or run away in the face of danger (10: 8.10.12-13.14). Jesus describes himself: "I am the good shepherd. The good shepherd lays down his life for the sheep" (10: 11). The purpose for his self-sacrifice is that "they may have life and have it abundantly" (10: 10).

The Inner Journey in Narrative Form

Because of the use of images taken from space and time we need to be careful that we do not miss the inner journey, which is being narrated and the great conflict between light and darkness, the Son and the prince of this world, the symbol of evil (12: 31; 14: 30). The narrative interpretation of Jesus' life and work is full of activity. However this activity is the path to fullness, to a union with God, which enables Jesus in this Gospel to reiterate in many different ways his unity with God the Father (10: 30.38; 14: 10.20; 17: 21). This union is rooted in his obedience to the Father, the expression of his *bhakti* and self-surrender (15: 10; 14: 31). His death is the final expression of this self-emptying. Therefore he who always had the fullness of God within the mystery of God as the Word has the same fullness as Jesus Christ which he can share with all who believe.

Colossians 1: 19

We turn to two other texts, which affirm that Jesus as the risen Lord has been gifted with the fullness of God. The first text is a hymn:

> He is the image of the invisible God
> the first born of all creation;
> for in him all things in heaven and on earth were created
> things visible and invisible,
> whether thrones or dominions, or rulers or powers,
> all things have been created through him and for him.
> He himself is before all things
> and in him all things hold together.
>
> He is the head of the body, the church;
> he is the beginning, the first born from the dead,
> So that he might come to have first place in everything.
> For in him all the fullness [*Plerôma*] of God was pleased to dwell,
> and through him God was pleased to reconcile to himself all things
> whether on earth or in heaven,
> by making peace through his blood on the cross.
>
> — Colossians 1: 15-20

This hymn is framed by reminders to the community of what God has done for them through his beloved Son. He speaks of rescue from the power of darkness and transfer into the kingdom of his beloved Son, redemption and forgiveness of sins (1: 13-14). He also applies the image of reconciliation effected through the death of Jesus concretely to the community. He reminds them:

> And you, once estranged and hostile in mind, doing evil deeds, he has now reconciled in his fleshly body [in the body of his flesh] through death so as to present you holy and blameless and irreproachable before him. . . .
>
> — 1: 21-22

The writer wishes to remind his community of the central place of Jesus Christ in the whole story of God's action in the cosmos and human history. Readers are invited by the writer to note the varied ways in which totality is expressed in the hymn and the use of prepositions. As all begins and ends with God the Father he uses "by/with/through/" when describing Christ's role. The total fullness of God is related to Jesus, being both the beginning and the first born from the dead, namely to his resurrection, the great new beginning for the human family. Dunn relating the statement to Jesus' ministry comments:

> The importance of the language is to indicate that the completeness of God's self-revelation was focused in Christ, that the wholeness of God's interaction with the universe is summed up in Christ.[8]

This fullness of God is also related to his death on the cross by which God reconciles the world to himself. The relationship between the death on the cross and the fullness of God is not

---

8. James D.G. Dunn, *The Epistle to the Colossians and to Philemon*, Grand Rapids: Wm. B. Eerdemans, 1996, 101.

so explicit in this text. The letter also does not tell the story of Jesus' obedience and self-emptying which accompany his fullness. The focus is on the central place of Jesus Christ within the action of God, which embraces the whole cosmos and human history, creation and redemption. We note in the text the absolute use of *Plerôma* and the additional emphatic adjective, "all."

Colossians 2: 9

The purpose of this deliberate emphasis on the person of Jesus Christ becomes clear when we come to the next text:

> See to it that no one takes you captive through philosophy and empty deceit, according to human tradition, according to the elemental spirits of the universe, and not according to Christ. For in him the whole fullness [Plerôma] of deity dwells bodily and you have come to fullness [verbal form] in him, who is the head of every ruler and authority.
>
> — Col 2: 8-10

The context is a series of warning. The tone of warning is a thread, which appears in 1: 23 and is taken up again in 1: 28 and runs through to 2: 8. This warning forms a frame since specific aspects of unacceptable conduct in the community are dealt with in detail (2: 16-23) after the writer has developed how Christ in whom the fullness of deity dwells is the source of fullness for the community (2: 9-15). Teachings which are influencing the community are referred to as popular bazaar teaching (philosophy) and empty deceit whose source is human reflection and a world-view of power which resides in celestial powers ("elemental spirits of the universe") which are supposed to rule human life.[9]

---

9. The meaning of the phrase "elementary spirits" is disputed. Dunn (*op. cit.*, 149-150) indicates how the normal meaning of elemental substance of which the cosmos was thought to be made could →

Before this passage the writer has also developed briefly the central place Christ has in God's plan for the human family with specific emphasis on his concern for the Gentiles. He has stated that "the mystery of God," namely God's hidden plan for human history culminates in Christ "in whom are hidden all the treasures of wisdom and knowledge" (Col 2: 2-3; 1: 27). Against this background we consider the statement that "the whole fullness of deity dwells in Christ bodily [in his humanity]." The writer is affirming that God has given his own fullness to Jesus who is both human and divine. Access to the divine is through Jesus Christ. He underlines the fact that the human Jesus is just what God is. Commenting on the use of the term *Plerôma* Delling states:

> The *Plerôma* [the text uses Greek] statements in Col. present the full unity of the work of God and Christ in such a way that the distinctness of person is preserved and yet monotheism is not imperilled. God works through Christ in His whole fullness (1: 19) and in his full deity (2: 9).[10]

Again the writer does not narrate the path on which Jesus had to travel and the quality of life he had to live to be faithful to this gift of divine fullness.

→ have already referred to heavenly bodies. The world-view behind a lot of astrology today would be akin to the probable meaning of the phrase. For this reason in this writing and in Ephesians there is a polemic against the power of these heavenly spirits referred to as "thrones, dominions, rulers, authorities" (Col 1: 16; 2: 10.15; Eph 1: 21; Rom 8: 38; 1 Cor 15: 24). These are more likely to be cosmic forces and could include at times human rulers. Paul and these writers want to affirm Christ's dominion over all powers, which can in any way influence human life and history. In consequence the believer does not need to pay any heed to the influence of these forces as they have been liberated from their influence by God and Jesus Christ (Col 1: 13; 2: 15.20).

10. Delling, 'Plerôma,' *TDNT*, p. 304.

The Path to Fullness for the Community

What is probably more important for our theme is the statement that the community "has come to fullness of life in union with him." He uses the perfect form of the verb *Plerôm* (to fill) from which verb is derived the noun *Plerôma*. Using various images of the ceremony of initiation into the community and the consequent transformation which has been effected (2: 11-15), the writer excludes a whole world of religious practices and rituals (2: 16-23). He proceeds to describe the genuine path to the realization of the initial gift of "fullness" and the promised total fullness (3: 1-17). He wants the community to become "mature in Christ" (1: 28). He uses the images of "put to death," "strip off," "get rid of" and "clothe yourself with" and describes a life caught up in the conflict between light and darkness (3: 5-17). He urges them to "set your mind on" and contrasts a way of life which is characterized by "things which are above" in contrast to "things that are on earth" (3: 2). I shall quote the whole passage, which describes the world of self-emptying and fullness.

> Put to death, therefore, whatever in you is earthly: fornication, impurity, passion, evil desire, and greed (which is idolatry). On account of these the wrath of God is coming on those who are disobedient. There are the ways you also once followed, when you were living that life. But now you must get rid of all such things — anger, wrath, malice, slander, and abusive language from your mouth. Do not lie to one another, seeing that you have stripped off the old self with its practices and have clothed yourselves in knowledge according to the image of its creator. In that renewal there is no longer Greek and Jew, circumcised and uncircumcised, barbarian and Scythian, slave and free; ***but Christ is all and in all.***

> As God's chosen ones, holy and beloved, clothe yourselves with compassion, kindness, humility, meekness, and patience. Bear with one another and if anyone has a complaint against another, forgive each other; just as the Lord has forgiven you, so you also must forgive. Above all, clothe yourselves with love, which binds everything together in perfect harmony. And let ***peace of Christ rule*** in your hearts, to which indeed you were called in the one body. And be thankful. Let the word of ***Christ dwell in you*** richly; teach and admonish one another in all wisdom and with gratitude in your hearts sing psalms, hymns and spiritual songs to God. And whatever you do, in word or deed, do everything in the name of the Lord Jesus, giving thanks to God the Father through him.
>
> — Col 3: 5-17

Christ as the Christian Maṇḍala

I am suggesting that in these passages Jesus Christ with the fullness of God is the Christian *maṇḍala*.[11] Presented before the believer he acts as the source of healing and wholeness. This is because he himself has confronted and conquered evil

---

11. I am using this idea within the background of the *maṇḍala* as "a symbolic diagram used in the performance of sacred rites and as an instrument of meditation. The *maṇḍala* is basically a representation of the universe, a consecrated area that serves as a receptacle for the gods and as a collection point of the universal forces. Man (the microcosm) by mentally "entering" the *maṇḍala* (a visual symbol of the macrocosm) and "proceeding" towards its centre, is by analogy guided through the cosmic processes of disintegration and reintegration." I would see Christ as a type of *vajra-dhātu* form which is representative of the many into one. *Maṇḍala* in *The New Encyclopedia Britannica* (Micropaedia) vol. VI, Chicago, 1980, pp. 555-56. Cf. also Peter Gaefke and E. Dale Sanders, *maṇḍala* in *The Encyclopedia of Religion*, ed. Mircea Eliade, vol. 9, Macmillian, New York, 1987, pp. 153-58. I am aware to an extent of the many differences.

in his life and especially in his death on the Cross and the fullness of God came to a visible and full flowering in his resurrection and glorification. The believer is to come to, to gaze upon, to see, to grow in knowledge of and to believe in Jesus Christ. In this way the believer journeys to wholeness. Jesus Christ is the source of reconciliation, peace, forgiveness and life.

Plerôma and the Community of Believers (Ephesians 3: 19, 4: 13 and 1: 23)

The texts we have considered concern the fullness of divinity which Christ in one sense had and yet acquired in his pilgrimage on earth especially through his death on the Cross. The resurrection, exultation or glorification are symbols of this fullness. Now we turn to texts that speak of the fullness gifted to the community of believers. We shall quote the first text which is a prayer and concerns the *Plerôma* of God and the believing community:

> For this reason I bow my knees before the Father, from whom every family in heaven and on earth takes its name. I pray that according to the riches of his glory, he may grant that you may be strengthened in your inner being with power through ***his Spirit*** and that ***Christ may dwell in your hearts*** through faith, as you are being rooted and grounded in love. I pray that you may have the power to comprehend with all the saints, what is the breadth and length and height and depth, and to know that love of Christ what surpasses knowledge, so that you may be filled ***with all the fullness*** [*Plerôma*] ***of God***.
>
> — Eph 3: 14-19

We could say that, within the language world of the writers of Colossians and Ephesians, this text describes the final outcome of the contemplation of the Christian *maṇḍala*.

The writer enumerates a series of gifts, which he wants to flow from the Father and the riches of his glory (vital being). The dwelling of the Spirit in the inner world of the believers is to strengthen them with life-giving and sustaining power. Christ is to dwell at the depth of their being (hearts) and they are to live, rooted and grounded in the mystery of God's love (or love for God). There are three final gifts, the comprehension of the unsearchable riches of God and his universal plan and commitment as expressed in Christ (cf. 3: 8.6.9-11), the knowledge of the unfathomable love of Christ which is the expression of the Father's love. The ultimate consequence of all these gifts and the final gift is that the believer be filled with (unto) all the fullness of God (*Plerôma*) namely the totality of what God can communicate and share with the human. The Spirit's presence and Christ's indwelling are not just aspects of this but other expressions of this same reality.

Believer to Grow to the Fullness of Christ — Ephesians 4: 13

The following text is also concerned with the effects on believers of union with Christ. The total text will give a sense of the context and the argument of the writer.

> I therefore, the prisoner in the Lord, beg you to lead a life worthy of the calling to which you have been called. With all humility and gentleness, with patience, bearing with one another in love, make every effort to maintain the unity of the Spirit in the bond of peace. There is only one body and one Spirit, just you were called to the one hope of your calling, one Lord, one faith, one baptism, one God and Father of all, who is above all and through all and in all.
>
> But each of us was given grace according to the measure of Christ's gift. Therefore it is said: "When he ascended on high he made captivity itself a captive; he gave gifts to his

> people." (When it says, "He ascended," what does it mean but that he had also descended into the lower parts of the earth? He who descended is the same one who ascended far above all the heavens, ***so that he might fill all things***.)
>
> The gifts he gave were that some would be apostles, some prophets, some evangelists, some pastors and teachers, to equip the saint for the work of ministry, for building up the body of Christ, until all of us come to the unity of the faith and of the knowledge of the Son of God, to maturity, to the measure of the stature ***of the fullness* [*Plerôma*] *of Christ***. [Another translation could be: to the age in which we are filled to receive the fullness of Christ/or the full stature of Christ].
>
> We must no longer be children tossed to and fro and blown about by every wind of doctrine, by people's trickery, by their craftiness in deceitful scheming. But speaking the truth in love, we must grow up in every way into him who is ***the head***, into Christ, from whom the whole body joined and knit together by every ligament with which it is equipped, as each part is working properly, promotes the body's growth in building itself up in love.
>
> — Eph 4: 1-16

Within his very long exhortation to appropriate behaviour (4: 1-6: 20), the writer first addresses himself to the problem of unity, listing essential virtues and describing the foundations of this unity (4: 1-6). The unity is endangered not only by the diversity of gifts of leadership but more specifically by the divisive nature of the teaching of some and the lack of orthodoxy.

In a few words and in a picturesque way the writer summarizes the story of Jesus' life, his descent with special emphasis on his death (into the lower parts of the earth) and his ascent which symbolized his victory over all enemies and his universal Lordship (fill all things [4: 8-10]). This Christ has endowed his community with gifts of leadership. He enumerates four goals in the exercise of the service of leadership: unity of faith (unity created by faith), the knowledge of the Son of God (experiential knowledge) and maturity to become a full-grown person. The final goal is that measure of maturity (inner growth) that the community may possess the fullness (*Plerôma*) that belongs to Christ.

Briefly describing the problem in explicit terms (children tossed to and fro . . . .) he states the essential characteristic of teaching as "speaking the truth in love." The goal is described by means of the metaphor of the head and body and the healthy growth and profound unity proper to the body based ultimately on love. This is another way of speaking of the "measure of maturity of the fullness of Christ." The term "head" is another symbol of fullness.

With much detail and at greater length than the writer of Colossians, this author addresses the problem of the conflict between evil and good in the life of believers. With various images he returns to description of a way of life dominated by ignorance and evil and the opposing way of life dominated by union with Christ and new attitudes and behaviour. Christ is again the *maṇḍala* who enables people to journey from evil to ever greater goodness and fullness.

The Church to share in the Fullness of Christ, its Head — Ephesians 1: 23

The final text in which our term occurs is found at the beginning of this letter. We will again give the larger text, another of the writer's prayers.

> I have heard of your faith in the Lord Jesus and your love toward all the saints, and for this reason I do not cease to give thanks for you as I remember you in my prayers. I pray

> that the God of our Lord Jesus Christ, the Father of glory, may give you a spirit of wisdom and revelation as you come to know him, so that, with the eyes of your heart enlightened, you may know what is the hope to which he has called you, what are the riches of his glorious inheritance among the saints, and what is the immeasurable greatness of his power for us who believe, according to the working of his great power. God put this power to work in Christ when he raised him from the dead and ***seated him at his right hand*** in the heavenly places, far above all rule and authority and power and dominion, and above every name that is named, not only in this age but also in the age to come. And ***he put all things under his feet*** and has made him ***the head over all things*** for the Church, which is his body, ***the fullness (Plerôma) of him (filled by him) who fills all in every way.***
>
> — Eph 1: 15-23

The writer prays that the experience of God be accompanied by life-giving insight with the result that the "eyes of the heart" be permanently enlightened. The fruit of this enlightenment is a type of "knowledge." He lists the interrelated aspects of this knowledge:

(a) the hope at the heart of their being chosen as God's people (your calling);

(b) the riches of the divine inheritance promised to the saints;

(c) the immeasurable greatness of God's power which is at work in believers.

The measure of this great power is its manifestations. Therefore he describes the manifestations of this immeasurable and transformative power. They are:

(a) the resurrection of Christ from the dead;

(b) God's seating him at his right hand in the highest

heaven (This is the symbol of total sovereignty over all cosmic powers, whatever they be, both in the present and the future. He shares in God's own absolute dominion.)

(c) God's placing all things under his feet, another symbol of absolute sovereignty;

(d) God making Christ head over all things, another figurative expression of absolute sovereignty.

Finally the writer now spells out the relationship between this Christ and the community of believers, the Church. The symbol of "head" leads him to describe this community as the "body" of which Christ in glory is the Head (Eph 1: 10 [verbal expression]; 4: 15; 5: 23; Col 1: 18). This leads him to use another figure to describe this relationship, namely the *Plerôma* with the sense of the Church sharing in the fullness of Christ who is described as the one "who fills all things in all possible ways." He takes up again the repeated images of absolute sovereignty which are other expressions of fullness. The Church is filled with all the presence, power, riches and activity of Christ. The head is the source of life to the body and the power that dominates and guides and promotes the unity of the body.

The text both describes the nature of the community of believers filled with the power of Christ and also indicates the pilgrimage to which the community is called. We saw this in 4: 13 more explicitly, less explicitly in 3: 19. The implications of the continuous pilgrimage "to become what it is" are spelt out with much detail in the long exhortation 4: 1-6: 20. The community is assured of the power of Christ accompanying it in this journey.

With this we have surveyed the few significant texts in Christian foundational writings which use the term *Plerôma.*

Were we to pay greater attention to these texts and the whole writing in which they occur we would note other expressions of this same idea of ultimacy and fullness using other symbols. We turn to one text in particular and to some other symbols mainly in the writings of Paul.

The Writings of Paul
The Choice of Emptiness — Gift of Fullness

We turn now to Paul's own letters. The term *Plerôma* does not occur in the sense that we have been studying. However, he has other ways to describe the fullness of Christ. More importantly he traces for us the journey of Jesus to the gift of fullness from the Father. There is an underlying pattern in Paul's basic story of Jesus. It begins with the choice of emptiness and concludes with the affirmation of the gift of fullness from God and the overflow of his fullness to whoever in the human community open themselves to this mystery of God's love. The "narrative" of Jesus journey in Paul's writings is very brief with the focus on his entrance into human history and solidarity with the sinfulness of this situation. This solidarity comes to its most graphic expression in his death. His resurrection and lordship and the outpouring of the Spirit give expression to his fullness. We shall quote the most concise textual expression and then examine some texts. Paul writes to a rather wealthy community who are tight fisted and reluctant to participate in a collection for the poor in the communities in Jerusalem. The major basis for generosity is the life of Jesus Christ. He writes:

> For you know the generous act of our Lord Jesus Christ, that though ***he was rich***, yet for your sake ***he became poor***, so that by ***his poverty you*** might become ***rich***.
>
> — 1 Corinthians 8: 9

In this figurative manner Paul summarizes a central insight. By the phrases "he became poor" and "his poverty" he refers to Jesus' becoming human, the quality of human solidarity and his death. There are a series of other texts that highlight one or other aspects of this story. We shall list them and then study a major text. The important texts are:

> But when the fullness (a use of Plerôma) of time had come, God sent his own Son, ***born of woman, born under the Law*** (in a slave state), in order ***to redeem those who were under the Law*** (in a slave state 4: 3.7.8-9), so that ***we might receive adoption as children*** (sons). . . . So you are no longer a slave but a child (son) and if a child then also an heir, through God (Gal 4: 4-5.7).

> ***Christ*** redeemed us from the curse of the law ***by becoming a curse for us*** — for it is written, "Cursed is everyone who hangs on a tree" (Cross) — in order that in Christ Jesus the blessing of Abraham might come to the Gentiles, so that ***we might receive the promise of the Spirit*** through faith (Gal 3: 13-14). [This text is complicated because of the allusions to themes in the Jewish scriptures].

> All this is from God, who reconciled us to himself through Christ and has given us the ministry of reconciliation; that is, in Christ God was reconciling the world to himself, not counting their trespasses against them, and entrusting the message of reconciliation to us. So we are ambassadors for Christ, since God is making his appeal through us; we entreat you on behalf of Christ, be reconciled to God. For our sake ***he made him to be sin*** who ***knew no sin***, so that in him ***we*** might become the ***righteousness of God*** (2 Corinthians 5: 18-21).

> For God has done what the law, weakened by the flesh, [the human under the power of sin] could not do: by sending ***his own Son in the likeness of sinful flesh*** and to deal with

> sin, he condemned sin in the flesh, so that the just requirements of the law might be fulfilled ***in us***, [we may be obedient to God's law] who walk not according to the flesh but ***according to the Spirit*** [The gift given by God through Jesus Christ who died and was raised].

In each of these texts the solidarity of Jesus — the Son of God — with the human situation and his emptiness are stated in various apt figurative ways according to the contexts. Normally this is related to his death. His resurrection — exaltation, namely his consequent fullness and his prior obedience are not mentioned in these texts. The effects of his solidarity with the human family, namely various types of fullness, are also stated, again in ways appropriate to the context and the writer's argument.

These texts could be graphically illustrated by means of the *mandorla*. The *mandorla* is constructed by two circles that intercept and form an almond shape. The most perfect *mandorla* is when the two circles perfectly overlap and become one circle. One circle would represent the person of Jesus, the archetype of goodness and the other circle would represent universal human evil. By fully immersing himself into the situation of human evil and yet remaining totally good, as the person totally obedient to God his Father, he transforms evil into goodness. His fullness enables him to identify so radically with evil and at the same time transform evil into good and create a new type of fullness for the human family. There is here the paradigm of paradox.

The Classical Text — Emptiness to Fullness — Phil 2: 6-11

We turn now to a classical text that focuses only on the journey of Jesus Christ to fullness. We quote the hymnic text in full.

> Let the same mind be in you that was in Christ Jesus,

who, though he was in ***the form of God***
did not regard equality with God
as something to be exploited
but ***emptied himself*** taking ***the form of a slave***
being born of human likeness.

And being found in human form,
he humbled himself
and became obedient to the point of death —
even the death on a cross.
Therefore God also ***highly exalted him***
and ***gave him*** the ***name that is above every name,***
so that in the name of Jesus every knee should bend
in heaven and on earth and under the earth,
and every tongue should confess
that Jesus Christ is ***Lord,***
to the glory of God the Father

— Philippians 2: 6-11

This is a classical text.[12] We note the two major parts, the second beginning with "therefore" and describing with specific images God's response to the decisions of Jesus Christ. In the first part we have two stages in the process of emptying. The stark contrast between "form of God" and "form of slave" vividly describes the decisive journey of the one who was like God. Two contrasting verbs also express this extraordinary decision, "exploit" and "empty." The decision not to exploit but to empty explain each other. Being human is not stated to be a negative reality. The second stage in the process of self-

---

12. I wish to only mention here a book in which the *kenosis* (emptying) of the Son is studied in dialogue with some Buddhist scholars. Donald W. Mitchell, *Spirituality and Emptiness. The Dynamics of Spiritual Life in Buddhism and Christianity*, Mahwah, Paulist Press, 1991. I have not incorporated ideas from the author into this written paper.

emptying focuses on one moment in Jesus' life. The major verb is "he humbled himself" and this comes to expression in obedience, that obedience which is related to the acceptance of death, and even that specific form of death involved in crucification. This form of death was most humiliating and degrading of the human person. The writer draws our attention to the inner world of Jesus and to his inner relationship to God.

The consequent description of gifted fullness is very vivid. God "super-exalts" the obedient man. This is spelt out in terms of the gift of a unique name indicative of universal [note the use of "every"] sovereignty that is acknowledged by the whole universe in court like fashion (profound bow and acclamation). The name that expresses this fullness is *Lord,* the name, which that religious tradition reserved for God alone.

A Path for the Believer

The fruitfulness of this life for the community is not elaborated except in the exhortation to a life of renunciation of the self. Paul writes:

> Do nothing from selfish ambition or conceit, but in humility regard others as better than yourselves. Let each of you look not to your own interests, but to the interests of others. . . .
>
> — 2: 3-4

He also traces the journey of his life with his eyes fixed on this Lord who finally will transform all the believers (Philippians, 3: 12-14.20-21).

Paul's Narrative of Jesus' Life

There are a whole series of other texts that implicitly presume the fullness gifted to Christ as a consequence of his life's journey marked by love and obedience and crowned in his death. I will not treat the texts in detail. However, before enumerating these texts I shall briefly describe the fundamental framework of the story of Jesus which Paul tells in various ways.

At the origin and end of the story is God, called the Father of our Lord Jesus Christ, who through out human history has interacted with the human family. The Jewish account of these interactions forms the background for the particular story of the one Jew, Jesus of Nazareth. God who always acts and reveals his Self through mediators/mediations is the great "actor" who achieves his purpose "by," "in" or "through" Jesus Christ. The key event in the life of Jesus is his death and resurrection. Jesus' key and essential attitude is obedience to God and love for others. The world into which Jesus is sent and with which he must be in solidarity is the human family and the cosmos under the power of Sin and Death and destined to condemnation and total death. Sin and Death are personified as universal, destructive and unconquerable powers that enslave the whole human family unless God acts. He describes the human person with the term "flesh" when he wishes to speak of the domination of Sin over the human.

Other Expressions of Fullness

Paul describes the fullness gifted by God to Christ with various symbolic expressions. The indwelling *Plerôma* of God in Jesus Christ is one such expression. There are many others. God makes Jesus Christ "the Son of God in power" (Romans 1: 4), confers on him the most distinguished name of Lord (Philippians 2: 9) and places him at his own right hand with all things subject to him (Romans 8: 34; 1 Corinthians 15: 25). God made him a "life giving spirit" and gifts the Spirit through him (1 Corinthians 15: 45; Romans 8: 2. 9; 2 Corinthians 1: 21). He gives the exhaustive expression of his own love in and through Jesus Christ (Romans 8: 39; 5: 8) who is the second

Adam (1 Corinthians 15: 21-21.45). The Son of God, Jesus Christ is the "yes" of God to all his promises (2 Corinthians 1: 20) and the very glory of God is to be seen in his face as he is the very image of God (2 Corinthians 4: 5-6). God reconciles all things to himself in Christ who is the source of the new creation (2 Corinthians 5: 18; Galatians 6: 15). The fullness of Christ is related to the victory of God over Evil and the transformation of the human race.

Paul uses many images from various socio-religious backgrounds to describe this victory of God and the transformation he effects through Jesus Christ in his death and resurrection. The inner reality of these effects is expressed in a temporal manner, namely as "already" in existence and as "not yet" in existence. The believer to be in the "already" state and to journey to the "not yet" state and receive the gift of the "not yet" must be united to Jesus Christ, be accompanied by him and empowered by His Spirit. The purpose of the believer's life's journey is to become who Jesus Christ has become. The loss of the self could be one description of "faith which energizes and expresses itself in love" (Gal 5: 6).

Paul describes the transforming activity of God in and through Jesus Christ in so many ways. He tells of God as justifying, redeeming, sanctifying, reconciling, recreating, bringing from death to life, bestowing the gift of being a child of God (adopted son), pouring his Spirit into the inner core of the believer's being, conforming believers to the image of the Son, making believers temples for his presence and his Spirit's presence, making them his own. . . . All these descriptions of recreation are indications of the fullness of Christ. The final destiny of the believer is to share as fully as possible in the Sonship of Jesus Christ, raised and glorified, restored fully to the image and likeness of God. There is a long journey, which is to be marked by obedience, love and hope. One of Paul's famous summaries of the *sādhanā* of the believer's life is expressed in terms of "faith which is coming to continuous expression through love" (Gal 5: 6).

There are other texts, which give expression to the fullness of Christ. Paul describes the risen Christ as the new Adam who is the source of life and not death for all (1 Cor 15: 21-23 and 45-49). Using an agricultural image he calls him the first fruits of the human community's journey to fullness (1 Corinthians 15: 23). He also describes him as having dominion over every evil power, including death (1 Corinthians 15: 25-26).

Another Writing and Ways of Describing Fullness

As the final part of this study we turn to a writing which pretends to be a letter and is really an extended "word of exhortation" (Hebrews 13: 22). This author uses two main descriptions of Jesus Christ to give expression to the quality of the person at the end of his journey, namely Son of God and High Priest. He also underlines his solidarity with the human community in graphic and moving ways (Heb 2: 1-18. 5: 5-10). I shall quote and comment on a few major texts.

> Long ago God spoke to our ancestors in many and various ways by the prophets, but in these last days he has spoken to us by ***a Son***, whom he appointed ***heir of all things***, through whom he also created the worlds. He is the ***reflection of God's glory and the exact imprint of God's very being***, and he sustains all things by his powerful word. When he had made purification for sins, ***he sat down at the right hand of the Majesty*** on high, having become as much superior to angels as the name he has inherited is more excellent than theirs. For to which of the angels did God ever say, "You are ***my Son***; today I have begotten you"? Or again, "I will be his Father, and he will be my Son"? (Hebrews 1: 1-5)

The writing opens with this rich and overloaded praise of the Son. Using various images he underlines the idea of fullness or the ultimate role of Jesus Christ. He is "heir of all things" and both the reflection and imprint of God's very being. He is partner to God both in creation itself and in the process of sustaining the whole universe. Again we find the image of the Son at the right hand of God. The writer tells the story of Jesus Christ both prior to his becoming like his brothers and sisters in all things (2: 17) and the story of the Son at the end of his journey when he re-enters, as it were, into God's presence. He is the reflection and imprint of God both prior to his human life and at the end of this human life. In this text we have rich expressions of fullness. This fullness is inseparable from the painful journey of suffering and obedience.

Jesus Christ enters God's presence in this writing as the High Priest. We shall not develop the Jewish background of the special sacrificial role of the High Priest once a year in the Temple, which forms the background of the image. We shall just look at pieces from larger text units, which have vivid and different ways of describing his fullness. He tells the story of his life. It comes to its climax when he is made perfect and consequently remains the source of life to others.

> In the days of his flesh, Jesus offered up prayers and supplications, with loud cries and tears, to the one who was able to save him from death, and he was heard because of his reverent submission. Although he was a Son, he learned obedience through what he suffered; and ***having been made perfect***, he became the source of eternal salvation for all who obey him (Heb 5: 7-9)

He emphasizes the once fzor all nature of Jesus' self sacrifice and its universal significance. These are strange ways to describe the reality implied in the use of *Plerôma*:

> And every priest stands day after day at his service, offering again and again the same sacrifices that can never take away sins. But when Christ had offered ***for all time a single sacrifice*** for sins, ***he sat down at the right hand of God,*** and since then has been waiting "until his enemies would be made a footstool for his feet." For by a ***single offering*** he has perfected ***for all time*** those who are sanctified.
>
> — Heb 10: 11-14

He underlines the fact that Christ entered into the very presence of God, a spatial image, and that he offered himself once for all, a temporal image. This is coupled with another temporal image which refers to the fullness of time, namely the end of the age. The whole purpose of this life was to be a sacrifice for sin for the many, namely for all according to Greek usage. Possessing the gift of fullness he is then at the end of all time the source of ultimate salvation for all who wait for him.

> For Christ did not enter a sanctuary made by human hands, a mere copy of the true one, but he entered into heaven itself, now to appear in the presence of God on our behalf. Nor was it to offer himself again and again, as the high priest enters the Holy Place year after year with blood that is not his own; for then he would have had to suffer again and again since the foundation of the world. But as it is, he has appeared ***once for all at the end of the age*** to remove sin by the sacrifice of himself. And just as it is appointed for mortals to die once, and after that the judgment, so Christ, having been offered once to bear the sins of many, will appear a second time, not to deal with sin, but to save those who are eagerly waiting for him.
>
> — Heb 9: 24-28

So we conclude this study with this strange world of imagery used in the background of Jewish sacrificial practice, of a major Jewish festival and a key figure in the religious world, the

High Priest. Journeying to fullness Jesus Christ as High Priest becomes the source of fullness to others in ways comparable to the thought of the writer of Colossians and Ephesians.

Plerôma defines the very being of God and of His Word and the Son. It is God's gift to Jesus of Nazareth at the end of his journey, lived in faith, which came to its climax in obedient love at his death. In his resurrection and exaltation God made him Lord, and Son of God in power. He is seated at God's right hand and filled with all the *Plerôma* of God. He remains the goal of the life of believers who are called to live and journey to fullness. They must follow Jesus Christ in ever growing emptiness of their self — accompanied and empowered by the Holy Spirit so that God Father may gift them with the *Plerôma* of Christ and therefore the *Plerôma* of God himself.

References

Delling G., *Plerôma* in *Theological Dictionary of the New Testament*, ed. G. Friedrich (tr. and ed. G.W. Bromiley), vol. VI, 1971, Grand Rapids: Wm. E. Eerdmans, pp. 298-305.

Dunn J.D.G., *The Epistles to the Colossians and to Philemon*, Grand Rapids: Wm. E. Eerdmans, 1996, pp. 100-01.

Ernst J., *Pleroma und Pleroma Christi*, Geschichte und Deutung eines Begriffs der paulinischen Antilegomena, Regensburg: Pustet, 1970.

Gaefke P., and Sanders Dale E., *Maṇḍalas* in *The Encyclopedia of Religion*, ed. Mircea Eliade, vol. 9, New York: Macmillian, 1987, pp. 153-58.

Lampe, G.W.H., *A Patristic Greek Lexicon*, Oxford: Clarendon Press, 1961-69, pp. 1094-95.

Liddel, H.G., Scott R., Stuart Jones H., *A Greek English Lexicon*, vol. II, Oxford: Clarendon Press, 1940, pp. 1420-21.

Lohse, E., *A Commentary on the Epistles to the Colossians and to Philemon*, Philadelphia: Fortress Press, 1971, pp. 57-58.

Mitchell D.W., *Spirituality and Emptiness,* The Dynamics of Spiritual Life in Buddhism and Christianity: Mahwah, Paulist Press, 1991.

Schippers, R., *Plerôma* in *Dictionary of New Testament Theology*, ed. C. Brown, vol. I, Exeter: Paternoster Press, 1975, pp. 733-41.

Schnackenburg, R., *The Gospel According to John*, London: Burns & Oates, vol. I, 1968, p. 275.

Thayer, J.H., *A Greek-English Lexicon of the New Testament*, 4th edn., Edinburgh: T.T. Clark, 1896.

Maṇḍala in *The New Encyclopedia Britannica* (Micropaedia), vol. VI, Chicago, 1980, pp. 555-56.

Abbreviations of New Testament Texts

Col	Colossians
Cor	Corinthians (1st and 2nd Letter)
Eph	Ephesians
Gal	Galatians
Heb	Letter to the Hebrews
Jn / John	Gospel of St. John
Phil	Philippians
Rom	Romans

5

Emptiness
Philosophy and Spirituality

Geshe Ngawang Samten

MANY pious persons believe that metaphysical study has nothing to do with spirituality, and most scientists say that metaphysical search undermines religious beliefs. Their assumptions have over the time, unfortunately, become axiomatic. But the Buddha ruled out opportunity of liberation for any one who neglects metaphysical investigation.

The entire enterprise of spirituality in Buddhism is oriented toward eliminating the defilements which are constituted by afflictive emotions. These emotions are rooted in the view that holds things to exist contrary to the way they do in reality. If we do not go to the foundational level, all the other approaches to achieve perpetual tranquillity or peace remain superficial endeavours. The Buddha and later *ācārya*s have emphatically stated that even though the virtuous actions — physical, vocal and mental — not associated with the refined view resulting from analytical insight into reality are meritorious and consequently alleviate suffering, they are by themselves mere palliative measures. Therefore, ontological speculation is mandatory for developing the insight which penetrates into the very ultimate nature of phenomena. Thus Ācārya Vasubandu says:

> Apart from the discernment of the *dharmas*, there is no means to extinguish the defilements, and it is by reason of the defilements that the beings wander in the ocean of cyclic existence. So it is with a view to this discernment that the Abhidharma has been taught by the Master.[1]

In Buddhism, soteriology and philosophy are inextricably intertwined fundamental strands. Each is incomplete without the other. Ārya Deva aptly puts the fact in his *Catuḥśataka:*

> Delusions pervade into every thing, just as the physical sense pervades the body; hence by conquering delusions, all afflictions are also conquered. When depending arising is realised, delusion does not arise; hence all efforts herein are only to explain that message.[2]

Striking a note of caution referring the above citation, Ācārya Tsonkhapa, who represents the Tibetan frame of mind, which potrays the heritage of the Indian Buddhist masters transmitted and received by the Tibetans with great integrity, reflects:

> Therefore, all the reasonings of the central way are factors of the eradication of the habit-pattern of misknowledge (*avidyā-dr̥ṣṭi*), the root of the cyclic existence. Hence, having identified how our own innate misknowledge (*sahajāvidyā*) maintains its hold, we should strive to terminate it, and should not amuse ourselves with expertise in mere hair-splitting with other philosophers.[3]

---

1. *Abhidharmakośakārikā*, 1: 3.
2. Here I follow the translation of Robert Thurman: Tsongkhapa, *The Speech of Gold: Reason and Enlightenment in the Tibetan Buddhism.* Delhi: Motilal Banarsidass, 1989, p. 310.
3. *Op. cit.*

Ācārya Candrakīrti emphasizes in his *Mādhyamakāvatāra* the reason why Ācārya Nāgārjuna exercises philosophical investigations in *Mūlamādhymakakārikā* and other treatises.

> (Ācārya Nāgārjuna) did not execute analysis in the treatise out of attachment for debate, but taught the fact in order to liberate (sentient beings).[4]

The primary ontological propositions apropos transience, and the inherent nonexistence of life and world, are the substrata of an entire complex structure of spirituality; and at the same time, elimination of suffering through extinguishing the defilements of mind, the fundamental characteristic of spirituality is, in turn, the substratum of the entire edifice of philosophy. This is because the process of self-purification is nothing but to disencumber oneself from the bondage of afflictive mind which is ultimately rooted in ignorance that, owing to its layers, projects fabricated nature on to self and world. This further occasions all the afflictive emotions which induce negative actions and finally results in suffering. This process is the set of cause and effect, the first two of the four noble truths, pertaining to involvement in *saṁsāra* — the truths of suffering and the truth of the origin of suffering. On the other hand, the two later truths, the truth of cessation and the truth of path can only be realized when, at the ground level, the correct view is ascertained through philosophical analysis, which eventually entails liberation from suffering by ceasing its causes through the practice of the path.

According to Buddhism, suffering is wider and deeper than is commonly understood. Not only are pain and unhappiness suffering, but transitory happiness, like enjoying a luxurious life, is also suffering, since the latter cannot necessarily occasion joy and often brings unhappiness.

4. Chapter VI, V. no. 118, Poussin ed., p. 231.

Moreover, whatever trivial and mundane joy there is inevitably changes into suffering. For example, swimming and sunbathing are regarded as pleasure but both turn into unhappiness when they go beyond a certain limit. If they were really in themselves sources of happiness people would enjoy them all the time, but this is not the case. We conclude that these objects are not *intrinsically* sources of happiness but instead are found pleasant in certain circumstances depending on our craving. Sometimes, something which is a source of great joy for some one becomes a source of displeasure for the same person. Such mundane joys therefore become suffering at some point.

The deepest sense of "suffering" is the contaminated aggregates of beings, which are originated from contaminated mind and actions and whose mere existence is conducive to further unhappiness. According to Buddhism, the psychophysical aggregates of unenlightened beings are vulnerable. Unless we care and protect our aggregates all the time they are susceptible to pain and agony, and even if we are constantly vigilant, there is much pain we cannot forestall. It is because the psychophysical aggregates are intrinsically contaminated as they are the products of contaminated actions induced by afflictive mind. The unwholesome physical and vocal actions are, of course, induced by negative mental forces: primarily attachment, hatred and ignorance. Even the wholesome actions of common beings are contaminated since they are grounded on ignorance, the misperception of reality. This is an important element in Buddhist philosophy. In order to bring about a radical change in the continuum of these aggregates that can free them from this contamination, efforts are made to free the present mind from contamination. The contamination is nothing but the afflictive mental states.

If we observe carefully our own and other lives revolving around us, we will instantly notice that there are constant conflicts, strives, and frictions. Mostly these are not visible outside; they remain suppressed and concealed within. However, these inner warfares are responsible for creating all ideological combat, family disputes, cold wars and world wars. We only notice conflicts and wars outside, but rarely know their origin. Most of us, in fact, falsely believe that conflicts and wars exist only at the physical level. We often rule out a possibility of another existence at a subtler level. As a result, even the origin of all the psychological and emotional conflicts have to be necessarily located on the physical and vocal level.

The Buddha, however, was diametrically opposed to this. More than 2500 years back, he proclaimed that all the miseries are originated at the mental level, and at the heart of all psychological and emotional conflicts there lies the fundamental misconception of reality. Being grounded on this, each and every one of us innately treats one's own self as the most important. Almost everything that we do is directly or indirectly directed towards quenching this selfish thirst.

The fundamental misconception with regard to the notion of self (*ātmā*) is considered to be the primary hindrance to comprehending reality as it permeates every domain of our cognition and distorts comprehension of the true mode of existence of object. In terms of the modes of influence, it is important to understand both forms of the notion of self or self grasping: the innate-self-grasping (*sahaja ātmagrāha*) and the intellectually-constructed-self-grasping (*parikalpita ātmagrāha*). The innate-self-grasping is not developed in this life; rather it is there right from birth continuing from the previous lives, or at least, is innate. But the intellectually-constructed-self-grasping is a conceptual elaboration of this more basic, instinctive self-grasping and strengthens it through its articulation in theories and dogmas.

Because the latter is strongly grounded in the former, every philosophical development and proposition advanced in this direction is governed by the innate self grasping and is manifestation of the former. Therefore, even if the intellectually developed self-grasping is severed, it does not reduce the innate self-grasping notion. For instance, even if the self-sufficient, substantial self, which is held as the inner agent "soul," construed as different from aggregates, is found non-existent and one subsequently meditates on it, the innate presumption of reality is not in the slightest reduced. Thus, so long as the self-grasping of the aggregates exists, there is no way to eliminate the afflictive emotions, desire and the like. Candrakīrti states in *Mādhyamakāvatāra*:

> When you understand selflessness through your practice, you do not realise the ultimate reality of form, etc. Greed, therefore, initiated on perception of form, will still arise, since you have not realised the ultimate nature of those objects.[5]

Ācārya Nāgārjuna highlights this point in his *Yuktiṣaṣṭikā,* which is hermeneutically traced back by Ācārya Candrakīrti:

> What could stop the great poison of affliction in those whose minds have the place? Even when they are in an indifferent state, they will be seized by the snake of affliction.[6]

Candrakīrti recapitulates the above statement in his commentary:

---

5. Chapter VI, V. no. 131, Poussin ed., p. 253.

6. *Yuktiṣaṣṭikā* verse: 52.

> It is completely impossible to eliminate affliction for those who, although they want to do so, still perceive an intrinsic reality in forms, etc.[7]

Holding to intrinsically identifiable real existence, which is concluded through an analysis of the meaning of conventional expression, is not the innate self-grasping, as it is arrived at through intellectual assumptions. It is the innate self-grasping which binds living beings in cyclic existence, and which therefore philosophical reasoning must principally refute. The innate self-grasping holds to the reality of internal and external things as if they existed in their own right, rather than merely established on the power of convention. When such self-grasping holds persons such as "Devadatta" in that way, it is called "personal self-grasping" and when it holds things such as "eyes" and "ears" in that way, it is called "phenomenal self-grasping." Thus, the two selves also can be understood not as different in terms of intrinsic nature, but different with reference to the objects involved. Candrakīrti explains this in his commentary on *Catuḥśataka:*

> As for "self," it is a characteristic of things that is not dependent on anything else. Its non-existence is selflessness. Selflessness again is understood as twofold because of the distinction between person and phenomena; namely personal selflessness and phenomenal selflessness.[8]

Although this innate self-grasping does not hold objects in this way as a consequence of analysis of the meaning of expressions, if the objects thus held were to exist in fact, they would have to be discoverable by the analytic cognition and reasoning which analyse the mode of existence of the referents

7. Thurman: 1989 p. 303.

8. I follow Thurman's translation with alteration in the definition of "self."

of conventional expressions. Therefore, one should not adhere to the notion that Sūtras and Śāstras negate only the intellectual self-grasping, in that they comprehensively apply an analytic approach. Rather their primary target of negation is innate self-grasping and its *object*. Although the intellectually constructed one is still secondary, since it fortifies the innate one, to attack it is the initial step.

The self-grasping about things is the seed of cyclic existence, and its abandonment requires the realization of selflessness, which itself is the realization of the intrinsic unreality of things. Therefore, actual holding to the truth of personal and phenomenal things is the afflictive misconception (*kliṣṭa avidyā*).

Candrakīrti clearly explicates the holding of things as truth to be afflictive misconception — the first of the twelve links of dependent origination — in his commentary to *Catuḥśataka*:

> Consciousness, attached to things under the influence of afflictive misconception which causes excess reification of intrinsic reality in things is the seed of the cyclic process. And, when it entirely ceases, it is established that cyclic existence ceases.[9]

Should we observe carefully, and closely analyse the existence of "I," it is sure that there cannot be any substantial entity apart from mere designation on the basis of the five psychophysical aggregates. We can do the most scientific experiment available employing sophisticated equipment, we can slice and dissect every part into pieces to see if there is any so-called "I," hidden somewhere in a mysterious place, if we like. Nor do any of the mental aggregates have the entity postulated as the self. The experiments performed over many

---

9. Commentary of *Catuḥśataka*, XIV, verse: 25.

centuries in this field have decisively proven that there is no independent thing called "I" that we grasp anywhere within these five aggregates. If we pin down each of these five aggregates in search of the so-called "I," everything falls apart like a sand castle.

Some consider the self or "I" to be the aggregates themselves; some consider the self to be a part of the aggregates; and some take it to be only the single aggregate or a form or mind. Suppose self is analogous to the psychophysical aggregates, then there would have to be plurality of selves, for there are many aggregates. Self or "I" is not a composite of five aggregates, for we grasp "I" as a singular unit existing by virtue of its own character. The self is not analogous to the shape of the psychophysical aggregates, for shape is only associated with form, which implies that the other aggregates, like sensations, could not be equated with the self, because they are not associated with any shape. The self is not form, nor does the self possess form. The self is not "in" form, and form is not "in" the self. All five aggregates have to be understood from these four alternatives.

In short, the nature of self or "I" is not unlike a table in this respect. We do not consider a table to be different from its own parts, nor to be identical with its parts, nor to be in possession of its parts, nor is the table "in" the parts, nor are the parts "in" table, nor is the table the mere composite of its parts, nor is the table the shape of those parts.

Therefore, the self or "I" does not exist in the way we generally suppose. The self is empty of its essential existence. It does not have a self-sufficient existence. Just as a table is simply designated on the basis of its parts, so is the self or "I" merely designated on the basis of these five psychophysical aggregates. Nothing more, nothing less. Thus, Mādhyamikas claim that not only self but all entities whatsoever are empty of any intrinsic reality at the ultimate level. Hence, emptiness of true existence is advocated as the fundamental mode of existence and reality. Moreover, its perception at the direct experiential level has tremendous therapeutic value. Not only does it heal emotional and psychological problems but it releases us from the clutches of every miserable bondage including passionate obsession, obsessive aversion and obsessive ignorance.

If all things are empty, does it mean that they do not exist at all? Does it mean that Mādhyamika philosophers are adopting a nihilistic approach? From the Mādhyamika perspective, the answer is certainly "no." Though all things are empty from the ultimate analytical perspective, things definitely exist conventionally. Since the existence of things remains unproven according to any of the ultimate analysis, it is merely designated. We can conclude thus, that everything lacks self-defining characteristics governing its existence. They all exist, but simply nominally.

Every entity of inner and external world is labelled for conventional identification. The name "table," for example, is designated as referring to a substance which has a top and supporting legs. Beyond that convention, there is no relation between the name and the object; and the value of this relation is limited to the identification of the object. However, it is common to think not only that the name is intrinsically associated with the object, but that the application of the name presupposes the existence of a concept or a universal of "tableness" as a substantial essence of table in virtue of grasping which we understand the name. This thought is the most common way of grasping the table as truly existent, that is, as having an essence. This is completely in contradiction to reality. Hence, Buddha shows the reality of things through the analytic approach of reasoning.

In this context it is important to note the differences between an object's existence being refuted by rational cognition and a thing's being unable to withstand analysis. The self is merely fabricated through misconception. Therefore, when it is analysed by the cognition analysing ultimate reality its existence is refuted. A car, for example, is unable to withstand the analysis, yet its empirical existence is not refuted by this analysis since it does conventionally exist.

Provided that all entities are designated we should not, however, take for granted, that all designated entities should exist nominally. A three-fold yardstick employed to determine whether something should be considered nominally or conventionally existent, is as follows: *First,* an entity must be well-known to the world, that is, to conventional cognition and faculties. *Second,* it must not be invalidated by other conventional valid cognition, and *third,* it must not be invalidated by a reasoning cognition analysing the ultimate.

The *first* qualification or clause "well-known to the world" excludes things like unicorn, the son of a barren woman, etc., from the class of conventional existents. The *second* criterion excludes, for example, a mirage being water, because the status of a mirage as water can be discredited by conventional authoritative cognition. The *third* criterion excludes inherent existence, self-defining characteristic, which must be repudiated by ultimate authoritative cognition.

Nominally existents or conventionally existent entities are authoritatively established from the perspective of nominally authoritative cognition. It is not the case that emptiness is like a destructive agent destroying all existent entities. The concept of emptiness neither annihilates nominal existents nor can it possibly destroy nominal existents. Instead, the status or the nominal existent entities are perfectly preserved through a correct understanding of emptiness and its implication. All apparent inconsistencies, such as tension between nominal existent entities and that of emptiness arise essentially from a misconception of either the ontological status of nominal entities or the implication of emptiness. Emptiness should not be understood as diametrically opposed to nominal existence. Emptiness and nominal existence, in fact, are intimately connected and mutually supportive. Whatever is empty of essence is nominally existent and vice versa. Wherever there is nominal existence, there is emptiness; wherever there is emptiness, there is nominal existence. Whatever is nominally existent, is itself dependently arisen; whatever is dependently arisen, is itself empty of essence. The Ācārya Nāgārjuna says:

> For him to whom emptiness makes sense,
> Everything makes sense.
> For him to whom emptiness does not make sense,
> Nothing makes sense.[10]

The philosophical implication of emptiness is neither nihilistic nor substantialistic. Thus, the Mādhyamika's notion of emptiness should be understood as the middle-way approach transcending speculations based on nihilism and substantialism.

Thus, by negating the extreme of substantialism or reificationism and by negating the extreme of nihilism the Mādhyamika school holds the middle view and compatibly establishes the two truths. In the middle-way school of thought, every object of knowledge is being classified into two categories: the conventional truth and the ultimate truth. Every object of knowledge must necessarily be either a conventional truth or an ultimate truth. No object of knowledge can be both conventional and ultimate. This is a precise enumeration of the objects of knowledge. It neither adds

---

10. *Mūlamādhyamikakārikā*, 24: 14.

unnecessary entities nor subtracts necessary entities. It just eliminates the possibility of any further division among objects of knowledge. Given that the two truths are mutually exclusive, it is essentially implausible for something to exist that either belongs to both the truths or belongs to neither of the two. This simply must be the case, for should a cognition affirm an entity as a conventional truth, a possibility of that entity itself being ultimate truth is severed. Similarly, should a cognition affirm an entity to be an ultimate truth, a possibility of that entity itself being conventional is severed. Thus, all truths must necessarily be subsumed under the two truths.

The two truths are closely related. They relate in such a way that they are neither the same nor different. In more traditional terms, the two truths are one entity *but different isolates*. For example, with regard to a table, a table itself is a conventional truth and the table's emptiness of *true existence* or emptiness of the "self-defining characteristic" of table is its ultimate truth. They are neither identical nor separate entities just like a conch-shell and its whiteness. However, whatever is conventionally existent, is itself empty of essence. In other words, whatever exists conventionally must necessarily be commensurate with emptiness of true existence, and whatever is emptiness of true existence must necessarily be commensurate with conventional existence. Emptiness of true existence and conventional existence are simply analogous in their nature. Emptiness of true existence is not different from conventional existence; in the same way conventional existence is not different from emptiness of true existence. Thus, they are not separate entities.

Just by understanding ultimate reality at the intellectual level without discrediting worldly convention the purpose of the study of philosophy is not completely served. Rather it is the initial step. The practitioner contemplates and develops this wisdom. Yet it is not fully developed even after contemplation. Thereafter, it is further developed by bringing it to the experiential level through meditation and thus developing the accomplished wisdom by means of which one directly — that is perceptually — cognizes the ultimate truth. When selflessness is directly cognized the ignorance of self-grasping is completely extirpated and thereby the grasping by the self of objects other than itself is also eliminated. Without these as the basis, craving, aversion and other afflictive mental aspects are also eliminated and hence the actions induced by these negative forces are no longer generated. As a result he is no longer born in cyclic existence, and hence suffering is no longer generated. Eventually, when the wisdom is strengthened further, the imprints of the negative mental forces — including the subtlest ones — are expelled; and then *nirvāṇa* is achieved. As Nāgārjuna says:

> When views of "self and being mine" are extinguished,
> with repect to the internal or external,
> the appropriator ceases.
> This having been ceased, birth is eliminated.
> Through the elimination of *karma* and affliction there is *nirvāṇa*.
> *Karma* and affliction come from conceptual thought.
> These come from mental fabrication.
> Fabrication ceases through emptiness.[11]

Through the elimination of *karma* and affliction there is *nirvāṇa*. *Karma* and affliction come from conceptual thought. These come from mental fabrication. Fabrication ceases through emptiness.[12]

---

11. *Mūlamādhyamakakārikā*, XVIII: 5.
12. *Ibid.*

Thus, the purpose of the philosophical venture in Buddhism is to get rid of the fabricated views we have about ourselves, about other beings and about inanimate objects. And spiritual practice in Buddhism is nothing but (a) the elimination of negative forces from the fundamental levels of mind. This can be done only through the realization of reality; (b) the development of positive forces like immeasurable compassion, immeasurable love extended to all sentient beings and the development of qualities like generosity, appropriate conduct, patience, etc., to perfection. These two aspects are equally indispensable: without either of the two, total enlightenment is not possible. But the elimination of these fabrications, and hence spiritual practice itself, is impossible without philosophical analysis.

Therefore, philosophy is not only studied but also practised. As it often happens to be an interesting and enjoyable domain of study, the Buddha and other philosophers often remind us not to allow philosophical study to remain at the intellectual level. This, they say, would be like a person who knows a lot about art, and can give an extensive and critical commentary on a painting but who cannot paint by himself. Another analogy presented in the literature is that a person who produces medicines but never takes the medicines himself even when he needs it. If we study philosophy with a deeper commitment, contemplating deeply, and implementing what we thereby learn in our lives, it can have tremendous transformative impact, reducing depression, tension, disappointment, and in the end giving us a deeper understanding of the meaning of life and of the fundamental nature of the world.

References

Candrakīrti, *Byan-chub-sems-dpahi rnal-rnal-hbyor spyod-pa bshi-brgya-pahi rgya-cher-hgrel-pa*, Sde-gde edition, Ya 30b-239a.

———, *Dbu-ma-la hjug-pa Ran-hgrel = Mādhyamakāvatārabhāṣyam*, Dharamsala: The Council of Cultural & Religious Affairs, 1968.

———, *Dbu-ma-tsing-gsal = Prasannapadā Mādhyamaka vṛttiḥ*, Dharamsala: The Council of Cultural & Religious Affairs, 1968.

———, *Mādhyamakaśāstra of Nāgārjuna with the Commentary: Prasannapadā of Chandrakīrti*, ed. P.L. Vaidya, Darbhanga: Mithila Institute, 1987.

Garfield, Jay L., *The Fundamental Wisdom of the Middle Way: Nāgārjuna's Mūlamādhyamakakārikā*, New York: Oxford University Press, 1995.

Huntington, C.W., with Namgyal Wangchen, *Emptiness to Emptiness: An Introduction to Early Indian Madhyamika*, Delhi: Motilal Banarsidass, 1989.

Lindtner, Chr., *Nāgārjuniana: Studies in the Writings and Philosophy of Nāgārjuna: Yuktiṣaṣṭikā*, 1982, Reprint, Delhi: Motilal Banarsidass, 1987.

Jackson, Roger R., *Is Enlightenment Possible? Dharmakirti and Rgyal tshab rje on Knowledge, Rebirth, No-Self and Liberation*, tr. and annotated, Ithaca: Snow Lion Publictions, 1993.

Nāgārjuna, *Nāgārjuna's Seventy Stanzas: A Buddhist Psychology of Emptiness, Śūnyatāsaptati*, comment. Sonam Rinchen, transl. and ed. David Ross Komito, and Tenzin Dorjee, Ithaca: Snow Lion Publications, 1987.

———, *Ston-pa-nid bdun-cu-pahi hgrel-pa = Śūnyatāsaptati*, Sde-dge Edition, Tsa 24a-27a.

Poussin, Louis De La Vallée, *Abhidharmakośabhāṣyam*, translated into English L.M. Pruden, 4 vols., Berkeley: Asian Humanities Press, 1988.

Rgyal-tshab Dar-ma-rin-chen, 1364-1432, *Yogic Deeds of Bodhisattvas: Gyel-tsap on Āryadeva's Four Hundred*, comment. Sonam Rinchen: tr. and ed. Ruth Sonam, Ithaca: Snow Lion Publications, 1994.

Tsongkhapa, 1357-1419, *Lam-rim-chen-mo*, Varanasi: Gelugpa Students Welfare Committee, 1993.

———, *The Great Treatise on the Stages of the Path to Enlightenment,* tr. The Lamrim Chenmo Translation Committee; ed. Joshua W.C. Cutler and Guy Newland, 3 vols., Ithaca: Snow Lion Publication, 2000.

———, *The Speech of Gold: Reason and Enlightenment in the Tibetan Buddhism,* tr. and ed. Robert A.F. Thurman, Delhi: Motilal Banarsidass, 1989.

———, *Tsa-se-tik-chen,* Varanasi: Gelugpa Students Welfare Committee, 1973.

Vasubandu, *Abhidharmakośa and Bhāṣya of Ācārya Vasubandhu with Sphuṭārtha Commentary of Ācārya Yaśomitra,* Critically ed. Swami Dwarikadas Sastri, 4 vols., Varanasi: Bauddha Bharati, 1987.

———, *Chos-mnon-pa-mzod-kyi bsad-pa,* Dharamsala: The Council of Cultural & Religious Affairs, 1968.

6

Concept of Fullness

Pūrṇatā in Kashmir Śaivism

M.L. Kokiloo

WE are proud of our great sages and seers who morally, spiritually and intellectually conquered the world through compassion, love and supernatural powers. The remarkable Indian sages, saints, and literary giants, right from the time of the divine sage Vasugupta (eighth century CE) of Kashmir and of Ādi Śaṅkara of Kaladi to the present day, spiritual luminaries have won the minds and hearts of millions of people in India and abroad. Their message is *vasudhaiva-kuṭumbakam*, "the entire world is our family," and "all humanity is one community." It is our prime duty to extol the wonder-words and deeds of the luminaries of by-gone days. The world-renowned Indian philosophers crusaded for universal peace, justice and brotherhood. Their spiritual preaching, indeed, inspired all types of seekers. People must follow them seriously and engage themselves in noble action and strive for unity with all their fellow beings. Yet intellectuals today are more busy promoting division than seeking unity and there are very few good people who seek to promote unity in diversity. The oneness of all mankind has to be realized.

Names and forms are many, but the inherent divinity in every one is the same. As we see there are different lamps and lights everywhere but the current that flows in them all is one and the same, similarly the divine spark in all human beings is one and the same, because the divine is common to all. There is no separate God for Varanasi and a separate God for New Delhi. All religions have one common divinity, one common super-consciousness. As is said by Vasugupta in the *Śiva-Sūtras: caitanyamātmā,* "one's own nature is universal consciousness."[1]

This sudden flash of universal or transcendental consciousness is identical with Bhairava, which is equivalent to *pūrṇatā* (fullness) or *anuttara* (unsurpassable). This word Bhairava has been lucidly explained by Ācārya Abhinavagupta in his immense treatise called *Tantrāloka*. The principal figure of Kashmir Śaivism, Abhinavagupta (tenth/eleventh century CE), was the greatest exponent of the philosophy of Śaivism, which lays more stress on practice than on logical discourse. It opposes the use of all sacred symbols and marks but recommends the life of a householder as well as the practice of Śaiva-Yoga for self-realization. It prohibits the suppression of one's emotions and instincts and proposes their sublimation. It prescribes the path of *bhukti* (worldly enjoyment) and *mukti* (liberation), both of which can be pursued side by side. It advocates the principle of devotion (*bhakti*), which makes it practicable and did not disturb the traditional religion of the masses. It also lays great emphasis on the practice of Śaiva-Yoga, which is the concentration of the mind in meditation whilst enjoying every means of sense pleasure. For initiation into such a Yoga, a master is required who can easily and spontaneously guide the mind and senses of his disciples and devotees so that the disciple attains that state in which, while engaged in worldly activities with awareness, he enjoys the divine bliss of Bhairava. In the Śaiva philosophy of Kashmir, *pūrṇa,* Bhairava or *anuttara* is not only the highest God above

1. *Śiva-Sūtra* I.1.

all gods but is, indeed, supreme consciousness and the reality of the entire universe.

In order to explain the term *Bhairava,* Abhinavagupta says:

viśvaṁ bibharti pūraṇa-dhāraṇa-yogena tena ca bhriyate ।
savimarśatayā rava-rūpataśca saṁsārabhīruhitakṛcca ॥
— *Tantrāloka,* I.96

Being in the form of fullness, (Bhairava) protects this whole universe, fills up this whole world and sustains it. Besides being full of *jñāna* and *kriyā* and by his real nature, he is helpful to those who are being carried away by the ferocious thought currents.

Having *pūrṇatā* (fullness) he unfolds the universe upon the screen of his own self by the power of his own will alone, neither by the will of another nor by means of any extraneous material cause, etc. He unfolds this universe like a city in a mirror, which, though one with the mirror, appears to be different from it.

The word *bhairava,* Abhinavagupta further says, contains three phonemes: *bh* which suggests *bharaṇāt; ra* which suggests *ramaṇatā;* and *va* which suggests *vamanatā. Bharaṇāt*: being full (*pūrṇa*) in every respect, Bhairava protects this whole world. *Ramaṇāt*: because of his *pūrṇatā* he is present in every object; *vamanāt*: because of his *pūrṇatā* he reabsorbs this whole universe in himself. Since the world process is already contained in *pūrṇa-anuttara,* he projects it out of himself. Kashmir Śaivism does not translate the word *sṛṣṭi* as creation. *Sṛṣṭi* is derived from the root *sṛj* which means "to project," "to pour forth," "to cast out," so that the word *sṛṣṭi* means "emanation" not "creation." *Saṁhāra* means "restoration" not "destruction," as there is no destruction of the world. Śiva reabsorbs it and then projects it out of himself.

To reaffirm Bhairava's surpassing *pūrṇatā* Abhinavagupta states that:

sṛṣṭi sthiti tirodhāna saṁhārānugrahādi ca ।
turyamityapi devasya bahuśaktitvajṛmbhitam ॥
— *Tantrāloka*, I.79

Emanation, maintenance, concealment, re-absorption, grace, etc., and integral awareness (*turyam*): all these are the unfoldment of the various energies of the Lord.

This *pūrṇatā* (fullness) is defined as *baindavīkalā*. It is the freedom of Parama Śiva (Supreme Śiva) by which the knower always remains the knower and is never reduced to the known. This *pūrṇatā* is termed *bindu*, which is indicated by a dot on a letter and symbolizes the fact that Śiva, in spite of the manifestation of the universe, remains undivided. This undividedness is described as *ghanībhūtā śakti* (compacted emissional force). It is *cidghanatā* (the mass of consciousness) in which lie all the 118 worlds (*bhuvanas*).

It is pertinent to mention here that according to Kashmir Śaivism there are 118 *bhuvanas*. My Master I.S. Lakshman Joo Maharaj explained that the whole manifestation is divided into five phases (*kalās*). The lowest is *nivṛtti-kalā*, which has sixteen *bhuvanas*. *Pratiṣṭhā-kalā* consists of fifty-six *bhuvanas*. *Vidyā-kalā* contains twenty-eight *bhuvanas*. *Śantā-kalā* contains eighteen *bhuvanas*, while *śāntātīta-kalā* has no *bhuvana*. Thirty-six *tattvas* (elements) are also found in these phases (*kalās*). The first phase, *nivṛtti-kalā*, consists of *pṛthivī tattva*. The second phase, *pratiṣṭhā-kalā*, extends from *jala tattva* to *prakṛti tattva*. The third phase, *vidyā-kalā*, extends from *puruṣa tattva* to *māyā tattva*. The fourth phase, *śāntā-kalā*, contains three *tattvas*: *śuddha vidyā*, *Īśvara* and *Sadāśiva*. The fifth phase, *śāntātīta-kalā*, consists of Śiva and Śakti *tattva*.

In the *Svacchanda Tantra,* a very important Śaivāgama from Kashmir, it is said: *kulam śaktiriti proktam akulaṁśiva ucyate.* "*Kula* means *śakti* and *akula* means Śiva." *Kula* the totality, the entire manifestation, the divine manifesting power, is *śakti.* He who remains one and does not negate his fullness in the total manifestation is *akula,* i.e., Śiva.

The great Sanskrit grammarian, Pāṇini, defines the term *pratyāhāra* by the phrase *ādirantyena sahitā,* which means that several phonemes are encapsulated into one word by combining the first phoneme with the final phoneme. So *a,* the first phoneme of the Sanskrit alphabet together with *ha* the last phoneme — which suggests *aham,* "I" or "self" — includes all the phonemes of the Sanskrit alphabet. Since each phoneme indicates an object, so *aham* implies all objects of the universe. Thus the whole universe lies in Śiva in an undifferentiated state. This is the fullness (*pūrṇatā*) of Śiva.

About *pūrṇatā,* Abhinavagupta says the following:

yatra ko'pi vyavacchedo nāsti yadviśvataḥ sphurat ।
yadanāhata saṁvitti paramāmṛta bṛṁhitam ॥

yatrāsti bhāvanādīnāṁ na muhyā kāpi saṁgatiḥ ।
tadeva jagadānandam asmabhyaṁ śambhurūcivān ॥
— *Tantrāloka,* V.50cd-52ab

> Where there is no limitation because of its flashing forth all round; where the consciousness alone expresses itself because it remains always unattached; where the nectar of divine joy expands and increases; where meditations or imagination has nothing to do: that is *jagadānanda,* universal bliss.

In short the universe appears as a form of the bliss of the Self in its state of *pūrṇatā.* Explaining the state of *pūrṇatā* further, Abhinavagupta says:

pūrṇe'vadhānaṁ nahi nāma yuktaṁ ।
nāpūrṇam abhyeti ca satyabhāvam ॥
— *Tantrāloka,* II.12

There is no attempt to maintain alertness or onepointedness in the state of *pūrṇa,* because *pūrṇa* itself is alertness or super consciousness. One who has not achieved the state of *pūrṇa* cannot achieve true nature.

So it is futile to expect that meditation or imagination can be helpful in witnessing one's real nature in the state of supreme fullness.

ye'pi sākṣādupāyena tadrūpaṁ praviviñcate ।
nūnaṁ te sūryasaṁvittyai khadyotādhitsavo jaḍāḥ ॥
— *Tantrāloka,* II.14

Those who advocate attaining fullness by external means are fools, for they seek to find glow-worms in the bright light of the sun.

saṁvittattvaṁ svaprakāśam ityasmin kiṁ nu yuktibhiḥ ।
tadabhāve bhavedviśvaṁ jaḍatvādaprakāśakam ॥
— *Tantrāloka,* II.10

The state of supreme consciousness is self-luminous. It is improper to explain it in manifold ways. If [consciousness were not self-luminous] every thing would be insentient and without light.

How can an incomplete part be expected to exist in the state of fullness? If we presume that an incomplete part is also fully luminous then the incomplete part cannot exist. Another fullness or supreme consciousness cannot co-exist because the radiant fullness is one and absolute.

Thus the highest self-revelation is full in every respect. It is neither just *śakti,* the highest energy, because it is not dependent on other, nor is it the highest Lord because He has an independent nature. It is full, complete, in all respects. Full is always full. As is said in our ancient scriptures:

> *oṁ pūrṇamadaḥ pūrṇamidaṁ pūrṇātpūrṇamudacyate* ।
> *pūrṇasya pūrṇamādāya pūrṇamevāvaśiṣyate* ॥
> — *Īśopaniṣad*

> He is whole without parts. He is *pūrṇa*. He is called complete whole. If any thing is taken out of Him that also is complete and whole. What remains is complete and whole, if added that also is complete and whole.

Further it is said:

> *divyo hyamūrtaḥ puruṣaḥ sabāhyābhyantaro hyajaḥ* ।
> *aprāṇo hyamanāḥ śubhro hyakṣarāt parataḥ paraḥ* ॥
> — *Muṇḍakopaniṣad*, II.1. 2

> The divine consciousness which is without form pervades all forms and creatures. Totally full and complete internally and externally, without need of life or organs of perception and intelligence, enlightened and without any decay, it needs no elements of nature and is beyond the universe: such is *para* (the Supreme).

Śiva is fullness (*pūrṇatā*) and is beyond human comprehension, perception and intelligence. Swami Īśvara Svarūpa Lakṣmaṇa Joo Maharāj, my esteemed master of Kashmir Bhūmi, a Śaivite of the first order, a treasure-trove of Kashmir Śaivism and the last Śaiva *yogī*, who had both scriptural and practical knowledge together, used to say: "A mouse is not concerned with the size of a mountain of sweetmeat; it takes away just a bit of it, because that is sufficient for a mouse." Bhairava is whole. Even this limited aspect that human wisdom can perceive is whole and complete and is sufficient to liberate us from the shackles of mortality, sorrow and ignorance. As is said in Śaiva scriptures:

vigalati bhavadaurgatyaṁ mokṣaśrīḥ śrayati hṛtkajaṁ kacati ।
prasarati paramānando yatra tadīśārcanaṁ jayati ॥

By meditating on the fullness of Bhairava, the misery of this universe is put to an end, the wealth of salvation is owned, the lotus of the heart blossoms and the blissful state flows in from all sides. Let this type of worship be always glorified.

The realization of fullness is the principal means of carrying the boat of the body across the endless sea of this world. If you think even for a moment that you are incomplete, then you are caught up in *ajñāna* (ignorance). In the *Tantrāloka* it is said:

malamajñānamicchanti saṁsārāṅkurakāraṇam ।
— *Tantrāloka*, IX.99

Impurity (*mala*) is ignorance (*ajñāna*) and it is the cause of *saṁsāra*.

In Śaiva terms that is known as "the primary limiting condition" (*āṇava mala*). Because of it, the individual considers himself incomplete (*apūrṇa*), cut-off from the universal consciousness. This impurity (*āṇava mala*) is the root cause of *saṁsāra* or *māyīya mala*, "which brings about the consciousness of difference" (*bhinna-vedya-prathā*) which is expressed in such phrases as "this is mine" and "this is not mine." The root of this *māyīya mala* is *kārma mala*, which consists of the mental impressions (*vāsanā*) that carry an individual from one life to another. By this impurity we are tainted for many births to come. Thus, the realization simply of fullness saves an individual because it dispels limitation or contraction and enables the limited, individual person (*jīva*) to be free from all good and bad actions. In the *Spanda Kārikā*, Vasugupta states:

nijāśuddhyāsamarthasya kartavyeṣvabhilāṣiṇaḥ ।
yadā kṣobhaḥ pralīyeta tadā syāt paramaṁ padam ॥
— *Spanda Kārikā*, I.9

> By your own inborn impurities you are attached to various actions. When fullness is experienced, the highest state comes into being and the restless condition of unfulfilled numberless desires ceases.

This fullness, the ultimate reality, is the pre-existent cause and essence and identity of everything. It abounds in bliss and consciousness and is endowed with sovereignty of will, omniscience and omnipotence. It is everything and yet beyond everything. It is both immanent (*viśvamaya*) and transcendent (*viśvottīrṇa*). Time, form and space do not limit it because fullness is all. It is not bound by any physical laws. This freedom from all restrictions is the *svatantratā* of fullness. It gives life and existence to everything in this universe. It is pure consciousness. About *paripūrṇatā* the *Svacchanda Tantra* states:

> *malakarmakalādyaistu nirmuktaśca yadā priye* ।
> *sarvādhvasamatītaśca māyāmohojjhitaścayaḥ* ॥
>
> *nirmalatvaṁ yadā yāti padaṁ paramamavyayam* ।
> *paramātmā tadā devi procyate prabhuravyayaḥ* ॥
> — *Svacchanda Tantra*, XI.89-90
>
> [Lord Śiva addresses Pārvatī]: "O Beloved! The person who is free from three types of impurities, who is beyond all *adhvā* (pathways), who is devoid of *māyā* and attachment: after attaining complete purity, he achieves the supreme peace, which is everlasting, O Devī! That everlasting, omnipotent Lord is called *Paripūrṇaparamātmā*.

In order to define the importance of fullness (*pūrṇatā*) Bhaṭṭa Vāmadeva states:

> *tyajetkṣetraṁ tathā tīrthaṁ yāvat brahmaṇi no viśet* ।
> *tadviditvā śvapāko'pi matsamo nātra saṁśayaḥ* ॥
> — *Janma-maraṇa-vicāra*

> A place of pilgrimage or sacred site has importance so long as you have not achieved fullness. After knowing fullness even a scoundrel gains entry into God-consciousness.

This same fact is confirmed by Abhinavagupta in his *Paramārthasāra:*

> *tīrthe śvapacagṛhe vā naṣṭasmṛtirapi parityajan deham* ।
> *jñānasamakālamuktaḥ kaivalyaṁ yāti hataśokaḥ* ॥
> — *Paramārthasāra,* 83

> An aspirant after gaining entry to the state of fullness, becomes liberated even whether he dies at a place of pilgrimage or in a sweeper's house; even if he has forgotten what he knew, he becomes free of all sufferings.

In our scriptures it is said:

> *pradeśo'pi brahmaṇaḥ sārvarūpyaṁ anatikrāntaśca avikalpyaśca* ।[2]

> Even a little space in the world is the form of fullness of the creator, insurmountable and unimaginable.

In the Śaiva texts also it is said:

> *ekaikatra ca tattve'pi ṣaṭtriṁśattattva rūpatā* ।

> In the series of thirty-six elements, from Śiva *tattva* to earth (*prithivī*) *tattva*, all elements exist in each *tattva*.

So it becomes evident that every particle of this world is the form of fullness (*pūrṇatā*).

While explaining verse 5 of Abhinavagupta's *Paramārthasāra*, Yogarāja says:

---

2. Quoted in various passages of Abhinavagupta's *Parātrīśikā Vivaraṇa* and Jayaratha's *Viveka* on the *Tantrāloka*, 3.46; 4.98; 12.5.

> *eṣa eva ca bhagavān śivaḥ svātantryāt bhoktā-bhogya lakṣaṇaṁ pramātā-prameya yugalakaṁ krīḍanakamiva samutthāpayati, yadapekṣayā ayaṁ bhedapradhāno vyavahāra tasmāt etadeva parameśvarasya svātantrya niratiśayaṁ yat pūrṇasvarūpatā parityāgena svātmani prasphuran saḥ cidānandaikaghanaḥ śiva eva* ।
>
> Lord Śiva by his unimpeded free will kicks this transformed subjective objective world like a toy and thus causes differentiated feeling everywhere. But it is because of his supremacy of unimpeded free will that he does not discard his fullness and sustains it. He jumps in *apūrṇatā*.

In his *Īśvara Pratyabhijña Vimarśinī,* Abhinavagupta supports the above statement by explaining that because of the Lord's fullness this whole variegated universe shines within him just as the reflection of a city is visible in a mirror.

The word *brahma* implies "fullness" because it means *sarvaṁ bṛhattvāt bṛhanīyatāt vā brahma,* i.e., because he is full everything is with him. He is full so he is named as *paraṁ.* Bhartṛhari says:

> *yadādau ca yadante ca yanmadhye tasya satyatā* ।
>
> His truthfulness is found at the beginning, at the end and at the centre.

Utpaladeva of Kashmir was the teacher of Abhinavagupta's teacher. In his unparalleled composition *Śivastotrāvalī* (Garland of songs to Śiva), he says:

> Whatever is not, let that be nothing to me. Whatever is, let that be everything to me. In this way may you be found and worshipped by me in all states. — 12.29
>
> Those who long for you they discover you in every object because you are full. So while beholding different objects, I

clearly see you and you alone. He, who without hesitation views this world only as your form, is eternally joyful. Why then the fear? — 13.16

Because —

harireva jagat jagat eva hariḥ harito jagato nahi bhinnamaṇuḥ ।
iti yasya matiḥ paramārthagatiḥ sa naro bhavasāgaramuddharati ॥
— *Swami Ram*

Hari (the Lord) is the universe, the universe is Hari, so how can an individual be other than Hari. One who has developed this sort of thinking, he alone attains the state of superconsciousness and this type of individual crosses this fearful worldly ocean.

The person who knows this truth of fullness is the real knower of *Śiva tattva*. As the *Vijñāna Bhairava* says:

yatra yatra mano yāti bāhye vābhyantare pi'vā ।
tatra tatra śivāvasthā vyāpakatvāt kva yāsyati ॥ 116 ॥

(The Lord Śiva addresses Pārvatī) O dear one, wherever our mind goes, externally or internally there is the state of fullness. So by going here and there our mind at last will rest at fullness.

By entering in that state of fullness the faculties are filled with radiant joy. They flourish under the impact of the whole wheel of energies. They are filled with the grace of the inner self, which is unique, intense and always fresh. In this unlimited state of fullness an aspirant feels more and more astonishment and becomes one with the supreme divine consciousness, the sea of repose. In this state of fullness, all distinctions and diversities are absent, being and non-being are identified, time is merged in eternity, individuality in universality and finitude in infinity. Fullness is the beginning and the end of this phenomenal universe. It is termed as *bodhābdhi* (the sea of supreme knowledge). In the Doctrine of Recognition (*pratyabhijñā*) it is said that from knowing that this whole universe is one's glory, one becomes established in the state of fullness even though various thoughts are present.

In the second chapter of the *Tantrāloka,* fullness is described as follows:

> The principle of highest self-revelation is synonym of fullness. It is neither the highest energy namely *śakti* because it is not dependent, nor is it the highest Lord, because of His being of independent nature. It is full and complete in all respects. Full is always full. This fullness is beyond the related cause and effects of the universe. It is not object of contemplation because there is no contemplator, and vice-versa. It is unworship-pable as there is no worshipper. It is neither *mantra* nor the reciter of *mantra* nor the deity for whom *mantra* is recited. It is neither initiator nor initiation nor initiated. This type of state is called fullness and that fullness is *Maheśvara,* the highest Lord full of all glories (summary).

In fact, the root cause of duality cannot exist in the state of fullness. The *Bharga Śikhā* confirms this point: [3]

> *na sannacāsatsadasanna ca tannobhyojjhitam* ।
> *durvijñeyā hi sāvasthā kimapyetadanuttaram* ॥
>
> *ayamityavabhāso hi yo bhāvo'vacchidātmakaḥ* ।
> *sa eva ghaṭavat loke saṁstathā naiṣa bhairavaḥ* ॥

> In this world whatever we perceive we call it by the name of 'this' or 'that,' as for example 'this *ghaṭaḥ* (pot)' or 'this *paṭaḥ* (cloth)' etc. but the highest self consciousness, which is called fullness, is neither *sat-asat* (being or non-being) and is both *sat* and *asat*. This sort of state is beyond comprehension. If this supreme fullness is neither *sat-asat* and is both *sat-asat*, then it must transcend both.

---

3. Quoted in *Tantrāloka,* II.28-29.

To remove any uncertainty on this point, Abhinavagupta says that this fullness is present not in appearance only but in non-appearance also. It cannot be defined because it is *anuttara* (unsurpassable). As is said:

> *tato'pi paramaṁ jñānam-upāyādivivarjitam* ।
> *ānandaśakti viśrāntam-anuttaramihocyate* ॥
>
> — *Tantrāloka*, 1.242
>
> *Anuttara* is that supreme knowledge, attained without any means, which rests in the energy of bliss.

> *ayaṁ raso yena manāgavāptaḥ svatantra ceṣṭāniratasya tasya* ।
> *samādhiyoga vratamantra mudrā japādi caryā viṣavat vibhāti* ॥[4]
>
> Whosoever has tasted this state even in a minor way, all types of meditation such as *samādhi*, *yoga*, fasts, *mantras*, *mudrās* (hand gestures), *japa* (recitation), etc., appear as harmful.

In fact, every element of the emanation is "full." Even in rocks, in plants, in beasts, in human beings, in the gods, this "I" is found secretly in seed form. It is said *yathā brahmāṇḍe tathā piṇḍe* which can be translated to mean: "Just as his fullness is evident in this whole cosmos, similarly it is evident in each and every physical form also." God is called omnipotent, omniscient and omnipresent, because from the cosmos to the minutest atom everything is penetrated by his fullness.

From the Hindu point of view there are eighty-four lakh of species in this universe. An individual, who by dint of his good actions takes the form of a human being, carries the impressions of every previous birth. Every impression of every birth is the centre of fullness in its own way. A man can go downwards and assume numberless forms and can go

4. Quoted by Jayaratha in his *Viveka* on *Tantrāloka*, III.270.

upwards also to come near to God. This is the meaning of his *bahusyāṁ* (presence in manifold forms). When we say *eko 'ham* (I am all alone) we take his fullness for granted. Then why should the *bahusyāṁ*-form be construed as incomplete (*apūrṇa*) because that is the inseparable part of His first half: *eko 'ham*.

In the *Bhagavad-Gītā*, Lord Kṛṣṇa clearly states: *vāsudevaḥ sarvamiti*, which means: "Whatever is found in this world is Vāsudeva." Furthermore, in the tenth chapter of this very sacred book Vāsudeva manifests His fullness in all beings and non-beings to Arjuna and emphasizes finally that: "there is nothing in this world which can exist without my fullness" or *mayi protaṁ jagatsarvaṁ sūtre maṇigaṇā iva*, "this whole universe dwells in me just like beads of rosary are strung one after another on a thread." Again in the eleventh chapter, at the request of Arjuna, Vāsudeva manifests his form of fullness (*virāṭ rūpa*). There he explains in detail the secret of fullness to his friend who has become a *jñānī*.

In the *Yajurveda* Rudra's glory is extolled in the following way:

> *yo rudro agnau yo'psu ya oṣadhīṣu yo vanaspatiṣu* ।
> *yo rudro viśvā bhuvanāviveśa tasmai rudrāya namo'stu devāḥ* ॥
> — *Taittirīya Saṁhitā*, V.5.9.3

> O Gods! Pay obeisance to that Rudra [i.e. Śiva] who is ever present in fire, in water, in herbs, in plants and who pervades all the worlds with his fullness.

The *Ṛgveda's Vāksūkta* (X.125) warns that those who do not accept the Lord's fullness will have to face His wrath. In the *Īśopaniṣad* (1) also it is explained that:

> *īśāvāsyamidaṁ sarvaṁ yatkiṁ ca jagatyāṁ jagat* ॥

> Whatever is found in this world, whether moving or stationery, is penetrated by the fullness of the Lord.

The Upaniṣads also support the state of fullness by saying that:

> *tameva bhāntaṁ cānubhāti sarvaṁ tasya bhāsā sarvamidaṁ vibhāti* ॥
>
> — *Kaṭha Upaniṣad*, 5.15

> When that effulgent light of fullness shines, all becomes luminous by means of his effulgence.

Somānanda, the founder of the Doctrine of Recognition (*pratyabhijñā*) explains fullness in his only surviving work *Śivadṛṣṭi*:

> *jñāte śivatve sarvasthe pratipattyā dṛḍhātmanā* ।
> *karaṇena nāsti kṛtyaṁ kvāpi bhāvanayāpi vā* ॥ VII.6

> If fullness, the stete Śiva of residing in every one, is made known truly or by determination, or by certain proofs, or by studying Śāstras or by master's explanation, then other means such as *karaṇa* or *bhāvanā* (contemplation) become redundant.

If fullness is known even once, all other means of verification become irrelevant. As we have already explained, this fullness is described as the highest state (*anuttara*), which is the all-pervading, eternal and self-evident self-consciousness. It is never less or more in its form. Moreover, there is no agency superior to it or separate from it. Therefore, this fullness or *pūrṇatva* is present at every moment, pervasive in everything and visible to all. It is like one's heartbeat, which is concealed in the seeker's innermost part. It is the vibrating energy to which the world process owes its existence. It is the highest reality. It is the mass of consciousness and bliss. It is sovereign in emanation, maintenance, and absorption. It does not depend upon any extraneous condition. *Pūrṇatva* involves *svātantrya* which is "the absolute spontaneous free will" of the divine consciousness. It is not conditioned by anything outside itself. This fullness of pure consciousness is like a waveless ocean and is full of bliss. It is a state in which the entire universe appears as the Self. The Tantras also explain that *pūrṇatva* is the final reality in both the transcendental as well as immanent state.

sarvātītaṁ paraṁ tattvaṁ sarvaṁ vyāpya vyavasthitam ॥

The *Svacchanda Tantra* describes the six phases of *śūnyatā* (void) and describes the ultimate *śūnyatā* as the unsurpassable being (*anuttara*) or fullness (*pūrṇatva*) or transcendence (*viśvottīrṇa*), as the highest and last reality, which is in reality *aśūnya*, as is said 'the void is non-void' (*aśūnyaṁ śūnyamityuktam*). This is not emptiness in the ordinary sense of the term, but a positive being (*sattāmātra*) from which emerge infinite universes and into which they are reabsorbed. This *śūnya* contains everything in itself and materializes itself in the concrete form of this physical and subtle universe. As is said in *Svacchanda Tantra*:

tatra tatra paraṁ śūnyaṁ sarvaṁ vyāpya vyavasthitam ।
tadeva bhavati sthūlaṁ sthūlopādhivaśāt priye ॥

Thus, this *pūrṇatva* is free from all limiting conditions, absolutely free from all objectivity. It is *cit kriyā* (consciousness as activity) and *cit kartṛtā* (consciousness as agent).

References

TEXTS AND TRANSLATIONS

Abbrev. KSTS — Kashmir Series of Texts and Studies (Srinagar)

Abhinavagupta, *Parātrīśikā Vivaraṇa, The Secret of Tantric Mysticism*, Sanskrit text ed. Swami Lakshman Joo, English tr. Jaideva Singh, ed. by Bettina Bäumer, New Delhi: Motilal Banarsidass, 1st ed. 1988.

———, *La lumière sur les Tantras, chapitre 1 à 5 du Tantrāloka*, French tr. by Lilian Silburn and André Padoux, Paris (ed. De Boccard), 1998.

———, *Tantrāloka*, 1st edn., Srinagar: KSTS, 1918-1938, 2nd edn., New Delhi: Motilal Banarsidass, 1987 (8 vols).

Bailly, Constantina Rhodes, *Shaiva Devotional Songs of Kashmir*, A Translation and Study of Utpaladeva's *Shivastotravali*, Albany, N.Y.: SUNY Press, 1987.

Dyczkowski, Mark, The *Stanzas on Vibration, The Spandakārikā with four Commentaries*, Varanasi: Indica Books, 1994.

Mālinīvijayottara Tantram, ed. Madhusudan Kaul Shastri, Bombay: KSTS, 1922.

Netra Tantra with Comment. Kṣemarāja, ed. Madhusudan Kaul Shastri, Bombay: KSTS, 1926, 1939 (2 vols).

Raniero Gnoli, *Luce delle Sacre Scritture (Tantrāloka) di Abhinavagupta* (Italian transl.), Torino: UTET, 1972, 2nd ed., 1999.

Singh, Jaideva, *Śiva Sūtras, The Yoga of Supreme Identity*, New Delhi: Motilal Banarsidass, 1979.

———, *Pratyabhijñāhṛdayam, The Secret of Self-recognition*, (Kṣemarāja), New Delhi: Motilal Banarsidass, 1st edn., 1963.

———, *Spanda-Kārikās, The Divine Creative Pulsation*, New Delhi: Motilal Banarsidass, 1st edn., 1980.

Somānanda, *The Śivadṛṣṭi*, with the Vṛtti by Utpaladeva, ed. Madhusudan Kaul Shastri, Srinagar: KSTS, 1934.

Svacchanda Tantra with Comment. by Kṣemarāja, Bombay: KSTS, 1921-1935 (6 vols).

Torella, Raffaele, *The Īśvarapratyabhijñākārikā of Utpaladeva with the Author's Vṛtti*, New Delhi: Motilal Banarsidass, 2002.

Utpaladeva, *The Īśvarapratyabhijñā* with the Vimarśinī by Abhinavagupta, Bombay: KSTS, 1921 (3 vols).

Utpaladevācārya, *The Śivastrotrāvalī*, with the Commentary of Kṣemarāja, ed. with Hindi commentary by Swami Lakshmana Joo, Jammu-Srinagar-New Delhi: Ishwar Ashram Trust, 2000.

STUDIES

Bäumer, Bettina, *Abhinavagupta, Wege ins Licht*, Zürich: Benziger, 1992.

———, *Trika. Grundthemen des Kaschmirischen Śivaismus*, Junsbruck, Tyrolia, 2003.

Dyczkowski, Mark, *The Doctrine of Vibration*, Albany, N.Y.: SUNY Press, 1987.

———, *The Canon of the Śaivāgama and the Kubjikā Tantras of the Western Kaula Tradition*, New Delhi: Motilal Banarsidass, 1989.

Lakshman Joo, Swami, *The Awakening of Supreme Consciousness*, ed. Jankinath Kaul, New Delhi: Utpal Publ., 1998.

———, *Kashmir Śaivism, The Secret Supreme*, New Delhi: Sri Satguru Publications, 1991 (1st edn. 1988).

Silburn, Lilian: *Kuṇḍalinī, The Energy of the Depths*, Albany: SUNY Press, 1988.

7

The Nothingness of God and its Explosive Metaphors

Alois M. Haas

God is inexpressible, and for this reason Christian tradition has often used the term "nothing" to refer to him. As a preliminary definition, the word "nothing" can be defined as the denial of any statement that restricts God or focuses too exclusively on any one of his attributes. Again and again in the history of Christian spirituality we encounter powerful statements about God's fundamental namelessness, expressed perhaps most forcefully in the work of Dionysius the Areopagite.[1] Thus, concerning the Godhead, Dionysius laments what he calls the "ignorance of God's transcendence that exceeds all reason and being."[2]

It is in fact Dionysius who is the originator of all later statements referring to God as "nothing." He is, as it were, the chief witness in the Christian spiritual tradition, to the concept of the divine nothing. In words of great clarity, Dionysius explains that the "supradivine light," "although it

1. Dionyius Areopagita: *De divinis nominibus* (abbr. *DN*) I, 2; *De mystica theologia* (abbr. MT) I, 3 and elsewhere; quoted by K. Ruh: *Geschichte der abendländischen Mystik*, vol. 3, p. 28.
2. *DN* I, 1; cp. B.R. Suchla, *Corpus Dionysiacum I*, Berlin, 1990, pp. 107-231.

is the origin of all being, nevertheless is itself nothing, because it is removed from all things by its transcendence of all concepts."[3] The fact that God is "being beyond being" leads to him being called "nameless yet also with every name."[4] God is seen not only "in everything but also far from everything"[5] — a paradox which is reflected in the ways of perceiving God. As Dionysius says:

> We see God not only through knowledge but also through ignorance. Although there is spiritual comprehension of him, understanding, knowledge, contact, sense perception, opinion, concept, naming and so on, nevertheless he is neither comprehended, nor explained, nor named. He is nothing existing, but he is also seen in anything existing. He is 'all in all' (I Corinthians 15: 28) and yet he is nothing anywhere. He is seen in all by all and yet he is seen in nothing by anyone. With good reason we say this about God, and on the basis of all existence he is praised as in harmony with all of which he is the cause.[6]

Through his *De mystica theologia*[7] Dionysius explains the idea of the nothing of God by allowing the negation "God is nothing in all" to be applied even to non-being.[8] In a longer

---

3. *DN* I, 5, Suchla 26, 593c, p. 31f.
4. *DN* I, 5, Suchla 26, 596a, p. 2f.
5. *DN* VII, 3, Suchla 80, 872a, p. 4f.
6. *DN* VII, 3, Suchla 80, pp. 6-14.
7. MT = Pseudo-Dionysius-Areopagita: *Über die Mystische Theologie und Briefe*. Eingeleitet, übersetzt und mit Anmerkungen versehen von Adolf Martin Ritter, Stuttgart 1994 (Bibl. der Griechischen Literatur, Bd. 40). Cp. A.M. Ritter: *Corpus Dionysiacum* II, Berlin 1991, pp. 141-50.
8. This idea is especially emphasized by M. Nambara: *Die Idee des absoluten Nichts in der deutschen Mystik und seine Entsprechungen im Buddhismus*, in: *Archiv für Begriffsgeschichte* 6 (1990) pp. 143- →

passage where Dionysius is discussing God's transcendental nature, this powerful proposition is expressed with great clarity:

> Taking this further we may say that the (original) cause is neither soul nor spirit; imagination, opinion, reason or thought cannot be ascribed to it, nor can it be equated with reason and thought, nor can it be expressed or even thought. It is neither number nor order, neither great nor small, neither equality nor inequality, neither similarity nor difference. It does not have a fixed position, nor does it move, neither does it rest. Power cannot be ascribed to it, nor is it identical with power or light. It is neither alive, nor identical with life, or with light. It is also not being, not eternity, not time. It can be neither grasped by thought nor known. It is also not to be equated with truth, dominion or wisdom. It is neither one nor oneness, neither godhead nor goodness. It is also not spirit in the sense by which we understand the expression, nor is it to be equated with fatherhood or sonhood or with anything else of which we or any other being have knowledge. It pertains neither to the sphere of being nor of non-being. . . . It eludes every form of definition, naming or knowing. It is not to be equated with either light or darkness, with falsehood or with truth. It can neither be promised nor denied anything.[9]

The background to all these statements is to be found in the ideas of Proclus on the One, which according to him can be described as "the nothing all of which it causes and maintains within its own being." As one scholar has put it:

→ 319; because it is here that "a notable relationship of the thought of Dionysius with Buddhism" is reflected, because "absolute Nothing consists precisely in the negation of being as well as non-being" (p. 182).

9. MT V. Ritter, *Corpus Dionysiacum II*, 79, 1045D, 1-1048A, 15.

> The negations demonstrate what the One itself is *not* and thus point to its radical otherness or absolute difference, to its being beyond being and thus to its 'transcendence' over every individual being and over being as a whole.[10]

The rigorous speculation on nothing adopted by Dionysius from Neoplatonism found its clearest expression in the work of John Scotus (Eriugena) in the ninth century. Although Eriugena speaks the language of the Christian doctrine of creation, there is little to show that he understands the idea of *creatio ex nihilo* any differently than the Neoplatonist concept of the emanation of all things from the One. In the *Periphyseon* he states explicitly that the *nihil*, the nothing out of which God creates his own nature, is God himself, and by creating all other things God also creates himself.[11] This theme had its own fascination, not only for Christian mystics[12] but also for Islamic and Jewish thinkers who combined it with apophatic speculation on the nature of God. In the fourteenth century it passed into writings in the German vernacular. A typical

---

10. W. Beierwaltes, *Dionysius Areopagita — ein christlicher Proklos?*, in: T. Kobusch/B. Mojsisch (eds.), *Platon in der abendländischen Geistesgeschichte. Neue Forschungen zum Platonismus*, Darmstadt 1997, 71-100; 73 (footnote 5). Beierwaltes shows clearly that the christian negative theology cannot be only traced back to Philo of Alexandria.

11. *Periphyseon* III, 23, 689 A 15-B2. Cp. H.A. Armstrong: *Negative Theology*, in, Armstrong, *Plotinian and Christian Studies*, London 1979, p. 179.

12. G. Scholem, *Schöpfung aus Nichts und Selbstverschränkung Gottes*, in: Scholem, *Über einige Grundbegriffe des Judentums*, Frankfurt/M. 1970, pp. 53-89; Scholem has described the most important phases and phenomena of this "reinterpretation of the creation out of nothing" (p. 68ff.); H.A. Wolfson: *Studies in the History of Philosophy and Religion*, vol. 1, Harvard 1979; H. Deku: *Wahrheit und Unwahrheit der Tradition. Metaphysische Reflexionen*, in: W. Beierwaltes (ed.): *De nihilo*, St. Ottilien 1986, pp. 221-46.

expression of the theme in such writings is the version in the mystical handbook known as the *Theologia Deutsch*:

> The piecemeal or the unperfected is that which has, or will have, its origin in the perfect — just as a beam or ray flows out from the sun or a light — and it is that which appears as some object or another and is termed 'creature.' And of all these parts, none is the perfect whole. Therefore also the perfect whole is not one of these parts. The parts are knowable, recognizable and expressible. The perfect whole is for all creatures unrecognizable, unfathomable and inexpressible, in so far as they are part of creation. Therefore we call the perfect whole 'nothing,' for it is none of these things.[13]

As a result of these ideas, the great figures of what is known as "German Mysticism" came to represent God as "the Nothing." This is true above all of Meister Eckhart and Heinrich Seuse, but also of such mystics as Marguerite Porete,[14] who is remarkably close to Meister Eckhart on this issue.

An ambivalent description of Meister Eckhart's attitude is given by the Japanese scholar Minoru Nambara. According to him, it is uncertain whether Eckhart describes God as Nothing in the same strict sense as prescribed by Dionysius.[15] More recently, however, it has been established that Meister

---

13. *Der Franckforter, Theologia deutsch.* In nhd. Übersetzung hg. und mit einer Einleitung versehen von Alois M. Haas, Einsiedelen 1980.

14. Cp. S. Köbele, *Bilder der unbegriffenen Wahrheit. Zur Struktur mystischer Rede im Spannungsfeld von Latein und Volkssprache,* Tübingen/Basel, 1993.

15. Cp. Nambara, *Die Idee des absoluten Nichts,* p. 193ff. Quint (*Meister Eckharts Predigten,* vol. 3, Stuttgart 1976, p. 212, footnote 1) has corrected this opinion and pointed out that the sermon of Meister Eckhart quoted in the following ensures a designation of God as "nothing."

Eckhart explicitly refers to the Nothingness of God in his Sermon 71 on Acts 9: 8 (*Surrexit autem Saulus de terra apertisque oculis nihil videbat* — "Saul stood up from the ground and with his eyes open, he saw nothing").[16] Speaking of St. Paul at his conversion on the road to Damascus, Eckhart plays on the expression "see nothing," which normally would mean "to become blind," but is interpreted here as "see Nothing;" in other words, an explicit reference to the Nothing of God, even if the definition of the term "nothing" is not restricted to this one semantic possibility, but also includes the nothingness of created things as well as other variations on the meaning of the word "nothing." At the very least, the primary meaning of "nothing" in Paul's conversion vision comes out very clearly as being God himself.

Its other meanings are as follows: firstly, Paul's vision is concerned with nothing but God; secondly, in the presence of the divine light, for all creatures nothing but God is visible; and finally, in the divine vision, things appear as nothing.[17]

In explaining his ideas on the nothing of God, Eckhart expressly refers back to Dionysius. The full passage is as follows:

> 'Paul stood up from the ground and with his eyes open he saw nothing.' I cannot see what is one, but he saw nothing, which was God. God is a nothing and God is a something. Whatever is something is also nothing. Whatever God is, He is fully. Therefore, the enlightened Dionysius, whenever he writes about God, he says: 'He is being beyond being. He

---

16. Cp. J. Quint, *Meister Eckharts Predigten*, vol. 3, Stuttgart 1976, (Meister Eckhart, *Die deutschen und lateinischen Werke, Die deutschen Werke* (abbr. *DW*) pp. 211-31.

17. Cp. *DW* 3, p. 211, 5ff. Regarding Eckhart's complex speculation about nothing, cp. B.J. Lanzetta: *Three Categories of Nothingness in Eckhart*, in: The Journal of Religion 72 (1992) pp. 248-68.

> is life beyond life. He is light beyond light.' He does not add any 'this' or 'that' to Him, and he thus intimates that He is an unknown something which is even further away. If someone sees something, or if something comes to your knowledge, then that thing is not God, for this reason: because He is neither 'this' nor 'that.' Whoever claims God is here or He is there — do not believe them! The light which is God shines in the darkness (John 1: 5). God is a *true* light; whoever would see it must be blind and must keep God apart from every 'something.' A master has said: Whoever speaks of God in the form of a simile, speaks of Him in an impure manner. But whoever speaks of God with nothing, speaks correctly about Him. When the soul comes into the One and enters in with a pure rejection of her self, then she finds God there as in a nothing. There is a story of a waking dream in which a person dreamed that he had become pregnant with nothing, just like a woman with child, and in this nothing God was born, and *He* was the fruit of nothing. God was born in the nothing.[18]

The allusion to Dionysius is clear and obvious here, and it draws on an undiminished tradition of Christian speculation on Nothing. It is also clear that this identification of God with Nothing is applied by Eckhart not only in the apophatic context of Dionysian thinking, but is also applied to the Dionysian *via eminentiae* in discourse about God, i.e., the way of speaking about God in terms of eminence.[19]

---

18. *DW* 3, p. 222, 11 — p. 225, 1.

19. The question whether Dionysius knows a third way of defining God, besides the *via cataphatica* and *apophatica*, namely a *via superlationis* or *eminentiae*, is controversial. Cp. V. Lossky, *Theologie negative et connaissance de Dieu chez Maître Eckhart* (Etudes de Philosophie Mediévale XLVIII), Paris 1960. Cp. Lossky, *La notion des 'analogies' chez Denys le Pseudo-Areopagite*, in Archives d'Histoire Doctrinale et Littéraire du Moyen-Age 5 (1930), pp. 279-309.

Another writer with reflections on the nothingness of God is Heinrich Seuse, in his *Büchlein der Wahrheit* (Little Book of Truth), where he recounts an experience of oneness that stayed with him over a period of ten weeks. His main point is the experience of truth in what he calls the *unbekennen*,[20] or "unknowing," which is expressed above all in the following insoluble paradox: *Ein ewiges niht und sin zitlichu gewordenheit*[21] (an eternal nothing and its temporal becoming), which signifies exactly the mystical unity of the human being with God. It is the role of the tranquil person to recognize himself as

> one with him who is a nothing among all things that can be conceived or expressed in words; and this nothing is called by convention 'God,' and it is in itself the most substantial being of all. And here the human being finds himself at one with this Nothing, and this Nothing is known without any activity of knowing at all.[22]

This personal allegory of truth implies significantly that hidden depths lie behind such a way of speaking. After a reference to Dionysius the Areopagite, who again is the main starting point for the discussion on the Nothing of God,[23] there is a move to break through the level of rational thought: the unity of man with God is in the strict sense of the word unthinkable, and therefore also inexpressible, despite the many teachers and books which attempt to teach otherwise. The Nothing is not to be comprehended by reason; even if the comprehension is considered to be identical with *vernunft* (i.e., reason or

---

20. H. Seuse, *Deutsche Schriften* (abbr. *B*), ed. Karl Bihlmeyer, Stuttgart 1907 (reprint Frankfurt/M. 1961) p. 341, 15f.
21. *B*, p. 341, 8f.
22. *B*, p. 342, 6-11.
23. Cp. *De div. nom.* I, 4-6; VII, 3; Suchla 23-27; 589D-596C; 80; 869D-872B. Cp. also *De myst. theol.* I,3; Ritter 76; 1001A.

rationality), with *wesen* (being), or with *niessen* (enjoyment), this reconstruction is still far too human-centred and insufficient. As Seuse says: *der kreftiger entwordenliche inschlag in das niht entschleht in dem grunde allen unterscheid* (the empowering and divesting move to the Nothing fundamentally frees from all differences), so that *daz ewig niht* (the eternal Nothing) can become a lived experience even during a person's lifetime, leading finally to perfection only in the eternity of heavenly bliss. In this way, the *geberlich niht* (the fertile, creative Nothing) is a divine power within the human being which leads towards unity and the removal of all difference, a result which is realized by the human being as an experience of unity and self-abnegation.

In Spanish mysticism, as far as I can see, it is quite clear that God can be described as the Nothing, although the idea is not expressed with quite the same frankness as it is in the Rhineland mystics. Among the Spanish mystics, John of the Cross writes the most incisively and consistently on the nothing/everything issue in the experience of God, but he is reluctant to describe God himself as Nothing. Erhard Meier writes:

> John of the Cross lays great emphasis on the immensity of God's being as opposed to the world, so much so that in the thoroughly positive drift of his thoughts he is unable to entertain any negative ideas of the nothing. This is clear from the basic tenor of his writings. . . . It should also be noted that the train of thought starts with eternity of God's being and only then considers the world, with the result that from this viewpoint the *world* itself is seen to be nothing. To follow this reversed way of thinking, if God is comparable to nothing, and therefore also not comparable to the world, then *vis-a-vis* God the world is quite simply nothing. What else could it be? Here too nothingness is not rendered independent, with its own value, but is quite clearly related

> to the comparison with God. In other words, nothingness is to be regarded as a *tertium comparationis* and not as a primary definition in relation to the world or to God.[24]

One way of reading John of the Cross is this: all the energy of his speculation on negation is referred back to the world and the human being, so that the human being can simply "plunge" into this nothing "as the only possible medium," "if you wish to come closer to God."[25] From such a perspective it is a very small step to regarding God himself as the nothingness of all restrictive concepts that limit him in any way, and John's strong Dionysian emphasis[26] on the apophasis of God encourages us to take such a step. What he declares to be faith is surrounded with a plethora of negative definitions. For faith "speaks to us of things we have never seen or heard, not even by analogy, for nothing can be compared to them."[27] From such an attitude to faith, which focuses wholly on its mysterious character, John of the Cross develops a specific form of negation which is determined by the enslaved nature of human existence, by human alienation from the world of objects, and by things in

---

24. E. Meier, *Struktur und Wesen der Negation in den mystischen Schriften des Johannes vom Kreuz*, Altenberge, 1982, p. 38f.
25. *Ibid.*, p. 39.
26. Cp. Eulogio de la Vierge du Carmel, Saint Jean de la Croix, DSp 3, Paris 1957, pp. 399-408; W. Völker, *Kontemplation und Ekstase bei Pseudo-Dionysius Areopagita*, Wiesbaden 1958.
27. I quote the works of Juan de la Cruz in the following way: S (*Subida del Monte Carmelo*); N (*Noche Oscura*); CE (*Cantico Espiritual*); L (*Llama de Amor Viva*); C (*Cartas*, "letters"); P (*Poesias*, "poems"); R (*Cautelas*, "rules"); C (*Cosejas a un Religioso*, "recommendations for a monk"); maxims (*Avisos y Sentencias Espirituales*, "spiritual thoughts and maxims"). Spanish edition: *Crisogono de Jesus/Matias del Nito Jesus/ Lucinio del SS. Sacramento, Vida y Obras de San Juan de la Cruz*, 4th edn., Madrid 1992.

themselves.[28] One famous poem from the *Subida del Monte Carmelo* (The Ascent of Mount Carmel) expresses well the tense dialectics of *todo/nada*:

> To come to enjoy everything
> seek enjoyment in nothing.
> To come to possess everything
> seek to possess nothing.
> To come to be everything
> seek to be nothing.
> To come to know everything
> seek to know nothing.
> To come to what you do not taste
> go to where you taste nothing.
> To come to what you do not know
> go to where you know nothing.
> To come to what you do not own
> go to where you own nothing.
> To become what you are not
> go to where you are nothing.

These verses aim to illustrate the ascent to the summit of contemplation and deal with both the night of senses and the night of spirit. In an extant fragment addressed to a spiritual daughter (Magdalena del Espiritu Santo) John has depicted this mountain.[29] The fragment is complemented by a number of further verses that show how the whole cannot be prevented from reaching its culmination:

> If you linger somewhere
> you will never conquer the whole.

---

28. Cp. the annotations of the editors in: San Juan de la Cruz. *Obras Completas*, ed. Jose Vicente Rodriguez y Federico Ruiz Salvador, 4th edn., Madrid 1992.

29. This sketch is shown in the edition: San Juan de la Cruz, *Obras Completas*, p. 130.

To come wholly to the whole
you must leave the whole.
And if you come to where you can grasp the whole,
have it without wanting to have it.
For if you want to hold fast to only something of the whole,
so you will not have your treasure purely in God.[30]

In this way, an inner nakedness and humility is a necessary condition of fulfilment in everything; nothing and everything are mutual conditions in a single inner movement:

In this nakedness the spirit finds its rest and refreshment; it desires nothing, so that nothing forces it upwards or drives it downwards, for it rests in the centre of its humility. Only the desire for something can make the spirit tired.[31]

I now turn to Angelus Silesius, my last example of Dionysian influenced speculation on the Nothingness of God. Here the same idea of nothing/everything appears as in John of the Cross, but expressed in his own individual way:

Whoever desires everything, still has nothing.
Whoever desires nothing, has everything:
Whoever desires everything has not in fact gained a thing.
— VI, 86[32]

---

30. Original text in: San Juan de la Cruz. *Obras Completas*, p. 204.

31. 1 S 13,13, "En esta desnudez halla el alma espiritual su quietud y descanso, porque, no codiciando nada, nada le fatiga hacia arriba y nada le oprime hacia abajo, porque este en ele centro de su humildad. Porque, cuando algo codicia, en eso mismo se fatiga." See s.v. "nada" and "negación" in: Fr. Luis de San Jose, *Concordancias de las Obras y Escritos del Doctor de la Iglesia San Juan de la Cruz*, pp. 729-31 and 740-43; F. Ruiz: *Saint Jean de la Croix, mystique et maitre spirituel*, Paris 1995.

32. I quote Angelus Silesius (Johannes Scheffler) in the edition: Johannes Angelus Silesius, *Cherubinischer Wandersmann oder Geistreiche Sinn- und Schlussreime*. Ed. Louise Gnädinger, Zürich 1986.

Silesius takes this theme even further in a whole series of proverbs and sayings in which he places great emphasis on the nothingness of God as the condition for any human contact with him. It was of course apparent to Silesius even as a young man that the world is nothing in comparison to God; in one entry in an album, for instance, he calls the world *unum pulcherimum nihil* (a most beautiful nothing; cp. VI, 191). Even clearer, for him, is that in comparison to the world God is a Nothing in an extreme sense. A few examples illustrate the idea, which remained with him all his life:

> God is nothing and everything.
> God is nothing and everything without any sophistry!
>
> For can you name something which he is?
> Or something which he isn't? — V, 197

God is incomparable being, alongside of which nothing can be placed (IV, 154); he is All and Nothing:

> God is nothing and everything.
> God is a spirit, a fire, a being and a light.
> And yet at the same time he is also none of these.
> — IV, 38

As unsurpassable love, which he showed on the cross, God is the purely incomparable (III, 36); God is everything, the human being nothing (II, 180). Thus the categories of everything and nothing become interchangeable:

> Equality is seen by God.
> For whom Nothing is as Everything, and Everything as a Nothing.
> He is vouchsafed the countenance of the beloved.
> — II, 169

The human being must therefore be furnished with Nothing, poor in spirit (II, 148); for him or her it is indeed a "self-abnegation" that is required ("Whoever is negated more, has more divinity," II, 140). In the "deification," nothing and everything become interchangeable (I, 216); both man and God can come in equal measure under these categories:

> The human is the highest thing.
> Nothing seems high to me: I am the highest thing,
> because even God without me is himself reduced.
> — I, 204

The basic condition for all these ideas, which boldly extend the notion of deification, is the fundamental and unsurpassable Nothingness of God:

> God is nothing (created).
> God is truly nothing: and if he is something
> it is only insofar as he is in me, as he chooses me.
> — I, 200

> The Godhead is a nothing.
> The tender Godhead is a nothing and beyond a nothing:
> he who sees nothing in everything, believe, O human! he sees it!
> — I, 111

> God cannot be grasped.
> God is a pure nothing, untouched by now or here:
> the more you reach for him, the more he evades you.
> — I, 25

In brief, then, there are numerous proverbs and sayings in which paradoxically fundamental renunciation and a total self-abnegation (desire nothing: I, 76; demand nothing, like the saints: I, 169; not to desire to seek God: I, 1712; etc.) are demanded of human beings in order to find God. The attitude required can be understood as the paradoxical perception of God from the point of view of non-perception:

> God beyond creation.
> Go where you cannot go! Look where you cannot look!
> Hear where there is no sound or echo: then you will be where God speaks. — I, 199

> Silent prayer.
> God is above everything, so that nothing can be spoken:
> Therefore, best of all, pray to him in silence too.
>
> — I, 240

As Georg Simmel has put it in an enlightening essay on "Die Persönlichkeit Gottes" (The Personality of God), it is in the end not the idea of the mystics that God is "a Nothing;" for — as he says —

> The mystics only want to exclude definitions of him, which of necessity are bound to be somewhat onesided, limiting, or exclusive and which thus deny the omnipotence, omnipresence, and absolute nature of the divine principle. The divine 'Nothing' of the mystics means that God is nothing in particular, and for this very reason is the Whole.[33]

In other words, negation is practised for the sake of the all-pervasive being of God, to leave no space for any "humanization of the divine."[34] Such ideas have their exact

---

33. G. Simmel, *Die Persönlichkeit Gottes*, in: Simmel: Gesamtausgabe Vol. 14: *Hauptprobleme der Philosophie*, Frankfurt/M., 1996, pp. 349-66; 349.

34. *Ibid.*, 351. Simmel's conception of the "personality of God" establishes throughout an ultimate distance, in spite of the closeness of man to God, so that the Nothing of God does not lead to an emptiness which excludes all possibility of man to experience God, cp. *ibid* 357f. This statement is true for Christian mysticism as a whole. Cp. also J. Sudbrack: *Mystik*, Mainz 1988, pp. 97-112; *Mystik im Dialog*, Würzburg 1992, pp. 147ff.; *Mystische Spuren. Auf der Suche nach der christlichen Lebensgestalt*, Würzburg 1990, pp. 293ff.

equivalents in some of the reflections of Meister Eckhart, for instance in the idea that all human striving should have no other purpose save that of magnifying God[35] and that all negations of him and his being are, in the end, a *negatio negationis*,[36] undertaken for the sake of the higher, eternal nature of God's being (in the presence of which the human being is a nothing).[37] Along with silence[38] and unknowing, that is the *docta ignorantia* (*unbekant bekenntnisse*)[39] inherited from Augustine, we find a fundamental attitude depicted in which, at the very moment of the negation, an unlimited positive statement is implied. These are Meister Eckhart's words:

> And therefore (because the relation to God may not be disturbed by any images of knowledge from within), silence and stillness must be the rule, and the Father must speak there and give birth to his Son and work his works without any images. . . . Such (good and perfect) people should know that it is the best and most noble of actions for which we have come into this life, if you are silent and allow God to act and speak. When all powers are removed from their works and images, then this word is spoken. For this reason he said: 'In the midst of silence the heavenly Word was spoken to me' (Sap 18: 14ff.).[40]

---

35. *DW* 5, p. 199, 4-6.

36. Quotations see A.M. Haas, *Gott Leiden Gott Lieben, Zur volkssprachlichen Mystik im Mittelalter*, Frankfurt/M., 1989, p. 54, 161f., 181f., 221.

37. Quotations see: A.M. Haas, *Mystik als Aussage, Erfahrungs-, Denk- und Redeformen christlicher Mystik*, Frankfurt/M., 1996, p. 311f.

38. F. Pfeiffer, Predigt 1, in: J. Quint, *Deutsche Predigten und Traktate*, München 1955 (abbr. Qu), p. 419, l. 17ff.

39. F. Pfeiffer, *Meister Eckhart* (Deutsche Mystiker des 14. Jahrhunderts), vol. II, 2nd edn., Aalen, 1962, p. 8, l. 18. Augustinus, *Epistola ad Probam*, c. 15, *CSEL* 44, p. 72.

40. Qu p. 419, l. 17ff., l. 33ff.

Silence is a way of letting speech come and thus of letting go.

In his apophasis, Meister Eckhart reaches a point of the highest importance for a description of mysticism. If God is an *esse innominabile* (an unnameable being), which paradoxically (and fascinatingly) must also be called a *nomen innominabile*, then it will make no difference as far as God is concerned if the *nomen innominabile* is converted into a *nomen omninominabile*.[41] For whatever cannot be pinned down with names, is able to bear a multitude of names; but at the same time, God cannot be comprehended with a multiplicity of names. The potentially endless procedure of naming God with as many names as possible can have two possible interpretations. Firstly, it may be an attempt to quantify, to create the best possible concept of God amid the plethora of names. Alternatively, by means of the semantic competition it sets up between the many names, it may aim to abolish as completely as possible all attempts to conceptualize God, with the result that it puts an end to all imagery in the contemplation of God. In fact, in mystical texts there is a tendency to combine the two approaches. As Michael Egerding has said,

> . . . again and again in mystical texts, the conceptualization of God — sometimes by frequent naming, sometimes by radical naming — undergoes a process which leads to the relativization — and even to the abolition — of the conceptualization that has only just been achieved.[42]

Paradoxically, it is the very explosion of metaphorical richness which leads to an impression of the invisibility, unfathomability and hiddenness of God.

---

41. Cp. Lossky, *Theologie Negative*, p. 22ff. And 41ff.

42. M. Egerding, *Die Metaphorik der spätmittelalterlichen Mystik*, 2 vols., Paderborn 1997.

If and whenever mystics seek to grasp God by the richness and fullness of their images and metaphors, then it is in the very process of piling up names and metaphors that they prove the impossibility of finally fixing the name of God; just as Augustine says: *Si comprehendis, non est Deus.*[43] (If you understand, it is not God.)

Even more acute is the possibility which the speaker has of isolating the metaphor from its context of implication. The result is that it becomes much more difficult than with "contextually embedded types of metaphor"[44] to resolve the "semantic tension"[45] between the object of the image and the receptor of the image (in other words, between God himself and his image). This is likely to be seen in a negative light by those thinkers who operate within the normal functions of language. For poetics, on the other hand, with its highly developed feeling for nuances of style, it will be seen that in such contextually starved metaphors, language (or in Artaud's phrase "language as conjuration"[46]) must seize its opportunity.[47] Let us take an example from Mechthild of Magdeburg to clarify what is meant here. In her *Fließendes Licht der Gottheit*[48] (The Flowing Light of the Godhead), there occurs the following passage of praise to God:

---

43. Augustine, Sermo 117, c. 3, p. 5.

44. Egerding, *Metaphorik*, vol. I, p. 212.

45. *Ibid.*

46. A. Artaud, *Das Theater und sein Double*, München, 1996, p. 49.

47. Cp. Egerding, *Metaphorik*, vol. I, pp. 66-71.

48. Mechthild von Magdeburg: *Das fließende Licht der Gottheit*, ed. H. *Neumann*, vol. 1: München 1990, vol. 2, München 1993 (abbr. *N*). See also: Mechthild von Magdeburg, *Das fließende Licht der Gottheit*, translation and commentary by Margot Schmidt, Stuttgart/Bad Cannstatt 1995 (abbr. S).

> The least significant creature praises God in ten things.
> You burning mountain!
> You select sun!
> You full moon!
> You bottomless well!
> You unreachable heights!
> You brightness without measure!
> You wisdom without end!
> You mercy without hindrance!
> You strength without opposition!
> You crown of all honours!
> You are praised by the most insignificant of all you have created![49]

The doxology here, with its obvious indebtedness to invocations of God found in prayers, cannot be interpreted simply by its metaphorical function.[50] Through its genre and its rhetorical structure such a passage is connected to other similarly important contexts so that its interpretation is to a large extent given *a priori*. The praise of God expressed here in a series of ten images will probably engage today's literary historian in a point-by-point exposition. To a reader praying aloud at that time, however, such an interpretation would not have been of the greatest interest. The receptive situation for such a reader is described by Philo as follows: "Whatever bears comparison with all that may be thought about God must be viewed with the greater eyes of the soul."[51] These "greater eyes of the soul" — a Platonic term for the *nous* — provide an insight into the realization of the divine wisdom which is to a certain extent an expected language for the praying

---

49. S p. 16, l. 19-30; orginal text in: *N* I, p. 12, book I, chapt. 8, l. 1-5.

50. Cp. Egerding, *Metaphorik,* I, p. 211f.

51. F. Siegert, *Philon von Alexandrien. Über die Gottesbezeichnung "wohltätig verzehrendes Feuer" (De Deo),* Tübingen 1988 (WUNT 46) p. 33; cp. Commentary p. 40f.

follower of any religion. For this reason it is the associations that accompany the given semantic field which are significant rather than the individual metaphors. What seems to be just a vague outline description of God, by means of a gradual enumeration of ten statements of praise, is in fact the whole point of the expression, and not to be regarded as a defect.[52] The main thing is the greatness of God, which can be aimed through language, but not to be achieved through any unambiguous use of metaphors.

If a kind of explosive effect can be gained by a simple enumeration of metaphors, such an effect can be achieved in what has been called "Sprengmetaphorik" (explosive metaphors) by Hans Blumenberg. In the "explosive metaphor" in the strict sense of the term, the movement towards the unknown God is not propelled by groups of words but by content-filled definitions of specific metaphors. Blumenberg sees the origin of his "explosive metaphors" as follows:

> The negative theology of late antiquity and christianity, wherever it comes under Neoplatonic influence, created the need for a new language. Of course it could be said that a theology, which cannot state anything at all about God, does not need a language at all. But we need to make a fundamental distinction here between inability to speak and unwillingness to speak; this is what is meant by *docta ignorantia*. Negative theology does not represent a state of knowledge; rather it is a way, a praxis, a method of achieving a mode of behaviour. Even where negative theology is not propagated systematically, as with Augustine, we find those decisive 'metaphors which violate our visions.' (Ernst Robert Curtius).[53]

52. Egerding: *Metaphorik*, vol. I, p. 212 only retains the negative aspect.

53. H. Blumenberg: *Paradigmen zu einer Metaphorologie*, in: *Archiv für Begriffsgeschichte* 6 (1960) pp. 132-35.

In later passages Blumenberg categorizes the "truth" of explosive metaphors as being a pragmatic truth, "which can be termed 'mystical' in a general sense."[54] An example for him is Nicolas of Cusa's treatise *De docta ignorantia*, chapter 21, and its depiction of the infinite circle as a basic symbol of divine unity, and therefore also "a key symbol of theological thought and method."[55] Referring back to the famous second definition of God from the *Liber XXIV philosophorum* (Book of the Twenty-four Masters): *Deus est sphaera infinita cuius centrum est ubique, circumferentia nusquam,*[56] Blumenberg defines the process in the text as follows:

> The feature we refer to as *explosive metaphors* achieves more (than negative theology): it draws the vision into a *process* which at first may be followed (as for example, when you are asked to imagine the repeated doubling of the radius of an imaginary circle) until a point is reached at which you have to give up (for example when you have to imagine the largest radius you can, or indeed to imagine an infinite radius of an infinite circle), this point is then regarded as the 'giving up of the self.' The aim of all this is to turn the transcendence into a lived experience, as a limit to theoretical methods and thus as a challenge to various modes of realization. The explosive basis of this type of metaphor is the idea of eternity, the model for which comes from the formula regarded as hermetic in the 'Book of the Twenty-four Masters.'[57]

A parallel can be drawn between such statements and those of the theoretical linguist Ian T. Ramsey, who regards the

54. *Ibid.*, 135.

55. Blumenberg, *Paradigmen* 135.

56. *Le Livre des XXIV Philosophes*, Traduit du latin, edité et annoté par Françoise Hudry, Grenoble, 1989, pp. 93-96.

57. Blumenberg, *Paradigmen* 132f.

nature of religious and mystical language as being a combination of the "observable and more than observable."[58] The recipient is guided through a series of concretely imaginable geometric figures — particularly the line, triangle and circle — and through the exploding of their definitions is led on to a vision of endless eternity. By allowing the metaphor to deconstruct itself through paradox, it allows for the possibility of perceiving oneness and eternity.[59] The same method is explicitly followed by Meister Eckhart in the following passage of his Sermon 51:[60]

> I have often said: The shell must break and whatever is inside must come forth; for if you want to have the nut, you must first crack the shell. In the same way: if you want to find nature revealed, you must first crack all its parables, and the further you penetrate, the closer you will get to true being. When the soul finds the One in which all is one, then it remains in this single Oneness.[61]

Egerding is perhaps justified when he asks whether in the final analysis all metaphors can — from a particular point of view — be regarded as having an explosive effect.[62] In the case of statements about God I would like to reply in the affirmative, especially with regard to the way that through the translation of the metaphor the meaning is propelled towards the spiritual, infinite unity. In this respect, the

---

58. Cp. A.M. Haas, *Sermo mysticus. Studien zur Theologie und Sprache der deutschen Mystik*, Freiburg/Schweiz, 1979, 2nd edn. 1989, pp. 112, 131, 141, 321, 323.

59. Cp. Köbele, *Bilder der unbegriffenen Wahrheit*, pp. 58-63.

60. Cp. *ibid*.

61. Translation of: Quint in: N. Largier, *Meister Eckhart. Werke*, 2 vols., Frankfurt/M., 1993, Here vol. I, p. 545, l. 18-25.

62. Cp. Egerding, *Metaphorik* I, p. 53.

explosive metaphors of the sphere and the circle have been particularly effective in history[63] as a means of transfer to the dimension of eternity, a notable achievement of the language of metaphorical discourse. The circle whose centre is everywhere and whose circumference is nowhere *is* the epitome of the achieved vision of the eternity of God, a vision whose content is the nothingness of all concepts of the circle. In this way, the Nothing and the deconstructive application of the metaphor correspond in the most intimate of ways. The one is a prerequisite for the other, since the nothingness of God can be expressed in no other way than by its "explosive metaphors."

63. Cp. D. Mahncke, *Unendliche Sphäre und Allmittelpunkt* (orig. Halle 1937), Stuttgart-Bad Cannstatt 1966; G. Poulet, *Metamorphosen des Kreises in der Dichtung*, Frankfurt/M., 1966; M.M. Borrero, *La geometria mistica del alma en la literatura española del Siglo de Oro. Notas y puntualizaciones*, Madrid 1975; M.M.M. Lurker, *Der Kreis als Symbol im Denken, Glauben und künstlerischen Gestalten der Menschheit*, Tübingen 1981, p. 36ff.

8

Tāntric System in Buddhism

Wangchuk Dorje Negi

BUDDHA, after attaining enlightenment, turned the wheel of *dharma* in the world three times. He turned the first wheel of the *dharma* at Sārnāth, where he taught the "Four Noble Truths," emphasizing the true existence of all phenomena. This was based on the principles of Śrāvakayāna (Hīnayāna). The second turning of the wheel was at Gṛdhrakūṭa where he preached on *prajñāpāramitā*, emphasizing emptiness which refers to the non-existence of all phenomena or their emptiness of true existence. This was based on the tenet of Bodhisattvayāna or Mahāyāna. And the third turning occurred at various places such as Vaiśālī. At that time he taught the distinction between "what is true existence and what is not." However, while Buddha was preaching the *prajñāpāramitā*, he simultaneously emanated himself in the form of *kālacakra* at a place called Dhanyakaṭaka in south India. He also gave the *kālacakra* teaching to Sucandra who was the king of Shambala.[1] In general, the essence of Buddha's teachings are included in these three aspects of the mind: "Mind does not exist of its

1. *gṛdhrakūṭe yathāśāstrā prajñāpāramitānaye* ।
tathā mantranaye proktā śrīdhānye dharmadeśanā ॥ — *se.ṭī.pṛ*. 3

Sekoddeśaṭīkā of Nādapāda, ed. Mario E. Carilli, Baroda: Oriental Institute, 1941.

own," "its nature and experience are clear."[2] Hence, mind is temporarily deluded by adventitious afflictions; and this delusion is known as the cause of all suffering, and the path is the antidote to remove it. As soon as the path is well trained cessation which is known as the result is obtained, and "mind does not exist of its own" refers to wordness, and the clarity refers to the luminosity which is known as Buddha nature. The aforesaid Buddha nature permeates all sentient beings.

As mentioned in *Samādhirāja-Sūtra*.[3] "Tathāgatagarbha embraces and permeates all beings." It is also said in the *Mahāparinirvāṇa-Sūtra*:[4] "All sentient beings are endowed with the Tathāgatagarbha. Just as butter permeates milk, so does Tathāgatagarbha permeate all beings." This Tathāgatagarbha can be referred to in other words as well: Innate nature, primordial nature, Sāmantabhadra, Mahāmudrā, Great Consummation, Tantra, Great Śūnyatā, and so on. Hence, according to peoples' dispositions and ability, it is explained accordingly.

In this situation, we need to dig deep to find out about reality, since reality is more important than history and legend. If we turn the pages composed by some great individuals we will find that they have emphasized real matter and subject, not history and legend. Similarly, the matter of Tantra is the same. It is also something which can't be bound by history. Even these days, one who has the ability to meet the *bodhisattva* and Buddhahood, can also find a new and extraordinary system. So, the main thing is to see whether you have the ability to understand and practice it or not.

---

2. *taccittamacittam* । *prakṛtiścittasya prabhāsvarā* । — *Aṣṭasāhasrikā Prajñāpāramitā* pr. 3 Darbhaṅgā Saṁskaraṇa, 1960.
3. Toh. 127. This is quoted by Dakpo Rinpoche in his *Jewel Ornament of Liberation* p. 6, New Delhi: Sherab Gyaltsen, 1992.
4. Toh. 120, *Ibid.*, p. 7.

Now comes the real question: What is Tantra? Tantra literally means "continuity," "continuum." There is a continuous thread running since beginningless time. Usually we think of a thread as starting from somewhere. But according to Buddhism, the thread has no beginning, just as there is no beginning of time and space, and therefore the continuity is such a thread that does not even inherently exist but at the same time is continuous. As it is said in the *Guhyasamājatantra*:

> *Prabandham* is known as Tantra, of which there are three types: Base Tantra, Path Tantra and Result Tantra.
>
> *prabandhaṁ tantramākhyātaṁ tatprabandhaṁ tridhā bhavet* ǀ
> *ādhāraḥ prakṛtiścaiva asaṁhāryaprabhedataḥ* ǁ
>
> *prakṛtiścākṛterheturasaṁhāryaphalaṁ tathā* ǀ
> *ādhārastu upāyaśca trividhastantrārthasaṁgrahaḥ* ǁ
>
> — 18, 33-34[5]

(1) ***Base Tantra*** **:** Base Tantra is the seed of the Result Tantra, as it possesses the ability to bring forth fruit by connecting with other causes. If we analyse it properly we will find that the nature of the Base Tantra is clear, but is temporarily obstructed by adventitious defilements. Dharmakīrti says the nature of mind is clear light; the defilements are adventitious, and once the defilements don't subsist in the nature of the mind, it is possible to remove them through generating an antidote if we remove the very stage which we called Buddha. So, in view of the predicable matter, this mind is known as the Base Tantra. As said in the *Hevajratantra*:[6]

---

5. *Guhyasamāja Tantram*, ed. Svāmī Dvārikādāsa Śastrī, Varanasi: Bauddha Bhāratī Prakāśana, 1984.

6. *The Hevajra Tantra : A Critical Study* (Part 2), ed. D.L Snellgrove, Oriental Series Volume 6, London: Oxford University Press, 1980.

sattvā buddhā eva kintu āgantukamalāvṛtāḥ ı
tasyāpakarṣaṇāt sattvā buddhā eva na saṁśayaḥ ıı
— 6,3.9

In fact, the (mind of all) sentient beings are Buddha, but they are covered by adventitious defilements. If these are removed, then they will become real Buddhas.

(2) ***Path Tantra*** : The Path Tantra is said to be the path which causes one to remove the adventitious defilements in order to bring forth the nature of mind. As a seed needs water, sun, light, manure, etc., to bring forth its fruit, so does the Path Tantra need this method to bring forth the reality of mind. Therefore, initiations, instructions, oral transmissions are the Path Tantra which, too, are the mind.

(3) ***Result Tantra*** : This is the luminous stage from beginningless time in an invisible manner. Its main function is to make apparent the clear form, as a fruit of a tree which exists in its cause and conditions and an invisible manner, when it is ripened it comes into being. Likewise, depending on the "Path Tantra" our minds become clear from defilements and assume the forms of a Bodhi which is known as the "Result Tantra."

Generally the base Tantra is the inseparable subtle wind and luminosity which is the base of all appearance. I think this is the main crux of Tantra. Sometimes, this is referred as five wisdom winds or energy which can't be separated from the clarity and its dynamic nature. It is like the fire and its warmness, or flower and its odour. In Tibetan, we use the term *rlun-semes-dbyer-med*. This is Base Tantra which is continuous from beginningless time. Path Tantra is the generation stage, and completion stage which is of course not separate from Base Tantra. Base Tantra itself appears in divine clarity, Fruition as Result Tantra is through two stages of practice attending the two bodies (form and truth body) that is also not separate from Base Tantra. So, Base Tantra itself is Path, Path itself is Base, Base itself is Fruit or Fruit itself is Base. There is a state of inseparableness of body, speech and mind or the base, path and mind. As *Guhyasamāja* states :

> *kāyavākcittavajreṇa bhedābhedasvabhāvataḥ* ।
>
> — 18.38

The method for experiencing the very subtle wind (*prāṇa-vāyu*) and mind (*Rlun-semes-dbyer-med*) is explained fully in the teaching of secret higher Yoga Tantra. Why is this? It is because we can attain enlightenment in this very life if we depend upon this very subtle mind and its mounted wind. The very subtle mind is the substantial cause of the Truth Body of the Buddha, and the very subtle mind upon which it is mounted is the substantial cause of the Form Body of the Buddha. Without using the subtle mind it is not possible to attain the perfect enlightenment of Buddhahood. The ability of a mind to function depends upon its mounted wind. If the wind (breath or energy) is impure, the mind mounted upon it will also be impure. On the other hand, if it is a wisdom wind, the mind mounted upon it will also be a wisdom mind. The wind that flows within the right and left channels and that which flows throughout all the seventy-two thousand channels of the body, all cause dualistic conceptions to arise. The wind that flows within the central channel, however, is the wisdom wind, so called because the *yogīs* develop their wisdom minds from it. All wisdom minds must be mounted upon wisdom winds. It is essential to bring all the winds into the central channel. The only way to catch or control the mind is through catching their base. So, in this context, Rangjung Dorjee says:[7] "You can't find fire through cutting wood into pieces. It can

---

7. *Zabmo Snaṛdon*, p. 36, Published in Tibet 1850.

only be achieved by rubbing them together." Likewise, thought alone is not enough to enable one to realize the nature of mind, but we can know luminosity through practising inhalation and exhalation practice through vase meditation, as normative of the Vajrayāna practices, through generation and consummation stage.

Characteristic of Tantra Vehicle

In order to achieve Buddhahood we must know how to ascertain the two bases, how to practice the two paths. And relying on the practices, how to achieve the goal which is said to be the two bodies of Buddha. According to the perfection path, the base of all doctrines and practices are the two truths: Conventional Truth and Ultimate Truth. As mentioned in Nāgārjuna's *Mādhyamakaśāstra*:

> Doctrines taught by the Buddha
> Are perfectly founded on the two truths.[8]

At the same time he also mentioned how to attain the two bodies of the Buddha through the two paths. As mentioned in the *Ratnāvalī* (Precious Garland) (1):[9]

> The form body of the Buddha
> Arises from collected merit.
> The truth body in brief, O king;
> Arises from collected wisdom.

It can be explained that the collection of merits which principally assists in attaining the body of the Buddha is known as the Buddha's Form Body. On the other hand, the collection of wisdom which principally assists one in attaining a kind of

---

8. *dvesatye samupāśritya buddhānāṁ dharma deśanā* ।

9. *buddhānāṁ rūpakāyastu puṇyasaṁbhārato bhavet* ॥
dharmakāyasamāsena jñāna saṁbhārato nṛpaḥ ॥ — 3.13

body is known as Truth Body. The nature of ultimate truth is similar to the perfection vehicle. The great Tibetan saint Mila Respa also said that in Tantra ultimate truth should not be different from the causal vehicle. If so, the ultimate truth will fall into contrived and thought perception. But the ultimate truth is beyond all thought. Nāgārjuna defines the ultimate nature thus:[10]

> Not dependent on another, peaceful and
> not fabricated by mental fabrication,
> not thought, without distinctions,
> that is the character of reality.
>
> — 18-19

> *aparapratyayaṁ śāntaṁ prapañcairaprapañcitam* ।
> *nirvikalpamanānārthametattattvasya lakṣaṇam* ॥
>
> — *Ma. Śā.*, 18.9

The state of peace transcending all fabrication is *śūnyatā*, voidness, Atīśa also says:

> Where emptiness is concerned there is not even one division.
> Thus, to conclude as the Buddha says,[11]
> Where there is no rejection, acceptance or
> grasping of any aspect of reality,
> There is meditation on the wisdom-gone-beyond.
> Non-contemplation and non-imagery are such meditations.[12]

Now in the division of perfection — vehicle and *mantra* — vehicle is made by method. As said before, the path is included

---

10. *Mādhyamakaśāstra* of Nāgārjuna, ed. P.L. Vaidya, The Mithila Institute, Darbhanga, 1987.

11. This is quoted by Dagpo Tashi Nanguyal in Mahamudra Pub.

12. *Abhisamayālaṁkāra*, 5.21, *draṣṭavya*, *Caryāgītikoṣa*, pr̥. 32, *tathā Caryāmelāpakapradīpa*, p. 102.

within the factor of method which is the very thing for achieving the Buddha's Form Body. Whereas the path included within the factor of wisdom (emptiness meditation) is the means for achieving Buddha's Truth Body, to achieve which one needs to cultivate a path which should be similar in aspect to a Truth Body. Both the perfection and *mantra* vehicle have a path of wisdom in which one cultivates a similitude of the Buddha's Truth Body. Similarly, in order to achieve a Form Body, one needs to cultivate a path that is similar in aspect to the Buddha's Form Body. Only *mantra* vehicle has this special method for achieving this fruit by cultivating paths which are similar in aspect to the Buddha's Form Body. That is why this vehicle is known as an effect-vehicle.

Synonyms of Mantrayāna

With respect to the "Secret Mantra Vehicle," the matter of Secret Mantra Vehicle is always hidden because it is achieved secretly and in hiding; it is not appropriate to be displayed like merchandise but should be practised secretly. If it is not so, instead of there being benefit there is a danger of harming beings due to generating misunderstanding. It is practised in order to achieve the activities of pacification, increase, power and wrath. These are not described in the "Perfect Vehicle." Hence, the vehicle in which the practices are performed in secrecy is known as the "Secret Mantra Vehicle." Generally, the word *mantra* refers to "mind protection." It protects our mind from ordinary appearances and conceptions. Here, mind refers to six types of consciousnesses which are to be freed or protected from the ordinary world. There are two factors in *mantra* training, pride in oneself as a deity and vivid appearance of that deity. Divine pride protects one from the pride of being ordinary, and divine vivid appearance protects one from ordinary appearance. Whatever appears to the senses is viewed as the sport of a deity; for instance, whatever forms are seen are viewed as the emanation of a deity and whatever sounds are heard are viewed as the *mantra* of deity. Through this transformation of attitude the pride of being a deity emerge. Such protection of mind together with its attendant pledge and vows are called the practice of *mantra*. As said in the *Guhyasamājatantra* also : Mind arising dependent on a sense and an object is said to be *mantra,* means protection by means of all *vajras* of the pledges and vows explained, free from the ways of the world, called "the practice of Mantra."

In another way we can explain that *man* is said to be knowledge of suchness, and *tra* the compassion that protects those sentient beings. As said in the *Guhyasamājatantra*:

> *pratītyotpadyate yadyadindriyairviṣayairmanaḥ* ।
> *tanmano mananaṁ khyātaṁ kārakatrāṇanārthataḥ* ॥ — 18.69

With respect to the Bodhisattva Vehicle, it is divided into two: a cause-vehicle of the grounds and perfection, and an effect-vehicle of secret *mantra*. Thus, "Secret Mantra Vehicle," "Effect Vehicle," and "Vajra Vehicle" are the synonyms of the Mantra Vehicle which is also called the "Method Vehicle." It is said that because of its indivisibility it is the Vajra Vehicle, because the effect itself became the path it is the Effect Vehicle; because of the greatness of its methods, it is the Method Vehicle. Because of its extreme secrecy, it is the Secret Vehicle. On the other hand Śraddhakaravarma says: [13] It is an Effect Vehicle because a path of imagination is practiced. In this the one assumes the aspects of the four, through purification. These are: (1) the abode where the Buddha resides after perfect enlightenment; (2) the body that is a manifestation of the wisdom-truth-body in the form of a residence and resident; (3) the resources that he enjoyed in the high status of

---

13. This is quoted by Tsongkapa in *The Great Exposition of Secret Mantrayāna*, p. 23 Pub. Dharmsala.

Buddhahood, and (4) the supreme activities of Buddhas ripening sentient beings. The similitude of these four factors of the effect state are cultivated in meditation. So this is called the Effect Vehicle.

Method Vehicle : Since the Mantra Vehicle has more varieties of methods or skillful means than the Perfection Vehicle, it is called the Method Vehicle.

As said by *Tripiṭakamālā*:[14]

ekārthatve'pyasaṁmohād bahūpāyādaduṣarāt ।
tīkṣṇendriyādhikārāñca mantraśāstraṁ viśiṣyate ॥
— *dra. a.va.saṁ.*, p. 32

Though the aim is the same, Mantra Vehicle is superior because of being for the non-obscured.

Having many skillful methods, no difficulties, and being designed for those of sharp faculties.

The objector himself asserts that this implies that the aim of attainment of the Mantra and Perfection Vehicle is the same, that is Buddhahood. The mere differences between these two *yāna*s (Vehicles) must be in terms of the causes or methods for attaining the effect — the state of Buddhahood.

Lateral Meanings of Four Schools of the Tāntric Tradition

Now I would like to explain the four Tantras: (1) Action Tantras are so called because the activities which are to be performed are predominant. (2) Performance Tantras are so called because activities and meditative stabilization are performed equally. (3) Yoga Tantras are so called because internal Yoga is very central. (4) And lastly, higher Yoga Tantras

14. *Advayavajrasaṁgraha*, ed. Haraprasāda Śāstrī, Gaekward Oriental Series-41, Baroda, 1927.

are so called because there are no higher yogas then this. On the other hand, Kong-Trul Rinpoche says,[15] those who have little capacity for meditation on suchness but are mainly involved in external activities are Action Tantras. Tantras are assigned as Performance if they teach internal meditative stabilization and external activities equally. The Tantra which explains the four *mudrā*s is generally called Yoga Tantra. The teaching concerning the sphere of purification, namely birth, death and intermediate state through generation and consummation is the Higher Yoga Tantra.

Higher Yoga Tantra should further be divided into three sub-classifications : Father, Mother and non-dual Tantra. According to Pad-ma-karpo's *General Presentation of Tantra Sets*,[16] the Tantra practised through five stages is known as Father Tantra. Like *Guhyasamāja*, the Tantra which is practicsed in two stages through the four *mudrā*s is known as Mother Tantra. It is mainly based on the *Hevajra Tantra*. And lastly, the Tantra which is practised though six Yogas is called a Non-dual Yoga Tantra such as Kālacakra Tantra Sādhanā.

The practice for the above-mentioned Tantra is not possible without having initiation. Buddha said practicing Tantra without obtaining initiation is like trying to extract oil from sand. Therefore, each Tantra has its own initiation.

Before doing practice of the path we need to have proper empowerment, scriptural transmission and explanations. These three are the main elements of Vajrayāna practice. These three transmissions must have been uninterrupted from your lineage *guru*. If an electric wire has been cut at a certain point, you will not receive light in your room. In the same way if the transmission had been interrupted you would not receive the

15. *Śes-bya Mdsad*, vol. II, p. 578, Pub in Tibet 1982.

16. *Collected Works*, vol. 11, Darjeeling: K.S.N. Khang, 1974.

blessing without which Vajrayāna cannot be effective. To practice Vajrayāna, ideally you should receive a complete empowerment, including four subdivisions: First the Vase Initiation by which your impure body is transformed into a pure, divine body. Second the Secret Initiation by which your impure speech is transformed into the pure speech of a deity, i.e., *mantra*. Third, the Wisdom Awareness Initiation, which transforms your impure mind into the pure mind of the deity, and lastly, through the Fourth Initiation body, speech and mind are simultaneously purified and the five Buddhas and the five primordial awarenesses are realized. Of course, initiation itself is not enough in order to be able to do the actual practice. For this you have to receive specific explanations. This is the only way to practice Vajrayāna. If you practice in this way you can achieve enlightenment in this very life. So the uninterrupted transmission of your root *guru* is like a lens, for example, and the Buddha's and *bodhisattva*'s blessings are like a sun. Even when the sun is very hot, it is not enough to burn a piece of paper or material on the ground, but if you place a lens between the sun and the paper or material, it will be burnt very quickly, even if the sun is the same as before. Therefore if we do according to *guru*'s instruction we can achieve the Buddhahood in this very life. So, Vajrayāna is a very quick way. These are a few of the characteristics of the Vajrayāna.

References[*]

Advayavajra Saṁgraha, ed. Haraprashada Shastri, Gaekwad Oriental Series 42, Baroda, 1927.

Abhisamayālaṁkāra Vṛtti Sphuṭārtha, ed. Ramashankara Tripathi, Bhota Bharati Granthamala, Sarnath, Varanasi: CIHTS, 1977.

Aṣṭasāhasrika Prajñāpāramitā, ed. P.L. Vaidya, Baudha Sanskrit Granthamala-4, Darbhanga: Mithila Vidyapitha, 1960.

Charyagiti Kosha, ed. Prabodhachandra Bagchi and Shantibhiksu Shastri, Shantiniketan: Viswabharati, 1956.

Caryāmelāpaka Pradīpam of Ācāryā Āryadeva, ed. Janardana Shastri Pandey, Rare Buddhist Texts Research Project, Sarnath: CIHTS, 2000.

Guhyasāmaja Tantram, Critically edited by Swami Dwarikadas Shastri, Varanasi: Baudhabharati, 1984.

The Hevajra Tantra: A Critical Study (part 2), D.L. Snellgrone, London Oriental Series, Vol. VI, London: Oxford University Press, 1980.

Jab-mo-nag-don published from Tibet, 1850.

Jewel Ornament of Liberation by Dakpo Rinpoche, New Delhi: Sherab Gyaltsen, 1992.

Jñeya Kosha (Tibetan edition) by Kongutal Rinpoche published by Mirig Petun Khang.

Mahāmudrā: The quintessence of mind and meditation by Dakpo Tashi Namgal, Boston: Sambhasha, 1986.

Mādhyamaka Śāstram, ed. P.L. Vaidya, Buddha Sanskrit Granthavali-10, Darbhanga: Mithila Vidyapitha, 1987.

Ratnāvalī, ed. P.L. Vaidya, Baudha Sanskrit Granthavali-10, Darbhanga: Mithila Vidyapitha, 1987.

Sekoddeshaṭīkā of Nādapāda (Naropa), ed. Mario E. Carilli, Baroda: Oriental Institute, 1941.

Sāmānya-tantram by Padma Karpo, Bhutan.

---

* By Anirban Dash.

9

Attaining the Form of the Void

Śūnya in the Vijñāna Bhairava

Bettina Bäumer

SOME of the basic Tantras of non-dualist Kashmir Śaivism describe the stages of spiritual experience as different forms of the Void, among them the *Svacchanda Tantra* and the *Vijñāna Bhairava*. The French scholar and mystic Lilian Silburn has published an article on "the seven voids," based mainly on the *Svacchanda Tantra*.[1] I want to focus attention on the *Vijñāna Bhairava*, the most practice-oriented Tantra of the non-dual Śaiva texts of Kashmir, which is called "the essence of the *Rudrayāmala* (Tantra)," and which is constantly referred to as authority by later writers. Abhinavagupta calls it "the Upaniṣad of the knowledge of Śiva" (*Śivavijñāna Upaniṣad*). Among the vast literature on Tāntric Yoga this text stands out by its directness, practicality and the immediacy of the mystical experience described. It teaches 112 methods of concentration, called *dhāraṇā*s or ways of Yoga, which involve the body, breath, mind, the universe and all levels of consciousness, from the most down-to-earth experience to the supreme level of awareness.

---

1. L. Silburn, "Les sept vacuités d'après le Śivaïsme du Cachemire." in: *Le Vide, Expérience spirituelle en Occident et en Orient*, Hermès 6, Paris, 1969, pp. 213-21.

In this paper I want to present the text from two points of view: an analysis of the language, in the context of *śūnya-pūrṇa;* and from the point of view of mystical experience. The relationship between language and mysticism has been thoroughly studied by Alois Haas.[2]

The logo of our Seminar is the wheel, *cakra,* an ancient Vedic and Buddhist symbol. It is not only the symbol for the place of this Seminar, Sārnāth, where the Buddha turned the *dharmacakra* for the first time, it was also the cross of Shantivanam which the two founders, Abhishiktananda and Monchanin, used to wear in the1950s.[3] It is thus a symbol which can bridge the three religions represented here. One of the most ancient Sanskrit words for void is *kha,* which means the nave of the wheel, the empty space which makes movement and dynamism possible. It also denotes the hollow of the sense-organs and the hollow of the channels in the body. Lilian Silburn had already noted the significant terminology of the void:

> [There is] the void in the depth of interiority — piercing through the phenomena in order to reach the Self — and the void of extension — the void of immensity which expands to the measure of the universe.
>
> The Śaivites denote the void of interiority by the term *kha,* the void of the nave of the cosmic wheel, of the conscious energies, and the void of the immensity by *vyoman,* the infinite firmament of Consciousness to which the first leads.

---

2. A.M. Haas, *Mystik als Aussage,* Frankfurt/M., 1996.
3. Swami Abhishiktananda, in whose name the seminar took place, founded the Ashram of Shantivanam near Kulitalai in Tamil Nadu in 1950 together with Jules Monchanin. Their symbol of the integration of Hinduism and Christianity was a wheel with a cross.

> Both are again divided into a passive void called *śūnya*, and a dynamic, unspeakable void, *anākhya*.
>
> — Le Vide, Hermès 6, p. 214

I may add to Silburn's observations that the Śaivites prefer the adjective *śūnya* to the abstract noun *śūnyatā*, and the adjective is often used in the sense of a noun. An analysis of the *Vijñāna Bhairava* also reveals another distinction: if *śūnya* denotes a state of consciousness, *laya*, merging, dissolution, absorption, indicates the dynamic, active aspect of the void, movement towards the void, absorption in the ultimate Reality. There are a number of important concepts, mostly in the form of adjectives, describing the spiritual state of emptiness, the most important being *nirvikalpa*, the thoughtfree state and *nirādhāra*, supportless.

This terminology already indicates some of the dimensions of the void as described in the *Vijñāna Bhairava*. We may straightaway go to the text.

Like most Śaivāgamas, the *Vijñāna Bhairava* is also presented in the form of a dialogue between Śiva and Śakti, or Bhairava and Bhairavī. This is not only a rhetorical frame, but has also a deeper significance. At the beginning of the text the Goddess asks Bhairava that, although she has studied all the (Yāmala) Tantras, she is not satisfied because her doubts have not yet been cleared (verse 1). According to Śaiva philosophy this means that the Goddess, whose very nature is knowledge (*jñānaśakti*) and the Word, especially the revealed word of the Āgamas (*vāc*), is pretending ignorance on behalf of those ignorant beings who need to be enlightened by divine revelation. By her questioning she thus leads the reader/ listener from a purely textual, theoretical knowledge of the Tantras to an experiential knowledge gained by the practice of the *dhāraṇā*s. At the end of the text the Goddess expresses her satisfaction by telling the great God (Mahādeva) that "today" she has been fully satisfied by understanding the essence of the Tantra, upon which she becomes one with Śiva. This narrative framework is couched in a very human language, but it implies that the Goddess, who stands here for every seeker, passes from a state of dissatisfaction, of ignorance, of emptiness, to a state of satisfaction, of knowledge, of non-dual fullness (*paritṛptāsmi*. . . , v. 161). This is explicitly stressed at the end of the *dhāraṇā*s, in a concluding verse:

> If anyone is established in any of the ways (described here), what he experiences is fulfilled day by day, until his spiritual satisfaction reaches its utmost fullness. v. 148
>
> — *sā atra tṛptir-atyanta-pūrṇatā*

But the way to reach this spiritual fullness and perfection is the way of complete emptying, of "attaining the form of the void" (*śūnyākāra*).

Although the text is practice-oriented, at the beginning it presents a clear theological conception which is underlying the spiritual experience. It is again expressed in the form of a dialogue, where the Goddess asks a series of questions regarding the nature of the Absolute (vv. 2-6), and Bhairava rejects all her conceptions, negating them all in a kind of negative theology (vv. 8-13), asserting the totally unlimited, inexpressible and indescribable nature of the Divine, Bhairava (v. 14). But far from being a negative experience, this Divine

> is filled internally with the bliss of one's own experience, and it is beyond the realm of thought. This state is always a state of Divine fullness. . . — *yāvasthā bharitākārā*. . . .
>
> His body of glory should be known as immaculate, universal fullness. — *vimalam viśvapūraṇam*
>
> — vv. 15-16

And, naturally, the question of the Goddess is concerned with the way how the transcendent Divine, which is beyond space, time and determination, can be realized in his fullness (vv. 22-23). The rest of the Tantra consists in an answer to her question.

We may now see the different dimensions of *śūnya* and the various approaches to this experience of the void.

1. An important meaning of *śūnya* is related to the intermediary space or time between any two things, happenings or experiences (also called *madhya*, or *sandhi*). An awareness of this gap or intermediary void is one of the most essential spiritual practices of the school.

The very first practice which is taught by Bhairava to Bhairavī concerns the most natural manifestation of all living beings, i.e., breath (*prāṇa*). The awareness has to be focused on the two voids, at the end of the breathing in and of the breathing out, and there itself the Supreme reveals itself (v. 25). This fundamental practice of awareness on two points leads to a unification in the thought-free centre:

> The Energy of Breath neither moves out nor enters within; when the centre unfolds by the dissolution of thoughts (*nirvikalpatayā*), then one attains the nature of Bhairava.
>
> — v. 26

Thus, the concentration on the two voids of breath terminates in the one centre, *madhya*, which is itself void and therefore gives access to the Supreme.

The same practice is extended to the middle or in-between of any two things or states, for which many examples are given:

> Meditating on the knowledge of two things or states one should rest in the middle. By abandoning both simultaneously, the Reality shines forth in the centre. — v. 61

Our perception normally moves from one object or mental state to another, but there are different practices — either to perceive both things and rest in the centre, or to stop the mind from moving to another object:

> When the awareness has abandoned one object and remains fixed without moving on to another object, then through the state in between (the two) the supreme realization will unfold. — v. 62

In relation to speech or *mantra*, the awareness of the void or silence between utterances should be developed:

> *praṇavādisamuccārāt plutānte śūnyabhāvanāt* ।
> *śūnyayā parayā śaktyā śūnyatām eti bhairavi* ॥ 39 ॥
>
> *yasya kasyāpi varṇasya pūrvāntāvanubhāvayet* ।
> *śūnyayā śūnyabhūto 'sau śūnyākāraḥ pumān bhavet* ॥ 40 ॥
>
> O Bhairavī, by uttering the *praṇava* (*mantra*) and by meditating on the void at the end of the protracted sound, one attains the state of the Void by means of the Supreme Energy of the Void. — v. 39
>
> One should meditate on the beginning and end of (the uttering of) any letter (or *mantra*). By becoming void due to the power of the void, one will reach the state of pure Void. — v. 40

Here there are clearly three levels of *śūnya,* one leading to the other: the meditation on the void is the condition (at the human level); the supreme Energy of the Void is the means; and the ultimate Reality is *śūnyatā* itself. Thus, it is an ascent of *nara-śakti-śiva,* all three being void: from the human through the Energy to the Divine.

The *dhāraṇā*s on the void — between any two breaths, two objects or experiences — are clearly aimed at overcoming our normal dualistic perception and at reaching a state of *nirvikalpa*, free from oscillating thoughts, and making the mind supportless (*nirālamba*, another characteristic of *śūnyatā*). This extends even to very ordinary experiences:

> At the beginning and end of sneezing, in a state of fear or sorrow, (standing) on top of an abyss or while fleeing from a battlefield, at the moment of intense curiosity, at the beginning or end of hunger; such a state comes close to the experience of Brahman. — v. 118

One verse which not only stands out by its imagery, but which is also quoted very frequently by later authors, is related to the sense-organs (although the term *indriya* does not occur):

> *śikhipakṣaiścitrarūpair maṇḍalaiḥ śūnyapañcakam* ।
> *dhyāyato 'nuttare śūnye praveśo hṛdaye bhavet* ॥ 32 ॥

> By meditating on the five voids of the senses which are like the various colours of the peacock's feathers, the *yogī* enters in the Heart of the absolute Void. — v. 32

The simile of the feathers of the peacock is rich in that it suggests at the same time the beauty experienced by means of the sense-organs, as well as the void, the openings of the senses, which are already described as *khāni* in the Upaniṣads.[4] The following verse is also significant:

> In the same way, if one concentrates one's awareness on anything, be it an empty space, a wall, or a worthy disciple, this (energy of concentration) will merge by itself and bestow grace. — v. 33

4. Cf. *Kaṭha Upaniṣad*, IV.1.

Here different aspects of the void are made the object of concentration.

An important practice consists in concentrating on the body as being void, both within and without. A whole series of *dhāraṇās* is directed at emptying the body, or rather the awareness of the body, of its apparent substance. These practices include: meditation on the inner space in the skull (v. 34), concentrating on the hollow of the central channel (*madhya-nāḍī,* i.e., *suṣumnā,* v. 35), meditation on the void below and above as well as in the heart (verses 44-45), and conceiving all the parts of the body as void (v. 47). The visualization used for attaining this aim is to conceive of the skin as an outer wall with nothing inside (v. 48), or to conceive the heart as two bowls in lotus-shape, one from below and the other from above, being empty in the middle (v. 49). This is a meditation on the empty space of the heart (*hṛdayākāśa*) which we find in the Upaniṣads. This is a process of interiorization. A summary *dhāraṇā* of these meditations on the body as void could be verse 43:

> One should meditate on the void in one's own body on all sides simultaneously. When the mind has become free from thoughts, one experiences everything as the Void.
>
> — v. 43

If *śūnya* pervading the body and all its parts refers to a static condition, its corresponding process is to meditate on the body as being consumed by the fire of Time (*kālāgni,* v. 52), and the same process is to be applied to the universe (v. 53). A similar *dhāraṇā* consists in meditating on the body as well as the universe in a reverse process of absorbing all the elements into ever subtler constituents (v. 54). The end result of these *dhāraṇās* is the supreme state of consciousness (*pumbhāvaḥ paramo bhavet,* v. 53; *ante vyajyate parā,* v. 54).

Meditation on cosmic space is the complementary aspect in the micro-macrocosmic scheme. It comprises the space outside the body, the unlimited sky (*ākāśa, vyoman*) and the all-pervasiveness of empty space which already in the Upaniṣads is the closest symbol of Brahman (v. 58).

It may not be easy to conceive at once the entire universe as void, but there are practical *dhāraṇās* leading to this experience:

> One should cast one's gaze on an open (stretch of) land devoid of trees, mountains, walls etc. When the state of the mind is fixed there, then the fluctuating thoughts dissolve.
>
> — v. 60[5]

Looking at the open sky is a way of entering the pure, non-dual consciousness (v. 84). Finally, the two meditations on the void of the body and of the universe have to merge in one realization:

> If one contemplates simultaneously that one's entire body or the world consists of nothing but Consciousness, then the mind becomes free from thoughts and the supreme awakening occurs. — v. 63

In fact, this micro-macrocosmic void corresponds to a state filled with bliss:

> (The *yogī*) should contemplate simultaneously on the whole world or his own body as filled with the bliss of the self. Then by his own blissful nectar he becomes united with the supreme bliss. — v.65

The thought-free void state is the very condition for experiencing the highest bliss.

---

5. This *dhāraṇā* can be related to the spirituality of the desert of the early Christian monks, called Desert Fathers.

Twice we find the term *śūnyālaya*: One comes as the result of a *dhāraṇā* where the attention is focused on an object and then withdrawn from it. It can be understood that the *yogī* then "becomes an abode of the Void" (or abides in the Void, which amounts to the same, v. 120). The second instance speaks of the true, i.e., spiritual *homa* or fire sacrifice, which consists in offering the elements, the senses and the objects of the senses in "the fire of the great Void" (*mahāśūnyālaye vahnau*, v. 149), which is the fire of pure Consciousness, where individual consciousness (*cetanā*) serves as the ladle.

The Buddhist philosophical concept of the emptiness of all things is not absent from the *Vijñāna Bhairava*:

> *ātmano nirvikārasya kva jñānaṁ kva ca vā kriyā* ।
> *jñānāyattā bahir-bhāvā ataḥ śūnyam-idaṁ jagat* ॥ 134 ॥
>
> How can the immutable Self have any knowledge or activity? All external objects depend on our knowledge of them. Therefore this world is void.

Meditation on the non-reality of things is enjoined to the *yogī* (v. 133), who therefore realizes the void nature of the world:

> *viśvam-etan-mahādevi śūnya-bhūtam vicintayet* ।
> *tatraiva ca mano līnaḥ tatas-tallaya-bhājanam* ॥ 58 ॥
>
> O Great Goddess! If one imagines this whole universe as being void, one's mind gets dissolved in it and one becomes worthy of merging in that (supreme Void).

And yet, the difference from Buddhism is that meditation on the void leads to a merging in the Ultimate Reality which, as in the Upaniṣads, is only indicated by *tat* "that" (*tallaya*).

The ultimate Reality, the Unsurpassable, is itself Void (*anuttara śūnya*, v. 32). It is understood to be Śiva or Bhairava, but the text rarely makes any theological statements. However, in one verse the equation is clearly expressed in the form of a meditation:

> *yadavedyaṁ yadagrāhyaṁ yac-chūnyaṁ yadabhāvagam* ।
> *tat-sarvaṁ bhairavaṁ bhāvyaṁ tadante bodha-sambhavaḥ* ॥127॥

> The unknowable, the ungraspable, the void, that which even pervades non-existence, contemplate on all this as Bhairava. At the end (of this contemplation) illumination will dawn.

This absolute Void is also called *advaya śūnya* (v. 89). Both the terms relating to the Absolute level, *anuttara* and *advaya*, are also central to the Buddhist Tantras. The difference is that the result of this particular practice is described as: *tatraiva ātmā prakāśate* (v. 89), i.e., in that very state of non-dual Void, the Self shines forth or reveals itself. At this level Śiva is described by negations culminating in *śūnya*.

We have spoken of different dimensions of *śūnya* (rarely *śūnyatā*), and the text itself consciously refers to these levels, as in the phrase: *śūnyayā parayā śaktyā śūnyatām eti bhairavī* (v. 39). Here it is by means of the supreme Śakti who is Herself the Energy of the Void that the (ultimate) state of the Void is attained. In terms of *trika* we can relate this to the Śakti and Śiva levels, whereas the *nara* or *aṇu* level is found in the physical experience of the void. In the very next verse these three levels are referred to:

> *śūnyayā śūnyabhūto'sau śūnyākāraḥ pumān bhavet* । — v. 40

> By the experience (or power) of the void he becomes void, and assumes the form of Void itself.

Thus *śūnya* is both, the means and the end. However, this end is not simply a negative state, for, as we have seen, the culmination of all the 112 *dhāraṇā*s is called a state of satisfaction (*tṛpti*, v. 148 and 161) which is described as utmost fullness (*atyanta-pūrṇatā*, v. 148).

Although this Tantra belongs to a very specific tradition, the non-dualist Kashmir Śaivism, it seems to me that it can be a real bridge of spiritual understanding between the Śaiva, the Tantric Buddhist and the Christian spiritual practice.

References

Abbrev. KSTS — Kashmir Series of Texts and Studies

Bäumer, Bettina, *Vijñāna Bhairava. Das göttliche Bewusstsein*, Grafing: Adyar, 2003 (2nd ed., 2004).

Lakshman Joo, Swami, *Vijñāna Bhairava: The Practice of Centring Awareness*, Varanasi: Indica, 2002.

Le Vijñānabhairava, texte traduit et commenté par Lilian Silburn, Paris (ed. de Boccard), 1983.

Vijñānabhairava, La conoscenza del Tremendo, Italian transl. Attilia Sironi (Introduction by R. Gnoli), Milano: Adelphi Ed., 1989.

The Vijñāna Bhairava with Commentary partly by Kṣemarāja and partly by Śivopadhyāya, ed. Mukunda Rama Shastri, Bombay 1918, (KSTS No. VIII) (Sanskrit).

Vijñāna Bhairava or Divine Consciousness, Sanskrit Text with English Translation, etc., by Jaideva Singh, New Delhi: Motilal Banarsidass, 1st ed., 1979.

Vijñāna Bhairavaḥ, ed. V.V. Dviveda (Sanskrit and Hindi transl.), New Delhi: Motilal Banarsidass, 1st edn. 1978 (2nd ed., 1984).

10

The Themes of Light and Dark in the Greek Fathers[1]

John R. Dupuche

THE conference has as its theme the three terms *śūnya, pūrṇa* and *plerôma*. The first two words are Sanskrit and rich in meaning. The third word, *Plerôma,* is Greek and means "fullness." However, the purpose of the conference is to set side by side in telling paradox, the two seemingly contradictory terms "void" and "fullness" and to hint that their apparent incompatibility points in fact to a transcendent Reality, which could be called *Plerôma*.

The term "void" has an equivalent in Greek: *kenos*, empty, which is used tellingly in the great hymn of Philippians 2.6-11 but is otherwise rarely used in the New Testament, and in any case does not have the variety of meanings of the word *śūnya*. The term "fullness" is expressed in Greek by the term *Plerôma* and its cognates but this term has been set aside as one of the themes of the Conference. It would not seem possible simply to provide a study on *kenos* and *Plerôma* which are the most obvious Greek equivalents of *śūnya* and *pūrṇa*.

---

1. This article is the written development of a verbal presentation given on 14 December 1999.

The Bible, which forms the background of the Fathers, has a variety of terms, however, which tend towards the same meaning. Thus for *śūnya* one might study the terms *bathys,* deep; *ptochos,* poor; *eleutheria,* freedom; *tapeinōsis,* lowliness; *skotia,* darkness; *aneu,* without; verbs such as *lyō* and *erimoō* and *kathairō,* to destroy; *lyō,* to free; the many verb forms that express the idea of leaving, or those that refer to rejecting. The term *pūrṇa* is reflected in words such as *phōs,* light; *doxa;* glory, splendour, praise, honour; *polys,* many; *plethos,* multitude; *megas,* great; *pas,* all; *holos,* whole; *eikōn,* image; or by verbs such as *pimplemi,* to fill, which is the cognate of *Plerôma*; *hyperballō,* to surpass; *perisseuō,* to have in abundance; *lampō,* to shine; *dynamoō,* to be able; *ischyō* to have the strength to; *hypsoō,* to exalt; *anabainō,* to go up; *egeirō*; to rise.[2] However, the mystical literature has above all used the striking images of light, *phōs;* and darkness, *skotia.*

It would seem more natural, therefore, to develop a short study on the terms "light" and "darkness," which provide the same paradoxical contrast as the terms "fullness" and "void." The term *Plerôma* will be understood to refer to the Reality which the paradox intimates.

It hardly needs to be said that this short study does not cover all the rich meaning of these terms but is given only to provide a suitable context for the many other papers in this volume.

The paper will look at three writers in particular: Gregory of Nyssa who stands at the head of the mystical tradition of both the Greek and Latin Churches; Pseudo-Dionysius who develops the apophatic tradition; and Gregory Palamas who is the last of the great Greek Doctors of the Church.

---

2. Darton, Michael (ed.), *Modern Concordance to the New Testament,* London, Darton: Longman & Todd, 1976.

I

Gregory of Nyssa (+ *c.* 395 CE) together with his brother Basil and his brother's friend, Gregory of Nazianzen, are classed as the "Cappadocian Fathers" who occupy a position of prime importance in the fourth century, which belongs to the so-called Golden Age of the Fathers situated in the first few centuries of the Christian Church. The thinking of these three bishops has exercised a profound influence on Christian theology.

Gregory of Nyssa is "one of the most powerful and most original thinkers ever known in the history of the Church."[3] He inspires the writings of Pseudo-Macarius and of Evagrius and is the chief inspiration for Dionysius the Areopagite.[4] Among his many writings on mysticism, such as the *Homilies on the Canticle of Canticles, De Instituto Christiano,* his greatest contribution is the *Life of Moses.* This work consists of two parts. The first part recounts, from the outside so to speak, the events of the people's escape from Egypt and their arrival at Mt Sinai, "the Mountain of God." The second part gives the inner meaning of the events which are thus seen to prefigure the spiritual journey of everyman. Gregory brings out in particularly striking fashion the juxtaposition of light and darkness. He emphasizes that paradox by phrases such as "wakeful sleep," "passion without passion,"[5] "ineffable gnosis,"[6] "sober

3. Bouyer, Louis, *A History of Christian Spirituality: Vol. I The Spirituality of the New Testament and the Fathers,* Tunbridge Wells: Burns & Oates, 1968, p. 350.

4. *Op. cit.,* p. 352.

5. Jean Daniélou, "Mystique de la ténèbre chez Grégoire de Nysse," in *Dictionnaire de spiritualité,* vol. II, part 2, pp. 1800-81.

6. *Contra Eunom,* III, i. 16, ed. Jaeger, I, ii, p. 7. 6ff. quoted in Bouyer, *A History. . . ,* vol. I, p. 362.

intoxication"[7] and "resplendent darkness."[8] The following quotation is justly famous:

> What is signified by Moses' entering into the darkness, and the vision he had of God therein? The present account seems, indeed, somewhat to contradict the theophany at the beginning [when Moses at the moment of his divine call sees God in the burning bush. Ex. 3.1 ff.]. Then it was in light and now it is in darkness that God appears. Do not think, however, that this is not in accordance with the normal succession of the spiritual realities we are considering. The text teaches us thereby that the religious gnosis (*tes eusebeias*) is light when it first begins to appear; for it is opposed to impiety which is darkness and darkness is dissipated by the enjoyment of the light. But the more the spirit (*nous*) in its march forward has attained, by an application always greater and more perfect, to an understanding of what the knowledge (*katanoesis*) of realities is and approaches nearer to contemplation the more it sees that the divine nature is invisible. Having left behind appearances, not only those perceived by the senses but those that the intelligence believes it sees, it goes continually further within until it penetrates, by the effort of the understanding, to the invisible and unknowable, where it sees God. The true knowledge (*eidesis*) of Him whom it seeks, indeed, and the true vision of Him consists in seeing that He is invisible, because He whom it seeks transcends all knowledge, completely separated by his incomprehensibility as by a dark cloud. This is why John, the one raised so high, who entered into this shining darkness, says that '. . . no one has ever seen God' [Jn 1.18], by this negation defining the gnosis of the divine essence as inaccessible not only to

---

7. *Fifth and Eleventh Homilies on the Canticle;* PG XLIV, 873 D and 990 B, quoted in *ibid.*

8. *Life of Moses;* PG, XLIV, 377 A, quoted in *op. cit.* p. 363.

> men but to every intellectual nature. When, therefore, Moses had progressed in gnosis, he declares that he sees God in darkness, that is to say that the divinity is essentially what transcends all gnosis and all comprehension.[9]

This play of light and dark is fascinating. What formerly appeared as light, i.e., the pleasing folly of a passing world, is now seen to be darkness, once the knowledge of the divine appears. This divine light, true and valid though it may be, is itself seen to be darkness, once a person moves further into the incomprehensibility of God. This incomprehensibility is darkness to the mind, for the mind cannot grasp it, yet it is a light since it is a far truer knowledge. It is a "shining darkness." What appears to be darkness is in fact light. What is deemed to be ignorance is the perfection of knowledge. It is the ultimate paradox.

The term "empty," *kenos,* is indeed used in the *Life of Moses* but only in the sense of the emptiness of a joy which is obtained by satisfying base desires.[10] It is the term "darkness," which has the richness of the word *śūnya.*

Although the mystic "sees God in darkness," this does not mean that he has reached the term of his search, for the divinity utterly transcends him and can never be attained. The spiritual life consists in the journeying, not in the arrival, for God is the infinite abyss or the utter void into which one is falling, so to speak, and this falling is the wonder, which is expressed in

---

9. Grégoire de Nysse *La vie de Moise, ou Traité de la perfection en matière de vertu*. Introduction, texte critique et traduction de Jean Daniélou, troisième édition, Paris, Les Editions du Cerf, 1968, pp. 211-13., Translation quoted from Bouyer, *A History*, vol. 1, pp. 363-64.

10. Cf. Grégoire de Nysse, *Vie de Moise,* p. 141, para. 60. line 5; and p. 141, para. 61. line 3.

St Paul's phrase "forgetting what is behind me and tending (*epekteinomenos*) towards what is ahead." (Phil. 3. 11.)

However, as Bouyer points out,[11] the mystical life cannot be expressed simply in terms of knowledge but must be formulated in terms of being, for knowledge derives from union. Gnosis is defined as participation (*metousia*) in God,[12] or "mutual compenetration, God coming into the soul and the soul being transported in God,"[13] since in the end it is love (*agape*) which holds all in unity.

> When in fact *agape* has excluded fear . . . all will be, in one another, one in the Perfect Dove [the Holy Spirit]. In this way encircled by the unity of the Holy Spirit as by the bond of peace all will be one single body and one single spirit.[14]

In fact this unity, *henoeidos,* is so complete that the distinction between subject and object, between what is done by one and what is done to one, i.e., action and passion, becomes in a sense inoperative.[15]

Although Pseudo-Macarius is a popularization of Gregory's teaching,[16] and although Ps.-Macarius continues with the imagery of light, he does not use the imagery of darkness which Gregory employed to such effect.[17]

---

11. Bouyer, *A History. . .*, vol. I, pp. 366-67.
12. *De infin.* PG XLVI 173C, quoted in Bouyer, *A History. . .*, vol. I, p. 367.
13. *Sixth Homily on the Canticle* PG XLIV 889 D, quoted in Bouyer, *A History. . .*, vol. I, p. 367.
14. *Fifteenth Homily on the Canticle* PG XIV, 1116CD, quoted in Bouyer, *A History. . .*, vol. I, p. 368.
15. Daniélou, "Mystique de la ténèbre," p. 1908.
16. Bouyer, *A History. . .*, vol. I, p. 352.
17. *Op. cit.*, p. 374.

II

Gregory of Nyssa profoundly influences the writing of Pseudo-Dionysius whom we wish next to consider. Although the majority of scholars consider that "Dionysius" belongs to the Syrian milieu of the sixth century, the matter is far from settled.[18] The *corpus* of Ps.-Dionysius consists principally of four works, *The Celestial Hierarchy, The Ecclesiastical Hierarchy, The Treatise on the Divine Names* and *The Mystical Theology*. In his *Celestial Hierarchy* he describes the whole panoply of beings in nine stages, extending from the highest, Being itself. From him derives the whole of created reality which he then draws back to himself, thus constituting a divine order, *taxis*, whose purpose is "assimilation to and union (*henōsis*) with God."[19] The hierarchy is not a static reality so much as a process. God is not disinterested in the order of beings, which flow from him, but rather out of pure love and generosity, *agapē*, he leads them to himself. Although beings have a desire, *eros*, for him and wish to attain a state which they do not yet enjoy, he has only *agapē* in which all beings are invited to share so that they too might have the same generous and selfless love. Each level of being is a varied manifestation of his total love and by attaining that same state of fullest love they acquire their own fullness. The "nothingness" of limited being is brought to the fullness of generous love so that the themes of fullness and emptiness and their interplay form the kernel of *The Celestial Hierarchy*. The same themes are also reflected in *The Ecclesiastical Hierarchy* which describes the various levels of the Church, from bishop to penitent, as engaged in a process by which the least illuminated, the least pure, are brought by *agapē* to the full flowering of their being, to their redemption. This great

---

18. *Op. cit.*, p. 397.

19. *Hierarchy Eccles*, PG 1.165A, quoted in *op. cit.*, p. 403.

process is best realized in the Eucharist which is the "reuniting, through Christ, together with the intelligible universe, of the whole human universe."[20] Thus the "full" and the "void" function as a great vibration in the two hierarchies, celestial and ecclesiastical.

The Greek word *mystikos*, mystical, at first simply means "hidden," without any more significance. Gradually, however, it acquires a spiritual sense until it refers to the experience of the inner meaning of things, in particular of the sacramental symbols.[21] In his *Mystical Theology*, Dionysius describes the ultimate reality in a prayer:

> O Trinity superessential, superdivine, supergood; *ephoros* of the theosophy of the Cherubim, lead us to that supreme height of mystical words that transcends understanding and manifestation, there where the simply absolute, unchangeable mysteries of theology are unveiled in the superluminous cloud of silence that initiates into hidden things, superresplendent in the deepest depths of darkness in a manner beyond any manifestation, which, wholly intangible and invisible, fills to overflowing with super-beautiful splendours our blinded spirits (*noas*). Such is my prayer.
>
> . . . indeed, it is purely by a free and absolute ecstasy out of yourself that you will be carried towards the superessential ray of the divine darkness.[22]

Ps.-Denis takes up the paradoxes of "superluminous cloud," "superresplendent in the deepest depths of darkness," "the superessential ray of the divine darkness," which are found in Gregory of Nyssa and before him in Philo and Clement

20. *Op. cit.*, p. 405.

21. *Op. cit.*, pp. 406-12.

22. *Theol. Mysti.* 1.1, PG III, pp. 997A-1000A, quoted in *op. cit.*, p. 412.

and Origen.[23] The stress on "super-" is explained by the *Treatise on the Divine Names* where he distinguishes between kataphatic knowledge and apophatic knowledge. The terms used of God in the Bible, such as "good," "loving," etc., while remaining true are radically inadequate. They do not define the indefinable but only very partially express it. The kataphatic statement must be joined to an apophatic statement, which denies that these terms are sufficient. The fullness of the statement must be joined by its emptying, so that the mystic proceeds beyond both the kataphatic and apophatic, beyond affirmation and negation, beyond light and dark, to a quite different level of knowledge, indeed to an experience, *theoria,* of the "super," to that which is beyond any knowledge. The mystic advances to the level of Being, to the state of communion with the divine, to a level of oneness of being, to an absorption in *agapē,* i.e., where the mystic dwells in the divine presence and receives the free communication of all that he is.[24] This is very different from the gnosis of Hermes, for example, which is just a knowledge of the divine realities in ourselves, for Denis is concerned with the knowledge that is utterly beyond because it is given. He is concerned with the moment of grace,[25] which is given especially in the sacraments.[26]

III

Gregory Palamas (*c.* 1296-1359)[27] lived first as a monk on Mt. Athos, and after various trials was made bishop of

---

23. *Op. cit.,* p. 412.

24. *Op. cit.,* p. 415.

25. René Roques, "La doctrine du Pseudo-Denys," in *Dictionnaire de spiritualité,* vol. III, Paris: Beauchesne, 1957, p. 275.

26. *Op. cit.,* p. 276 ff.

27. Palamas, Grégoire, *Défense des saints hésychastes.* Introduction, texte critique, traduction et notes par Jean Meyendorff. Second, revised and corrected edition, Louvain, 1973, vol. 1, pp. ix-x.

Thessalonica. In the context of a vigorous debate with his principal opponent, Barlaam of Calabria, he composed his famous works which show him to be the "last great spiritual writer of medieval Athos. And certainly its most powerful theologian,"[28] whose writings were received as the official doctrine of Byzantine Church in 1355.

While he knows the techniques of hesychasm[29] which Barlaam attacked[30] and which are so redolent of *Yoga,* he does not dwell on them.[31] Even though the text *La méthode de l'oraison hésychaste* was attributed to Simeon the New Theologian, — an important source of Gregory's teaching — the principal font of the mystical life is none other than the Holy Spirit.

> So, when the saints contemplate this divine light within themselves, seeing it by the divinising communion of the Spirit, through the mysterious visitation of perfecting illuminations, — then they behold the garment of their deification, their mind being glorified and filled by the grace of the Word, beautiful beyond measure in his splendour.[32]

There is first and foremost the interior transfiguration worked by the Spirit, made possible by the identity of the Christian with the Word made flesh. This takes a person into the darkness of the incomprehensible God and at the same time fills him with light. This knowledge does not remain hidden in the

---

28. Leclercq, Jean; Vandenbroucke, François; Bouyer, Louis, *A History of Christian Spirituality,* vol. II, *The Spirituality of the Middle Ages,* Tunbridge Wells: Burns & Oates, 1968, p. 585.
29. Palamas, *Défense* I.2.12 and II.2.2.
30. Meyendorff, "Palamas," p. 93.
31. Leclercq, *A History,* vol. II, p. 587.
32. Palamas, *Triads,* ed. with an introduction by John Meyendorff, translated by Nicholas Gendle. Preface by Jaroslav Pelikan. London: SPCK, 1983, p. 33.

depths of the soul but is revealed in all the faculties and senses. Thus, following the example of Maximos the Confessor and John Damascene,[33] Palamas refers to the Transfiguration of Jesus on Mount Thabor when his essential glory was made visible to the eyes of the disciples. This emphasis on the bodily effects of the inner transformation is one of Gregory's most valuable contributions. The interior darkness of the incomprehensible deity, which is also a fullness of light, is manifested as light in the body.

> In spiritual man, the grace of the Spirit, transmitted to the body through the soul, grants to the body also the experience of things divine. . . .[34]

It is thus a direct bodily experience of God himself.[35]

> For if it is in light that the light is seen, that which sees operates in a similar light, since this faculty has no other way in which to work. Having separated itself from all other beings, it becomes itself all light and is assimilated to what is sees, or rather, it is united to it without mingling, being itself light and seeing light through light. If it sees itself, it sees light; if it beholds the object of its vision, that too is light, and if it looks at the means by which it sees, again it is light. For such is the character of the union, that all is one, so that he who sees can distinguish neither the means nor the object nor its nature, but simply has the awareness of being light and of seeing a light distinct from every creature.[36]

The emphasis on experience which touches the heart and the psycho-somatic complex belongs to the tradition which stems

---

33. Meyendorff, "Palamas," p. 95.
34. Palamas, *Triads*, p. 51.
35. Leclercq, *A History*, vol. II, p. 587.
36. Palamas, *Triads*, pp. 65-66.

back to Pseudo-Macarius rather than to the "intellectual prayer" of Evagrius "free of all matter,"[37] a tradition reinforced in Symeon the New Theologian (*c.* AD 950-1022)[38] who does not so much know the contrast of light and dark but rather light and tears:

> One evening, when he was praying, and saying in spirit: "God, have mercy on me, a sinner," a divine light suddenly . . . shone on him from above and filled the room. The young man no longer knew whether he was in the house or under a roof, for on all sides he saw nothing but light: he was not even aware of being on earth. . . . He was one with this divine light and it seemed to him that he himself had become light and left the world altogether . . . he was filled with tears and unspeakable joy.[39]

Gregory's emphasis on the visibility of the uncreated splendour of God is one of the most controversial of elements in his teaching. Yet it follows from the notion of deification, the divine state, *theia hexis*. For if the whole person, body and soul and spirit is made to share in the divine nature, the body too must be able to perceive the divinity through its own faculties. To this effect Palamas quotes John Damascene, "the glory of the divinity has become also the glory of the body."[40]

At the same time Gregory is at pains to stress the utter transcendence of God, so that while the human being is divinised God remains utterly transcendent. This paradox is needed if Gregory is to maintain the sense both of immanence

---

37. Meyendorff, "Palamas," p. 94.

38. Leclercq, *A History,* vol. II, pp. 560 and 564.

39. *On Faith: Writings from the Philokalia,* pp. 145-46, quoted in Leclercq, *A History,* vol. II, p. 562.

40. *Homily In Transfigura.* 12, PG XCVI, 564B quoted in Palamas, *Triads,* p. 78. See also Palamas, *Défense* III.1.19, vol. II, p. 595.

and of transcendence. He achieves this aim by distinguishing between the essence and the uncreated energies of God[41] and rejects the jibe 'ditheist' made by Barlaam.[42] The prolegomena to this idea are found in Gregory of Nyssa who speaks of the divine inexhaustibility, and who teaches that progress in the redeemed condition does not consist in attaining some goal — for the goal is ever transcendent — but in tending towards it, in an *epekstasis* as we have seen.

In Christ, man enters in communion not with "the God of the philosophers and the savants," but with the One who — in human language — can only be called "more-than-God."[43] This gives rise to the frequent use of the prefix "super" such as in "superessential," *hyperousios*,[44] "supernatural," *hyperphyes.* God is entirely present and manifest in all his energies[45] and therefore in the dark and light and yet at the same time his divine essence surpasses the divine energies in the way "that the subject of an action surpasses its object."[46]

God is not only above knowledge but above non-knowledge.[47]

The terms of the conference are "void," "fullness" and "*Plerôma*." If Gregory Palamas were to review these terms,

---

41. This distinction had been foreshadowed by one of the Cappadocians, Gregory of Nazianzen. Daniélou, "Mystique de la ténèbre," p. 1873. It has striking resemblances to the distinction between Śiva and Śakti in Kashmir Śaivism, a subject for investigation which far exceeds the bounds of this brief essay.

42. Palamas, *Triads,* p. 81.

43. *Op. cit.*, p. 18.

44. *Op. cit.*, p. 81, p. 96, p. 100 *et passim.*

45. *Op. cit.*, p. 96.

46. *Op. cit.*, p. 97.

47. *Op. cit.*, p. 32.

might he not say that by the experience of a darkness which is light and a light which is beyond all knowledge and which is yet revealed in the body, the mystic enters into the knowledge of the One who is utterly transcendent and yet who is at the same time known, the One who is the *Plerôma* of all things? Or again, if the essence is ultimately unknowable, it is *śūnya*; yet through the energies it is manifest, *pūrṇa*; but both these are one in the *Plerôma*.

References

Bouyer, Louis, *A History of Christian Spirituality: Vol. I The Spirituality of the New Testament and the Fathers,* Tunbridge Wells: Burns & Oates, 1968, 541 pp.

Translation made by Mary P. Ryan of *La Spiritualité du Nouveau Testament et dès Pères,* Paris: Editions Montaigne, 1960.

Daniélou, Jean, "Mystique de la ténèbre chez Grégoire de Nysse," in *Dictionnaire de spiritualité,* vol. II, part 2, Paris: Beauchesne, pp. 1873-85.

Darton, Michael (ed.), *Modern Concordance to the New Testament.* London, Darton: Longman & Todd, 1976, xviii+786 pp. Based on the French *Concordance de la Bible, Nouveau Testament,* ed. Sr Jeanne d'Arc O.P., produced under the aegis of the *Association de la Concordance française de la Bible* by Editions du Cerf and Editions Desclée de Brouwer, 1970.

Gregoire de Nysse, *La vie de Moise, ou Traité de la perfection en matière de vertu,* Introduction, texte critique et traduction de Jean Daniélou. Troisième édition. Paris: Les Editions du Cerf, 1968, 352 pp. [Sources Chrétiennes 1]

Leclercq, Jean; Vandenbroucke, François; Bouyer, Louis, *A History of Christian Spirituality: Vol. 11, The Spirituality of the Middle Ages.* Tunbridge Wells: Burns & Oates, 1968, 602 pp., tr. The Benedictines of Holme Eden Abbey, of *La Spiritualité du Moyen Age,* Paris: Editions Montaigne, 1961.

Leon-Dufour, Xavier; Duplacy, Jean; Georges, Augustin; Grelot, Pierre; Guillet, Jacques; Marc-François, Lacan, *Vocabulaire de Théologie Biblique.* Paris: Les Editions du Cerf, 1966, 1158 pp.

Meyendorff, Jean, "Palamas" in *Dictionnaire de spiritualité,* vol. XII part 1, Paris: Beauchesne, 1984. pp. 81-107.

Palamas, Grégoire, *Défense des saints hésychastes,* Introduction, texte critique, traduction et notes par Jean Meyendorff. Second, revised and corrected edition. Louvain, 1973, vol. 1, I-Ll + 383 *bis* pp.; vol. 2, 384-767 pp. [Spicilegium Sacrum Lovaniense, fasc.30]

———, *Triads.* Edited with an introduction by John Meyendorff, tr. Nicholas Gendle, preface by Jaroslav Pelikan, London: SPCK, 1983, xiii+172 pp.

Pseudo-Dionysius, *The Complete Works,* tr. Colm Luibheid, foreword, notes and translation collaboration by Paul Rorem, preface by R. Roques, introductions by Jaroslav Pelikan, Jean Leclerq and Karlfried Froelich, New York: Paulist Pres, 1987, ix+318 pp.

Roques, René, "Contemplation, extase et ténèbre chez le Pseudo-Denys" in: *Dictionnaire de spiritualité,* vol. 2, part 2, Paris: Beauchesne, 1957, pp. 1885-1911.

———, "La doctrine du Pseudo-Denys," in *Dictionnaire de spiritualité,* vol. III, Paris: Beauchesne, 1957, pp. 264-86.

Symeon the New Theologian, *The Discourses,* tr. by C.J. de Catanzaro, introduction by George Maloney S.J., Preface by Basile Krivocheine. London: SPCK, 1980, pp. xvii, 396.

11

Śūnyatā in the Sahaja Practice of Buddhism

Suniti Kumar Pathak

AN appropriate English lexiconic equivalent of *śūnyatā* is not available because each word derives its meaning from its context. That is why it is so difficult to translate a word from one language to another. *Śūnya* in English is "void;" *śūnyatā* is "voidness" or "emptiness," in a literal sense. Is *śūnyatā* opposite to *pūrṇatā*? Definitely not. *Pūrṇa* in Upaniṣadic thought refers to fullness, totality or universality. Like *śūnyatā, pūrṇatā* remains inexplicable since the conceptual faculty of the human mind cannot define that which is. It cannot limit the all-extensive status of the universal mind where no individual object appears. *Śūnyatā* is likewise a mental status in which no particular object (*viṣaya*) is perceived, no thought construction (*vikalpa*) or contemplation (*bhāvanā*) or imagination (*kalpanā*) or functional dream (*svapna*) arises. *Śūnyatā,* like *pūrṇatā,* is beyond relative conditionality.[1] These two terms are neither synonymous nor contradictory.

---

1. *karmakleśakṣayānmokṣaḥ karmakleśa vikalpataḥ* ।
vikalpaḥ prapañcāt prapañcastu śūnyatāyāṁ nirudhyate ॥

— Nāgārjuna, *Mūlamadhyamaka-Kārikā*, 18.5.

"Liberation is the eradicating of stress caused by an action; the stress caused by an action is itself caused by the thought →

Again, *sa-ha-ja* is the untroubled state of the innate mind in which no disturbance arises.[2] In Buddhist esotericism that status of psychosomatic functionality (*niṣprapañca-caryā*[3]) consists not in numbers but in the retrovertive order of

---

→ construction (of holding as real that which is unreal); the thought construction itself is caused by the fluctuations of phenomena. The fluctuation of the phenomenal world ceases by means of *śūnyatā*."

2. *Dohākośa-vyākhyā*, p. 71 reads:

ahamapi śūnyaṁ vikalpa-gocaratvāt ।
jagadapi śūnyam vikalpa-mātram-eva ॥

tri-bhuvanamapi śūnyam ।
nirmale malarahite sahaje mahāsukham ।
na pāpam na puṇyaṁ sambhavati ॥

"I am *śūnyam* owing to thought construction [of I-ness which makes me to be existent]. The (changeable) world is also *śūnyam* for being (visualised as real) under thought construction. The three spheres [the world, the intermediate and the celestial] are also *śūnyam*; the great joy in *sahaja* which is devoid of filth, without vice or virtue, occurs there."

The *Hevajratantra* adds (1.10.17):

na rāga na virāga madhyam nāpalabhyate ।
trayāṇām varjanād eva sahajam bodhirucyate ॥

"*Sahaja* is called *bodhi*, as it is not alluring, not repulsive nor is in-between the two as it transcends all three."

3. The *Hevajratantra* commentary *Yogaratnamālā* (folios 21a, 23a-b) states:

guru-buddhānām ājñayā duṣkara-vrata-caraṇam caryā ।
. . . caryāpi trividhā kathitā-saprapañcatā, niṣprapañcatā, atiniṣprapañcatā ceti ॥

"*Caryā* is the observance of limited vows which the preceptor imposes in keeping with the teachings of the Buddhas. *Caryā* is also said to be of three sorts: observance of the phenomena, withdrawal from observance of the phenomena and observance of the higher withdrawal."

completion (*niṣpanna-krama*).[4] *Śūnyatā* tends to retrovert (*parāvṛtti*) the mind to its innate nature (*sva-bhāva*).[5] The empirical knowledge of external objects and the internal state of the introvertive mind merge interiorly. Thus "one plus one is one." In the retrovertive process (*parāvṛtti*) of becoming *sa-ha-ja*, the externalised consciousness (*pravṛtti vijñāna*) of the mind (*citta*) becomes still but not numb or inactive. Its functioning becomes motionless like an ocean with no wind to trouble its surface.[6]

---

4. *Hevajratantra* commentary *Yogaratnamālā* (fol.2b) reads:

   śrutaṁ sahajam-ityuktaṁ dvidhā-bhedena bheditam ।
   samvṛtam devatākāram-utpatti-krama-pakṣataḥ ॥

   vivṛtti-sukha-rūpaṁ tu niṣpanna-krama-pakṣataḥ ।
   satya-dvayaṁ samāśritya buddhānāṁ dharma-deśanā ॥

   "The *sahaja* teachings are divided into two kinds of truth, (conventional truth and beyond conventional truth). The teachings of the Buddhas appear to be in the two orders. The order of generation is related to the conventional truth in the divine form, while the order of completion manifests in the exposure of joy through higher esoteric status."

5. *Khasamatantra-ṭikā*, p. 231 reads:

   buddha-bodhi-lakṣaṇa bhagavān vajradharaḥ prakṛtyā kha-samaḥ । *prakṛtirasya svābhāvikāḥ kāyaḥ, tena kha-sama eva, nirābhāsānanta-suviśuddha-prakāśānāṁta thatā-svabhāvatvāt* ॥

   "The *vajradhara* who attains excellent merits, showing signs of the *bodhi* of the Buddha, becomes similar to the (cloudless) sky. That is the nature (of the individual) and its embodiment becomes of that of the self-existent. Therefore it is as empty as the sky. It has the nature of 'thatness,' which is unconditional, without impurity and infinite."

6. The *Ārya-laṅkāvatāra* reads:

   taraṅgā hyudadher-yāvat pavana-pratyayeritāḥ ।
   nṛtyamānāḥ pravartanto vyucchedaśca na vidyate ॥ 2.99 ॥

   ālayaughastathā nityaṁ viṣayapavaneritaḥ ।
   citnaistaraṅga-vijñānairnṛtyamānaḥ pravartate ॥ 2.100 ॥ →

A question arises: What is the nature (*svabhāva*) of the mind?

The mind is calm by nature, pure and crystal-like, transparent to the interior view.[7] As soon as it begins to grasp the objective world, it begins to function by means of faculties such as the sense-organs and other psychic faculties (*dhātvāyātana-indriyāṇi*) within the realms of desire, of form and the formless (*kāmaloka, rūpaloka, arūpaloka*). The mind becomes disturbed. Knowledge, led by active consciousness (*pravṛttijñāna*) of the external world, takes note of the minute and gross items through the internal perception (*manovijñāna*), which belongs to a sentient being (*sattva*).

According to the Buddhists, Śākyaputra Gautama, the Buddha Śākyamuni, is believed to have acquired the awakened mind (*bodhi*) which may be understood as the sublime mental state of an all-pervasive consciousness (*ālayavijñāna*) and in which the active processing of the sentient mind arises. The awakened mind may combine the externalized mental activity with the unwavering calmness of

---

→ "As the wind blows, the waves of an ocean move uninterruptedly in dancing. The immense consciousness, which is stored (like an ocean), is ruffled by wind-like objects; and for this reason diverse forms arise, as though dancing, in the functioning of the mind."

7. The *Jñanasiddhi*, p. 141 reads:

   svaccham hiraṇyagarbha sarva-sattvānāṁ cittaṁ śāntaṁ prabhāsvaram ।

   The *Dohākośa* commentary elucidates:

   citta-saṁjña dvividhā, laukikī, lokottara ca । *yallaukikam tad-vikalpa-lakṣaṇam, nirākāraṇīyaṁ* । *yallokottaram nirmalaṁ dharmakāya-lakṣaṇam sahaja-svarūpaṁ vā* ।

   "The two mental functions are the mundane and the supra-mundane. Mundane mental functions are characterized by thought construction, but they may be amended; the supra-mundane mental functions are pure, characterized by *dharmakāya* and *sahaja*."

the infinite mental ocean. No waves of thought disturb the quietude of the Buddha-mind, i.e., Buddhahood (*buddhatva*).[8] In the externalized aspect of the mind some thought did occur in his *bodhi*-mind, as the Buddhist texts occasionally record: *evam manasi ahosi* (such and such occurred in his mind). The retrovertive mind in a state of mental vacuum without an objective response is *śūnyatā*. The reality (*svabhāva*) of all-pervasive unlimited consciousness (*ālayavijñāna*) pervades the crystal-like transparent mind (*sphaṭikopama-svacchaṁ cittam*). He becomes the omniscient (*sarvajña*) and transcendent (*niṣyanda*) Buddha while living in external innate embodiment (*sahajakāya*). This is equivalent to the phenomenal essence-lessness of *dharmakāya* (the immanent unconditionality of phenomenal appearance).[9]

---

8. The *Ārya-laṅkāvatāra Sūtra* (2.179 and 181) reads:

   nāhaṁ nirvāṇaṁ bhāvena kriyayā lakṣaṇena ca ।
   vikalpa-hetu-vijñāne nirvṛtte nirvṛtto hyaham ॥ 179 ॥

   yathā kṣīṇe mahaughe taraṅgānāṁ-asambhavaḥ ।
   tathā vijñāna-vaicitraṁ niruddham na pravartate ॥ 181 ॥

   "I have attained *nirvāṇa* not by some existent reality, not by acts, not by some characteristic. I have attained *nirvāṇa* by the cessation of thought-construction and its cause(s). . . . As the waves cannot arise without the turbulent wind, varieties of consciousness are stilled in the person who attains *nirvāṇa*."

9. The *Advayavajra* states thus :

   asaṁskṛta-tathāgatātmakatvād dharma-kāya, pratibhāsamātratvāt-saṁbhoga-kāya, kalpita-nirmāṇa-kāyatvāt-nirmāṇa-kāya, kāya-tritayaikara-satvat svābhāvika-kāya.

   "*Dharma-kāya* is the embodiment out of unconditional, un-constituted Tathāgata characteristics; *sambhoga-kāya* is the effulgent embodiment refracted on (the universe); *nirmāṇa-kāya* is embodiment as imagined; and *svābhāvika-kāya*, the embodiment of the nature takes place by the unification of the above three."

In the esoteric order of contemplation, the manifestations of Buddhahood (*buddhatva*) are diverse. The Buddha in his human embodiment (*nirmāṇakāya*) involves the conglomeration of the aggregates (*skandha*) and their dissolution in *parinirvāṇa.* Through the visualization practiced by a competent esoteric practitioner, the effulgent manifestations of the cosmic radiant rays extend through all spheres, i.e., *sambhoga-kāya buddha.* Again, the essencelessness in the manifestation of both phenomenal and non-phenomenal spheres, whether they have form or no form, becomes *dharmakāya*, i.e., *tathāgata*, which manifests and non-manifests as well. In this way, the diverse states — *vajrakāya, sahajakāya, kālacakra buddha, svabhāva-kāya buddha* — seems to render the Buddhas multiple and mystic despite the understanding of *śūnyatā* as the core of Buddhahood (*buddhatva*). That is, the particular visualization of the universe in various spheres differs depending on the mental capacity of an individual practitioner. This is because the esoteric visualization depends on the order of generation (*utpanna krama*). *Buddhatva*, in the case of a competent (*samartha*) practitioner involves understanding the *śūnyatā-bodhi*, which is also described as *śūnyatā-śūnyatā.*[10]

A Buddhist practitioner, who aspires to reach the compassionate *bodhi*-mind (*bodhicitta*) practises the *bodhi*-way of life (*bodhi-caryā*) with an emphasis on the highest moral values. Among them *prajñāpāramitā*, "wisdom *par excellence*," is the highest state of the human mind (*manovijñāna*), as the

---

10. *Hevajratantra* commentary *Yogaratnamālā*, folio. 13b, reads:

prātibhāsa-svarūpaṁ cittam-ekāneka-svabhāva-rahitam ।
nirābhāsaṁ prabhāsvarā mayaṁ paśyet (*śūnyatā-bodhi*) ॥

"*Śūnyatābodhi* is a radiant enlightenment without refraction in which the accumulative mind evacuates the mental functions, in spite of experiencing (the bliss in reflection through higher esoteric achievement)."

Buddhists claim. The inseparable union (*avinābhāva*) of *karuṇā* (compassion) and *śūnyatā* awakened by wisdom (*prajñā-pāramitā*) leads a *bodhi*-being (*bodhisattva*) to undertake activity purely in order to render altruistic service for the benefit of those who suffer. In the Buddhist arts (*ādibuddha*), great compassion (*mahākaruṇika*) and *prajñāpāramitā* (manifest *śūnyatā*) are inseparable.[11]

A long path stretches from the state of an ordinary person to the state of a Bodhi-being (*bodhisattva*). It duplicates the historical growth of Buddhism from the *dharmacakra-pravartana* at Sarnath to the Post-Kaniṣka period of Indian history at the beginning of the Christian era. A practitioner is to follow the prescribed path (*mārga*) if he is to achieve the fruit (*phala*). The path prescribes the individual enterprise in spite of the altruistic fruition for many. Each person (*pudgala*) has a different psycho-physiological constitution so that the mental framework and physical capacity differ in each person. The condition of each individual varies. Furthermore, the actual condition (*saṁskṛta dharma*) of a person changes as they live out the effects of deeds performed previously. That fact substantiates the Buddhist doctrine of rebirth (*punarjanma*) in consequence of a

---

11. The *Prajñopāya-viniśeya-siddhi* of Anaṅgavajra reads:

yā ca samantabhadrā devatā śūnyatā-rūpātmikā, sā prajñāpāramitā caturdevī-jñānātmikā sphāraṇa-saṁharaṇa-vyavasthitā . . . I *The Aṣṭasiddhi*, p. 216.

"*Prajñāpāramitā*, which is divine manifestation of *śūnyatā*, brings benefit in all quarters and promulgates the knowledge, which belongs to the four divinities by the act of expansion and contraction."

See also the *Jñānasiddhi*, p. 135 which reads:

sarvadharma-niḥṣvabhāvatayā sarva-tathāgata-jñāna-parijñāna śūnyatā.

"*Śūnyatā* is the essencelessness of all phenomena and the accomplishment in knowing the knowledge about all *tathāgata*."

person's deeds (*karma*), irrespective of the momentary changes in the phenomena and physical constituents of a sentient or insentient being. As soon as an ordinary person becomes aware of the suffering caused by ignorance, he or she tends to work for the welfare of others. An altruistic attitude towards other sentient beings arouses compassion so that *bodhi*-awareness makes the person act. The observance of mindfulness (*smṛtyupasthāna*) during the transition from extroversion to introversion makes them visualize the nature of a phenomenon (*dharma*) as void (*śūnyam*) and without substantiality (*dharma-nairātmya*).[12] In the course of spiritual purification, a person understands the significance of dependent origination (*pratītyasamutpāda*) at which point the insubstantiality of the individual (*pudgala-nairātmya*) also disappears.

As a result of that, the methods (*naya*) of visualizing the nature (*svabhāva*) of the individual and others in the phenomenal world (*yathābhūta-jñāna-darśana*) do not appear to be similar. Many lineages of practitioners have arisen among the Buddhists in India (*bhāratavarṣa*) and elsewhere. Nevertheless, the fruit (*phala*) remains *nirvāṇa* after the elimination of ignorance (*avidyā*). *Nirvāṇa* is attained in different ways according to the condition of each individual but its power to eradicate suffering (*duḥkha*) has a profound social effect. Like a lamp, *nirvāṇa* dispels the suffering of others by awakening mental perception (*manovijñāna*) and filling others with bliss. When *śūnyatā*, i.e., *prajñāpāramitā*, is in inseparable union with

---

12. The four paths and their respective fruits have been taken into consideration by the practitioners from the beginning. The *Ārya-lankāvatāra* 2.130-131 reads:

srotāpattiphalaṁ caiva sakṛdāgāminastathā ।
anāgāmi-phalam caiva arhatvaṁ cittavibhramam ।
triyānām-ekayānāṁ ca ayānāṁ ca vadāmyaham ।
bālānāṁ manda-buddhānām-āryānām ca viviktatām ॥

karuṇā, bliss (*ānanda*) prevails. *Nirvāṇa* is attained. The attainment of bliss (*ānanda*), where suffering is eradicated, lies beyond the reach of Māra, who prompts everyone to allurement (*rāga*), malice (*dveṣa*) and delusion (*moha*). It is neither static nor uniform in experience. A *sahaja* practitioner aims at such bliss (*sahajānanda*) which is the attainment of the sublime state (*anuttara*) in order to make all sentient beings mentally and physically free from the pangs of misery. The spiritual joy (*muditā*) of *brahma-vihāra* is an extension of bliss.[13]

A *sahaja* practitioner endeavors to show compassion (*karuṇā*) towards the distressed, the hungry and the handicapped by bringing them to wisdom (*prajñā*). *Śūnyatā* is the state of the wise person who attains wisdom, which is an understanding of the essencelessness of the phenomenal existence and its attributes. He therefore pays no attention to the *smārtta* caste-divisions of touchable and untouchable, nor to ethnic groupings such as *ārya, anārya, kinnara, yakṣa, nāga, piśāca, drāviḍa, rākṣasa, bhūta,* etc., since he extends compassion (*karuṇā*) to all who are afflicted.

In course of practice *śūnyata* is attained step by step as a person experiences emptiness (*śūnyatā*) in each successive sphere. *Śūnyatā* is not the negation of existence but the experience of the void in the existent. *Śūnyatā* is not *māyā* (mirage) nor *śūnyam* (void) in the Vedāntin and the Mīmāṁsaka sense. The four dimensional existent in a dialectical exposition regarding *śūnyaṁ catuṣkoṭi vinirmuktam* remains unexplored unless the non-substantiality of phenomena (*dharmanairātmya*) is observed with fourfold mindfulness (*smṛtyupasthāna*). The first stage in understanding *śūnyatā* is as follows: one's physical

---

13. The four attitudes to be observed by a Buddhist are: (1) *maitrī* (friendliness), (2) *karuṇā* (compassion), (3) *muditā* (rejoicing in the joy of others), and (4) *upekṣā* (indifference to pleasure and pain).

body (*kāya*) and its conglomerated constituents are understood to be non-substantial because of their constant changeableness. The practitioner then begins to experience the non-substantiality of the phenomena belonging to physical, mental or even spiritual conditions. Multiple levels of experiencing *śūnyatā* are enumerated by the Buddhist authors starting from the internal essencelessness (*antardhā śūnyatā*) through to the eighteenth level, which is the essencelessness of the non-existent (*abhāva-śūnyatā*). According to the *śūnyatā yogakrama*, the nineteenth level is to understand the essencelessness of one's own nature (*svabhāva-śūnyatā*) and the twentieth, *parabhāva-śūnyatā*, is to experience the essencelessness of the existence of others.[14]

A *sahaja* practitioner lays emphasis on *śūnyatā yogakrama* along with the ancillary rituals, the observance of moral precepts (*śīladharma*) and the six-limbed Yoga (*ṣaḍaṅga*). This leads to achieving (*phala*) bliss (*ānanda*) by moving from introversion to retroversion (*parāvṛtti*) of reality (*svabhāva*). In the practice centred on the organs and nervous system of the body (*kāya-yoga*), *śūnyatā* links the six-petal plexus, *svādhiṣṭhāna*, to the multiple *uṣṇīṣa* plexuses by keeping the *sahaja* accomplishment constantly in view. The *siddhācārya* (accomplished masters) are able to reach *śūnyatā* in *sahaja* when wisdom (*prajñā*) and compassion (*karuṇā*) become inseparable.

The Vedic *ṛtam* is comparable to the all-pervasive *Brahman* as elaborated in the Upaniṣads. *Brahman* is also described as

---

14. The *śūnyatā* experience is developed among the practitioners through the four forms of mindfulness which are as follows: (1) mindfulness about physical condition; (2) mindfulness about the speech; (3) mindfulness of the mental status and their functioning; (4) mindfulness about the phenomenal world. In the process of appreciating the void, the manifold experiences eventually lead to the categorization of the *śūnyatā*. That requires a separate elaboration. (*Hevajratantra* commentary *Yogaratnamālā* folio 36a).

pūrṇam. Pūrṇam is the totality of the existent (*sat*) without limitation or deprivation. The Upaniṣadic *pūrṇam* is adopted by the Śaivites in their process of attaining total bliss (*pūrṇānanda*) where individual identity plays no part (*nirañjanam*). The Śaiva *yogī* attains a state of *śūnya* (*śūnyastha*) when he goes beyond time and desire. For him, the whole is omnipresent. The whole derives from the whole and the whole remains after the whole is removed. From the Śaiva point of view, *pūrṇaṁ* and *śūnyam,* in the context of *ṛtaṁ,* are non-exclusive.

Christianity understands the salvation of mankind in terms of "love." There are two types of love, like two cities. The city of Babylon, built on the love of self, involves a contempt for God. The city of Jerusalem, built on the love of God, involves a contempt of the self. This latter resembles the Buddhist concept of *karuṇā,* which ties in with *śūnyatā* and seeks the selfless service of sentient beings. In this connection the Gospel of John (1.14, 16) may be cited: "The Word (of God) was made flesh and dwelt among us, full of grace and truth. . . . And, from his fullness we have all received, grace upon grace." The outpouring of grace upon grace is the path of salvation.

A Buddhist, however, strives to achieve the state where, as a *sahaja siddha* (an accomplished one), he showers bliss (*ānanda*) upon all through the inseparable union of compassion (*karuṇā*) and wisdom (*prajñā*) or *śūnyatā.*

References

PALI & SANSKRIT ROOT-TEXTS

Abhidhammattha-sangaho, P.T.S., ed. Intro. Mrs. Rhys Davids (Eng. from *Compendium of Philosophy*), Sarnath: Central Institute of Higher Tibetan Studies, 1988.

Advayavajra Saṁgraha, ed. Haraprasad Shastri, Baroda: Gaekward Oriental Series, 1927.

Anaṅgavajra, *Prajñopāya-viniśeya-siddhi*. In *Guhyādi-aṣṭasiddhi-saṁgraha*, eds., S. Rinpoche & V.V. Dvivedi, Sarnath, 1987.

Ārya-laṅkāvatāra Sūtra, ed. P.L. Vaidya, Darbhanga edn.

Ārya Samādhirāja Sūtra, ed. P.L. Vaidya, Darbhanga edn.

Aṣṭasahasrikā prajñā-pāramitā, ed. P.L. Vaidya, Darbhanga edn., 1960.

Caryāgītikośa, eds. P.C. Bagchi & Shanti Bhiksu Shastri, Santiniketan: Visva-Bharati, 1956.

Dhammapada, ed. C.R. Lama, Sarnath, CIHTS, 1982.

Dohakośa, ed. P.C. Bagchi, Calcutta: Calcutta University, 1938.

Guhyādi-aṣṭasiddhi-saṁgraha (including the *Jñānasiddhi* of Indrabhūti and the *Prajñopāya-viniśeya-siddhi* of Anaṅga-vajra), eds. S. Rinpoche & V.V. Dvivedi, Sarnath, 1987.

Hevajratantra with the commentary *Yogaratnamālā*, ed. Snellgrove, Oxford: Oxford University Press, 1959.

Indrabhūti, *Jñānasiddhi*, in *Guhyādi-aṣṭasiddhi-saṁgraha*, eds. S. Rinpoche & V.V. Dvivedi, Sarnath, 1987.

Jñānodayatantram, eds. S. Rinpoche & V.V. Dvivedi, Sarnath, 1988.

Majjhima Nikāya, ed. Bhikkhu Jagadish Kashyap, Bihar Govt. Publ. 1958 [Nalanda edition].

Nāgārjuna, *Mūlamadhyamaka-Kārikā*, ed. P.L. Vaidya, Darbhanga edn., 1960.

Samyutta Nikāya, Bhikkhu Jagadish Kashyap, ed. Bihar Govt. Publ. 1954 [Nalanda edition].

Vasubandhu, *Abhidharmakośa* with his own commentary *Sputārtha* (Bandha Bhāratī Granthamālā), 1987.

Visuddhimaggo, ed. Bhikkhu Jagadish Kashyap, Bihar Govt. Publ. 1954 [Nalanda edition].

ENGLISH AND HINDI

de la Valleé Poussin, L., "Madhyamika" in *Encyclopaedia of Religion and Ethics*, VIII., New York, 1958, pp. 235-37.

Dutta, N., *Early Monastic Buddhism*, Calcutta, 1941.

Govinda, Anagarika, *The Psychological Attitude of Early Buddhist Philosophy.*, Patna University, 1937.

Junjeko Jakakusu, *The Essentials of Buddhist Philosophy*, Bombay: Asia Pubn. House, 1956.

Keith, A.B., *Buddhist Philosophy in India and Ceylon*, Oxford: Clarendon Press, 1923.

Murti, T.R.V., *The Central Philosophy of Buddhism: A Study of the Madhyamika System*, London, 1955.

Venkataramanan, K., *Nāgārjuna's Philosophy* (from the *Prajñāpāramitā-śāstra* in Chinese), Tokyo, 1962.

Yamakami, S., *Systems of the Buddhistic Thought*, Calcutta: Calcutta University, 1912.

12

Śūnya Sampādana
A Mystical Concept in Vīraśaivism

Rama Ghose

THERE are three prevalent forms of Śaivism in India, i.e., Kashmir Śaivism, Śaiva Siddhānta and Vīra Śaivism. The book *Śūnyasampādane* is the quintessence of the Vīra Śaiva philosophy. The presentation is mainly in the form of discourses between various saints. The central figure of *Śūnyasampādane* is Allam Prabhu, commonly known as Prabhudeva. He was a great mystic as well as an intellectual who took a leading part in revitalizing the reformative movement led by Basaveśvara through regular discourses regarding the mystery of the Ṣaṭsthala, the six steps of spiritual ascendance. The discussions by way of reply to questions regarding the mystery of the six steps of the spiritual journey have been compiled in the book *Śūnyasampādane* and listed as Vacana literature. The book was compiled by Śrī Gulura Siddhavīreśvara during fifteenth century. There are 21 chapters containing more than 1500 *vacanas*.

Vīraśaivism, like Advaita Vedānta, regards the highest Principle as *śūnya*. But there is a fundamental difference between the two regarding the expression of the Principle. Advaita Vedānta accepts the theory of illusion, i.e., *māyāvāda*, whereas Vīraśaivism believes that the world, as the emanation of God, is real and is evolved by a regular and orderly process.

In the beginning, there is Śiva alone in the state of complete void (*sarvaśūnya*) and without support (*nirālamba*). He is known as the *Brahman* without taint (*nirañjana Brahman*) and as the power indicated by the syllable *oṁ* (*nirañjana oṁkāra śakti*). The evolved Śūnya Liṅga is also known as the *niṣkala Brahman*, undifferentiated *Brahman*. Then Mahāliṅga was evolved from it and from Mahāliṅga came Sadāśiva of the five faces. From the five faces of Sadāśiva arose the five Sādākhyas and from them the five elements, viz., earth, water, light, air and ether. From his eyes and mind the sun and moon arose and from his hidden face (*gopya ātman*) his eight forms evolved. The universe, thus evolved from Sadāśiva, will be reabsorbed in him in the reverse order. The purpose of this two-fold process is nothing but his sport, an expression of bliss (*līlā*).

Reality is beyond comprehension and description. It is the Absolute, the infinite. It is beyond all positive and negative attributes and so is indicated by the word *śūnya*. It is described as only one (*ekam*), eternal (*nityam*), permanent (*śāśvatam*), beyond all contradiction (*dvandvātītam*) free from the three qualities (*triguṇa rāhityam*), always remaining as a witness of all actions (*sarvadā sākṣī bhūtam*), etc. It is perfect and complete in every respect and may be said to be identical with the Upaniṣadic word *pūrṇa* found the *Śāntipāṭha*:

> *oṁ pūrṇamadaḥ pūrṇamidaṁ pūrṇāt pūrṇamudacyate* ।
> *pūrṇasya pūrṇamādāya pūrṇamevāvaśiṣyate* ॥
>
> — *Īśa Upaniṣad*

Thus, the *śūnya* of the Vīraśaiva religion is not emptiness but rather is identical with the Upaniṣadic concept of *para-Brahman* or *paramātman* and is different from the *śūnya* of Mādhyamika Buddhism. The aim of *śaraṇa*, i.e., one who has taken refuge, is the attainment (*sampādana*) of this supreme state (*śūnya*). The book which records the attainment of this state by several *śaraṇa*s is named *Śūnya Sampādana*.

According to Vīraśaiva philosophy creation is the manifestation or emanation of the consciousness-force, which is nothing but the dynamic aspect of God and is the abiding God, identically one with Him. Evolution starts as soon as Śiva feels conscious of His being. His expression of bliss begins as soon as His awareness of His being in the form of "I am" comes to Him as a flash. Beyond that is the state where He is totally unaware of Himself. "As the waves are hid in the unruffled state of the sea, as the peacock's limbs and colour are inherent in its egg," so the entire creation, mobile as well as immobile, is inherent in Paraśiva or in the Godhead without form. It is indivisible, without a second, impartite existence-consciousness-bliss, eternal and perfect. It is at once naught and all, being and non-being. At this stage Śiva is *śūnya*, or Absolute Void in the sense of indescribability. Allam Prabhu has described this state in one of his *vacana*s:

O Lord, this is the true height of the form
of the undivided Absolute Divine:
it is neither form nor formlessness.
This undivided form of the Absolute:
it is neither of this [time] nor of timelessness;
it is neither of this [world] nor of the other world,
not touched by sorrow or by joy,
above all merit and all sin.
It is neither cause nor consequence,
not bound by duty or by works,
not worshipped nor the worshipper.
Thus being beyond all sense of twain,
He shines — our Guheśvaraliṅga!

— *vss* pt. I sec. I P. 1. v.2 (1931)

Another *śaraṇa*, Tōṇṭada Siddhaliṅgeśvara, supports his view:

Before time was or timelessness,
before the sprout
of Nāda, Bindu and Kalā appeared;

ere body or embodied beings came to be,
before soul or spirit,
before there was the slightest sign
of all the moving and unmoving things,
ere any of these existed at all,
Thou wert the Absolute, O Lord,
Mahāliṅga Guru Śivasiddheśvara!

— *Ṣaṭsthalajñāna sārāmṛta*, v.17 (1964)

Prabhu was mainly concerned to lead other seekers to spiritual perfection by revealing to them the true meaning of *Śūnya Sampādane,* which contains the quintessence of Prabhu's achievements and teachings. To realise *śūnya* is the sole aim and endeavour of the *śaraṇa*. The great *śaraṇa* Prabhu had realised the Truth known as *bayalu deha* or *śūnya kāya* through Śiva-yoga. He is the central character, the moving spirit of *Śūnya Sampādane.*

In the spiritual tradition of India, especially in Indian mysticism, the *guru* is considered to be the Absolute incarnate. Allam Prabhu explains how the *guru* and the disciple, though physically different, are identical at a higher level of spiritual consciousness. The *guru* bestows *liṅga* upon the disciple after fulfilling the ritualistic observation of institution called *liṅgadīkṣā*. In order to attain the realization of his identity with God, which is the sole aspiration of the devotee, *iṣṭaliṅga* is bestowed by the *guru* as a token of infinite grace. In the process of initiation, the *guru* draws out the divine consciousness inherent in the disciple by means of the connection between the head and the palm. He invokes that divine consciousness into the *iṣṭaliṅga* and installs the *liṅga* in the disciple's palm as a form of grace. The *iṣṭaliṅga,* worn upon the body, denotes a union of Śiva and *śakti*. Divine grace, descending from the higher level to the lower, manifests itself in the *iṣṭaliṅga* installed in the hand of the disciple. The devotee passes through the six-fold hierarchy (*ṣaṭsthala*) and realizes the oneness, the identity of *ātman* with the *liṅga*, i.e., Śiva. This is known technically in Vīraśaivism as *liṅgāṅga-sāmarasya*, i.e., enjoying the unity of the soul with the *liṅga*, the form of the Ultimate Principle. This goal is attainable only by the gradual maturation of devotion on the part of the *sādhaka* who ascends the six stages of spiritual attainment, namely: *bhakta, māheśvara, prasādi, prāṇaliṅgī, śaraṇa* and *aikya* by consantly observing the five virtuous disciplines or *pañcācāras*, i.e., *liṅgācāra, sadācāra, śivācāra, guṇācāra* and *bhṛtyācāra*, with the gracious help of the eight aids, i.e., the *aṣṭāvaraṇa* or eight protective auras, namely: the *guru, liṅga, jaṅgama, pādodaka, prasāda, bhasma, rudrākṣa* and *mantra*.

In the Vīraśaiva discipline, the word *sthala* stands for *liṅga* whereas *aṅga* denotes the soul. The syllable *stha* signifies that which is both the origin and the substratum from which everything evolves and has its being, whereas the phoneme *la* is pregnant with the idea of dissolution (*laya*). So, *sthala* is that from which the whole creation has emanated. Moreover, it signifies the substratum of all manifestations and again becomes the centre of involution, absorption. The word *aṅga* stands for the soul. The realization of the oneness or identity of Śiva and *jīva* is the purpose of life.

yasyāṅgaparijñānam nāṅgāṅgibhāvabodhanam ।
na tena labhyate muktirdūrasthā hi yataḥ śive ॥
— *Pārameśvarāgama*, VI.39

The person who does not come to know the inseparable relation between the *aṅga* and *aṅgī*, can never attain liberation.

The devotee, on the way to the final goal, has to proceed through and transcend the six aforesaid spiritual stages.

Transcendental Parama Śiva, being endowed with His own power, is known as *sthala*. Since the God and His power are one and the same, the power is also called "Existence-consciousness-bliss."

tadīyā paramāśaktiḥ saccidānanda lakṣaṇā ।
— *Siddhānta Śikhāmaṇi* 2.12

The power is divided into two, namely *liṅga* and *aṅgasthala,* for the manifestation and realization of his own nature. It divides Itself into two as the worshipper and the worshipped for the enjoyment of Its own bliss. *Kalā* based on the *liṅgasthala* named *śakti,* is the emanating power whereas the power based on *aṅga,* the soul, is manifested in the form of devotion and has the nature of *nivṛtti.* The *pravṛtti kalā* of the *liṅgasthala* emanates itself in the form of the world of manifestation whereas the *nivṛttikala* of *aṅgasthala* expresses itself as devotion, the most natural expression of the soul.

1. ***Bhaktasthala*** : The first stage of spiritual life, namely *bhaktasthala,* is the state in which the worshipper becomes attracted to all the rituals, rites, virtuous dispositions and outward observances of religion. There are fifty subdivisions of this state. The devotee performs all the prescribed injunctions regarding religious rites, penance, recitation of hymns, meditation and knowledge, etc.

śive bhaktiḥ samutpannā yasyāsau bhakta ucyate ।
tasyānuṣṭheyadharmāṇāmuktirbhaktasthalaṁ matam ॥
— *Siddhānta Śikhāmaṇi* 5.26

2. ***Māheśvarasthala*** : As the water of the sea is condensed and is transformed into a pearl, so also the firm vow assumes the form of deep devotion and thus the devotee ascends to the second stage of spiritual life, namely *māheśvarasthala.* Firm devotedness brings about a detachment from worldly objects. There are nine subdivisions of this stage, namely *māheśvara-praśaṅsā sthalam, liṅganiṣṭhā sthalam, pūrvāśrayanirāsana sthalam, advaitanirāsana sthalam, āhvananirāsana sthalam, aṣṭamūrtinirāsana*

sthalam, sarvagatvanirāsana sthalam, śivajaganmaya sthalam, bhaktadehikaliṅga sthalam. Discriminatory knowledge of real and unreal, purity of heart, detachment from the enjoyment of life, absorption in studying and realizing the Śaiva scriptures, praising Śiva, egolessness, absence of jealousy, greed and anger, contentment and constant commitment to the welfare of all beings are the main characteristics of Māheśvarasthala.

3. ***Prasādisthala*** : The *māheśvara yogī* who realizes the all-pervasiveness of Śiva is called a *prasādi*. When devotion has deepened and matured, the *sādhaka* comes to realize the existence of God in each and every object of the world. Thus the whole being of the *sādhaka* is immersed in the love of Śiva.

> *manaḥ prasādayogena prasādītyeṣa kathyate* ।
> — *Siddhānta Śikhāmaṇi* 11.2

Prasādi sthalam, gurumāhātmya sthalam, liṅgamāhātmya sthalam, jaṅgama māhātmya sthalam, bhakta māhātmya sthalam, śaraṇamāhātmya sthalam and *śivaprasāda māhātmya sthalam* are the seven subsections of this third stage. By regularly observing the procedures prescribed in the scriptures and the instruction of the *guru*, the *sādhaka* gradually ascends to higher and higher spiritual stages and achieves many auspicious qualities so that he is worthy of proceeding to the next stage.

4. ***Prāṇaliṅgīsthala*** : In this fourth stage of the *ṣaṭsthala*s the devotion becomes so intense that it assumes the new dimension of "experiencing devotion." As an insect, which remains in the closest association with a bee, turns into a bee, so also the *sādhaka* who maintains the most intimate union with Śiva through intense devotion becomes Śiva Himself.

> *kītobhramarayogena bhramaro bhavati dhruvam* ।
> *mānavaḥ śivayogena śivo bhavati niścayam* ॥
> — *Liṅga Purāṇa*, 21.95

In this fourth stage there are five sub-stages, namely, *prāṇaliṅgārcana, śivayoga samādhi, liṅga nijasthalam, aṅgaliṅgīsthalam* and *pañcāvantara sthalam*. The devotee, endowed with Śiva-consciousness, who is enlightened with the luminous *liṅga* in his heart is known as *prāṇaliṅgī sādhaka*. By an intense devotion with strong firmness, when the *sādhaka* practices penance with austerity, a light in the *mūlādhāra cakra* is illumined and gradually proceeds towards the *anāhata cakra* centred in the heart. The *liṅga* of Light, which is as large as a thumb, is installed in the middle of the twelve-petalled lotus. Since this luminous *liṅga* is empowered with the energy of *prāṇa* and is as large as a thumb, the Śaiva devotee names this luminosity *prāṇaliṅga* which is kindled like a lamp. All the mental faculties of the *sādhaka* are gradually dissolved in the light of *prāṇaliṅga* and he becomes immersed in the bliss of Śiva. The first three *sthalas*, namely, *bhakta, māheśvara* and *prasādi* are dominated by action whereas the fourth, i.e., *prāṇaliṅgīsthala*, is governed by *yoga* and *jñāna*. Awareness of the self as consciousness and bliss in the form of *prāṇaliṅga sthala* arises and consequently the *sādhaka* begins enquiring into the state of identity between *jīva* and Śiva. The luminous *prāṇaliṅga* is meditated upon in the six centres *of mūlādhāra, svādhiṣṭhāna, maṇipūra, anāhata, viśuddhi* and *ājñā*. In the *brahmarandhra* the thousand-petalled lotus should be contemplated and within that lotus an unblemished moonlight is to be imagined and then a subtle hole is to be meditated upon as the sacred mountain Kailāsa. The uncaused cause Śiva is adored on a seat. The accomplishment of such meditation is known as *śivayoga samādhi*. The *prāṇaliṅgī sādhaka* is fully immersed in the enjoyment of the consciousness-bliss produced by the unity of the soul and God in and through the *prāṇaliṅgī sthala*.

5. ***Śaraṇasthala*** : Realizing within his self the nature of Reality as consciousness-bliss, the *sādhaka* surrenders himself to the all-pervading consciousness-bliss. He takes refuge in the

highest blissful enjoyment with "blissful devotion," *ānanda-bhakti*. The *sādhaka* is so immersed in trans-empirical bliss that the analogy of conjugal intimacy is applied. The soul takes refuge in this and fully surrenders itself in order to achieve the non-dual state of perfection. *Tāmasanirāsana sthalam, nirdeśa sthalam* and *sīlasampādana sthalam* are the three subdivisions of *śaraṇa sthala* in which the *sattva guṇa* excels and the *rajas* and *tamas* are subdued. Thus the dispositions arising from the *sattva guṇa* namely *śama, dama, viveka*, non-attachment to objects, unflinching meditation, forgiveness, compassion, faith and devotion to Śiva, predominate. In this way the surrendered soul become full of *sattva guṇa* and completely devoid of *rajas* and *tamas*. In the last phase of *śaraṇa sthala*, the devotee attains the knowledge of the unity of the *jīva* and Śiva and remains in incessant meditation on Siva.

proktānandātmikā bhaktiriti vedāntavedibhiḥ ।
asyātmanastayā bhaktyā śaraṇasthalamāgatam ॥
— *Anubhava Sūtra* 5.79

6. *Aikyasthala* : In this final stage of the spiritual life, the *jīva* realizes complete identity with Śiva. The soul is immersed in the blissful consciousness of Śiva and so is known as *samarasa bhakta* like a river becoming one with the ocean. *Aikyam, ācārasampatti, ekabhajanam* and *sahabhojanam* are the four subdivisions of this final stage. In this stage, the *sādhaka* becomes devoid of sensuous pleasures, detached, pure, unblemished and attains the state of *śivo 'ham*. This is the state of complete union or identity with God transcending the duality of the *paśu-pati* attitude. No sense of discrimination remains.

jale jalamiva nyasta vahnau vahnirivārpitam ।
pare brahmaṇi līnātmā vibhāgena na dṛśyate ॥
— *Siddhānta Śikhāmaṇi*

> There remains no difference when water is mixed with water, fire with fire. So also no distinction is perceivable when the soul is immersed in God.

Since the *sādhaka* is fully renunciate he is beyond the state of affirmative and negative sanctions. Perceiving Śiva in everything and everything in Śiva, considering Śiva as the substratum and enjoying identity with Śiva, he is called Śiva-yogī and is known as *jīvanmukta*.

A state has been imagined which is beyond all relativity, positive or negative, *bhāvābhāvalayasthalam* (cf. *Siddhānta Śikhāmaṇi*). It is only the negation of all, *sarvaśūnya*; unmanifested, *nirābhāsī*, devoid of duality, *nirābhāsaṁ; sva para jñāna śūnyaṁ*.

> *nirvikāraṁ nirākāraṁ nityaṁ sīmāvivarjatam* ।
> *vyomavat parama brahma nirvikalpatayā sthitam* ॥
>
> — *Siddhānta Śikhāmaṇi* 20.63

> It is unchangeable, formless, eternal, endless, it has the nature of the void, it is transcendental, undifferentiated Brahman.

> *kevalaṁ saccidānanda prakāśādvaya-lakṣaṇam* ।
> *śūnyakalpaṁ parākāśaṁ parabrahma prakāśate* ॥
>
> — *Siddhānta Śikhāmaṇi*, 20.68

> It is non-dual, pure existence-consciousness-bliss, it has the nature of *Śūnya*, transcendental Absolute, the Para Brahman.

This indescribable state, which transcends the relation of knower and known, may be described as pure knowledge and so be termed *Śūnya-sthala*.

References

Anubhava Sūtra, Mysore: Oriental Research Institute, 1983.

Candrajñānāgama, tr. Rama Ghose, Varanasi: Shaiva Bharati Shodh Pratisthan, 1995.

Devaru, Malli, *Virasaiva Dharma ke Mula Tattva* (Hindi), Varanasi: Bharatiya Vidya Prakashan, 1991.

Dvivedi, V.V., *Nigamāgamīya Saṁskṛti*, Varanasi: Virasaiva Anusandhan Sansthana, 1992.

Karaṇāgama, ed. Ramachandra Pandey, Varanasi: Shaiva Bharati Shodh Pratisthan, 1994.

Liṅgadhāraṇa Candrikā, ed. V.V. Dvivedi, Varanasi: Shaiva Bharati Shodh Pratisthan, 1988.

Makuṭāgama, tr. Rama Ghose, Varanasi: Shaiva Bharati Shodh Pratisthan, 1996.

Nandimath, S.C., *A Handbook of Virasaivism*: New Delhi: MLBD, 1979.

Parameśvarāgama, ed. Rama Ghose, Varanasi: Shaiva Bharati Shodh Sansthan, 2004.

Śaktiviśiṣṭādvaita tattvatraya, ed. Chandrasekhar Shivacharya, Varanasi: Shaiva Bharati Shodh Sansthan, 1996.

Siddhānta Śikhāmaṇi, ed. Chandrashekhar Shivacharya, Varanasi: Shaiva Bharati Shodh Sansthan, 1993.

Siddhānta Śikhāmaṇi Samīkṣā, by Chandrashekhar Shivacharya, Varanasi, Shaiva Bharati Bhavan, 1989.

Sri Basaveśvara, *A Commemorative Volume*, Bangalore: Govt. of Mysore, 1967.

Sūkṣmāgama, ed. V.V. Dvivedi, Varanasi: Shaiva Bharati Shodh Pratisthan, 1994.

Śūnya Sampādane, ed. S.C. Nandimath, L.M.A. Meneges, R.C. Hiremath, Dharwad: Karnatak University, 1965.

Vīraśaiva Aṣṭavaraṇa Vijñāna, by Chandrashekhar Shivacharya, Guledgud, Karnataka: Sri Guru Amareshwar Prakashan.

13

Pūrṇam-Śūnya-Plerôma as Communion of Beings

Antony Kalliath

Introduction

"FULLNESS" is an archetype as well as an ideal in the religious traditions of the world. It is understood as the source from which the whole of reality is generated. Being estranged from the source, owing to sin, ignorance (*avidyā*) or suffering (*duḥkha*), reality finds itself in an existential situation of alienation. In this predicament, fullness is conceived as the ideal or destiny towards which reality is moving through the contingencies of time and space. In this context, salvation is conceived as a return to this fullness which thus becomes simultaneously both Alpha and Omega, the Beginning and the End.

However, the understanding of fullness varies according to the cultural insights of different religious traditions. At the same time we sense that there can ultimately be only one fullness, otherwise it becomes a contradiction in itself. It is a fact that, though we are born and brought up in different cultural and social situations there is an unity and harmony in our experience of fullness through our "connatural knowledge." In this regard scholarship does not count and even an illiterate person has the ontological competence to *know* fullness. Indeed the bedrock of our universal fellowship and solidarity beyond the boundaries of belief and ethnic identities is the collective participation in this fullness. Then fullness is, therefore, the ontological communion and confluence of beings. It is not a monolithic and absolute abstraction, but rather a web of life leading to "unity in diversity" and "harmony in plurality." It also sanctions and sustains "diversity in unity" and "plurality in harmony." Fullness does not involve unity with the consequent loss of plurality. Rather plurality is the inviolable constituent of unity. Therefore, fullness is neither unity at the cost of diversity nor diversity at the cost of unity. That is to say, fullness is the *simultaneity* of "one and many," complementing each other in a vibrant and creative communion of beings. Here we have the equation of "one" and "many," which is fullness. It is like a spectrum sustaining both the "one" and "many" which interact as interdependent and independent poles of reality. Fullness becomes a mere abstraction if reality is understood as exclusively referring to "one" or to "many." The *real* is the relation between these poles of reality. Fullness is, therefore, a *relation* which is the communion of beings. To put it differently, fullness is like a *maṇḍala* (spectrum) of beings engaged in covenantal communion of beings, in which both history and cosmos become text and context because humans are both cosmic and historical beings. Fullness is therefore life itself in its totality. That is to say, hopes and despair, joy and suffering, achievements and failures are all inviolable correlates of fullness. Despite the plurality of human facets and factors which may seem contradictory, there is an intense unity and harmony at the substratum of human experience. The different concepts of fullness point to this fundamental unity and communion of beings.

The following discussion is an attempt to interpret fullness — expressed as *pūrṇam* in Hinduism or *śūnya* in Buddhism or *plerōma* in Christianity — as the core experience of human fellowship and communion.

Pūrṇam — The Simultaneity of the One and the Many

In Hinduism, the word *pūrṇatā* has different meanings. In the Vedas it means "all-pervasive Reality." In the Vedic Saṁhitās, it refers to Viṣṇu's sustaining presence in creation or to the "fullness of wealth." In the *Atharvaveda, pūrṇam* is understood as the transcendent and immanent fullness of the supreme reality. It is "one whole" (*paripūrṇa*), *idam* and *adaḥ*, "here" and "beyond;" it is simultaneously manifest and unmanifest; it is ineffable and incomprehensible.

The philosophical understanding of *pūrṇam* blossoms in the *Īśa Upaniṣad*. It piles up infinities over infinities and identifies *ātman* and *Brahman* in an non-dual way.

> Fullness here, fullness there,
> From that which is fullness springs up fullness
> From fullness springs up fullness
> Fullness alone is everywhere
> Oṁ ! Peace ! Peace ! Peace!
>
> — *Īśa Upaniṣad,* Peace Invocation

Pūrṇatā is the "integral whole," embodying and transcending all changes and contradicitons. It is all-inclusive or integral fullness. "It can be compared to the *śūnya* (zero) which symbolizes infinity in the field of mathematics. Any addition does not make any change as it remains the immutable infinity."[1]

The non-dualistic schools link the transcendence of ultimate reality with its all-pervasive and all-inclusive nature in the concept of *pūrṇatā*. For example, in Śaṅkara's negative path

1. Deba Brata Sen Sharma, "Concept of Fullness or Pūrṇatva in Indian Philosophy" in this volume, p. 34ff.

the correspondence between the Unmanifest and the Manifest is achieved by identifying *Brahman* as the locus (*adhiṣṭhāna*) of *pūrṇatā* at the *pāramārthika* level, and thus the *prātibhāsika* (illusory) and *vyāvahārika* (phenomenal) aspects of reality are not excluded in an advaitic *pūrṇatva*. In this sense, it seems that the Advaita of Śaṅkara is neither monism nor dualism but a co-incidence of opposites; it is neither "this" nor "that" but is the organic interface between the Unmanifest and the Manifest. Instead of defining reality, Śaṅkara, in his negative path, sustains the "tension" of communion of the twin poles of reality, namely, One and Many. And this "communion" is *pūrṇatva*. Rāmānuja on the other hand, says that Īśvara (*saguṇa Brahman*), who holds everything together in identity, is the hub of both *cit* (consciousness) and *acit* (principle of matter).

The Advaita Śaivites of Kashmir conceive the *pūrṇam* as *śakti* (divine freedom), which is not an adjunct (*upādhi*) or attribute (*guṇa*) of Parama Śiva but is the very essence of God. This *śakti* or *caitanya* is a coincidence or an inclusive simultaneity and concurrence of the immanent and the transcendent, in which all contradictions and opposites attain *pūrṇatā* (or peace, *śānti*). This *pūrṇatā* is not a neutral or impersonal third person but is "Pure I" and, i.e., *svātmaviśrānta* in which both integrity and integration are reached. It is the ultimate goal.

While reviewing the various interpretations of fullness in the traditions of Hinduism, it seems to me that *pūrṇam* is more a symbol than a concept. It speaks of an awakening unto the Unmanifest which embodies and upholds the interrelatedness of its manifold manifestations. *Pūrṇam* is an inclusive communion of beings, and not something, extraneous to reality, which is to be "attained." *Pūrṇam* is the true reality (*satyasya satyam*) which has to be "evoked" or rather "invoked" in our *karma, jñāna and bhakti.*

Plerôma as Communion in Love and Justice

The best equivalent to the Sanskrit word *pūrṇam* in Biblical literature is the Greek word *plerôma* which means "fullness," "completeness," "sum total," "fulfilment." In New Testament literature *plerôma* has a Christic character which denotes the "fullness of God" in Christ (Col. 1: 19; 2: 9; Eph 1: 22-33; 3: 19; 4: 32). Jesus is "full of grace and spirit" (Jn 1: 14) and the Christian is called to the "fullness" realized in Jesus Christ. Hence, fullness of life is possible only in Jesus Christ (Col 2: 10) because "in him the fullness of God was pleased to dwell" (Col 1: 19).[2]

According to Christian teaching humans are created in the "image and likeness" of God (Gen 1: 26). Christ is "the image and glory of God" (1 Cor 11: 7), the "image of the invisible God and the first-born of all creation, for in him all things were created in heaven and on earth" (Col 1: 15). Moreover, in Christ "all things hold together" (Col 1: 17) and we are "renewed . . . after the image of God" (Col 3: 10). Finally all things are reconciled through Christ (Col 1: 20, 21). Therefore we can say that all things were created through him, sustained by him and destined for him. So Christ is simultaneously the source, the sustainer and the summit of the whole of reality. Hence, Christ is *plerôma*. The whole reality is thus born in the *plerôma* of Christ and moves in virtue of the *plerôma* of Christ and finally achieves the *plerôma* of Christ. In this way the whole of reality is vibrant with Christic mystery or rather with Christ himself. Abhishiktananda beautifully depicts the movement of reality toward the *plerôma* of Christ:

> From the beginning of time, the universe, including even its lowliest constituents of matter and life, has been drawn

2. See, "Plerôma," in *The Interpreter's Dictionary of the Bible*, Nashville: Abington Press, 1989, pp. 826-28.

> towards this *plerôma* . . . Christ is the crown of humanity, the keystone which holds together the whole fabric of creation. In him and through him everything attains to unity, and each human consciousness awakes to itself.[3]

St. Paul says that this Christic mystery, "the hope of glory," dwells *in us* (Col. 1: 27). It means that *plerôma* is not just a future reality but is a present reality to be actualized and celebrated here and now both at the deepest level of oneself and within the universal *koinonia* of the Spirit.[4]

Moreover, the mystery of *plerôma* can be expressed in terms of the Kingdom of God, which is the central theme of the New Testament. God's Reign is a new order of reality anchored in love and justice, in which "there cannot be Greek and Jew, circumcized and uncircumcized, barbarian, Scythian, slave, free man, but Christ is all and in all." (Col 3: 11). It is a new milieu in which "righteousness, and peace and joy" (Rom. 14: 17) reign. But God's reign is not an exclusively future reality but is both, a future and a present reality. According to Mark and Matthew, Jesus inaugurates his public ministry with the announcement of the nearness of God's reign (Mk. 1: 15; Mt. 4: 17). Jesus proclaims the Good News that the reign of God has drawn near and is in fact "upon" his listeners (Mt. 12: 28) and "within you" (Lk 17: 21). The Good News is that something totally new is happening — the irruption of a new era and a new order of life. However, throughout the New Testament there underlies an unresolved tension between the present and the future dimensions of God's reign. It has arrived and is yet to come. The tension between the "already" and the "not-yet" is the "force-field" which contains the Kingdom of

---

3. Swami Abhishiktananda, *Saccidananda : A Christian Approach to Advaitic Experience,* Delhi: ISPCK, 1984, p. 136.

4. *Ibid.*, 136.

God already realized in the person of Jesus Christ and the future Kingdom streaming into the present. This force-field is the arena of human-divine covenantal relationship which prepares for the final arrival of the reign of God. But first it is to be actualized in the historical situation, here and now, in one's life and in the society. The final fruition of the Kingdom is only the consummation of the human-divine collaboration already initiated in the ministry of Jesus and continued by his disciples.

Therefore, the Kingdom of God as *plerôma* is not a static concept but a continuous process occurring in society and in the individual, and it continues to the *eschaton*. Hence, we can say that Christian understanding of fullness (*plerôma*) is an organic process in which God and humans are covenantal partners, and co-operate to achieve it. The climax of the process of realization of the Kingdom is when Jesus finally delivers the Kingdom to God the Father who becomes "all in all" (1 Cor. 15: 28).

The *plerôma* as the final blossoming of the Kingdom of God is the communion of beings in love and fellowship which is rooted in "righteousness, peace and joy." It is a milieu of total reconciliation and restoration of all relationships in justice and peace. In Isaiah there is a beautiful portrayal of *plerôma* as the total communion of beings in a fellowship of harmony and happiness:

> The wolf shall dwell with the lamb, and the leopard shall lie down with the kid, and the calf and the lion and the fatling together, and little child shall lead them. The cow and the bear shall feed; their young shall lie down together, and the lion shall eat straw like the ox. The sucking child shall play over the hole of the asp, and weaned child shall put his hand on the adder's den.
>
> — *Isaiah*. 11: 6-8

Śūnya, the Spectrum of Communion of Beings

According to Nāgārjuna, the great philosopher of the Mahāyāna tradition of Buddhism, reality is *śūnyatā* ("void" or "emptiness") which corresponds to the *tathatā* (suchness) of Aśvaghoṣa, the founder of Mahāyāna Buddhism, who says that reality cannot be comprehended by concepts but can only be experienced as pure *suchness*. *Śūnya* or *tathatā* is not a nihilist expression, rather it implies the ineffableness of reality. That is to say, void is not naught but simply the absence of characteristics. "No-thing" means "there-is-no-thing." Where there is "no-thing" there is immense room for everything.

Therefore, *śūnya,* as the source of all life and creativity, gives birth to all forms of life in the phenomenal world. Therefore we can say that void is the womb of inexhaustible creative potential and a vortex of movement and energy. The ancient Sanskrit word for void is *kha*. It means the hub of the wheel, the motionless centre of a moving wheel. This still centre makes all movements and dynamism possible; it is the changeless centre of the changing world (*svastika*). *Śūnyatā* is the heart that holds the phenomenal world together in harmony and order. Hence it is the hub and web of reality.

The heart of the Mahāyāna tradition is its emphasis on the *bodhisattva* ideal, which replaces that of the *arhat* ("perfected," implying a state to be worked for) of Hīnayāna.[5] Whereas the *arhat* strives most earnestly for *nirvāṇa*, the saving knowledge which brings about the salvation of the individual, the *bodhisattva* refuses to accept the final release.

> Forasmuch as there is the will that all sentient beings should be altogether made free, I will not forsake my fellow creatures.[6]

---

5. Cf. Ananda K. Coomaraswamy, *Buddha and the Gospel of Buddhism*, New York: Harper Torchbooks, 1916, pp. 226-58.

6. *Avataṁśaka Sūtra.*

Bodhisattvas are those in whom the *bodhicitta* (the heart of wisdom) is fully expanded in *karuṇā* (compassion). It means that they dedicate all their life and activities to the task of saving the world; they do not merely contemplate but feel all the sorrow of the world. It is said of Gautama Buddha, for example, that there is no spot on earth where he has not in some past life sacrificed his life for the sake of others. According to Mahāyāna even the attainment of Buddhahood does not make one indifferent to the sufferings of the world. On the contrary, the work of salvation is carried on by the *bodhisattva* emanations of the supreme Buddhas. Therefore, the *boddhisattvas* are not living for the sake of their own complete *nirvāṇa*. Their course of life is undertaken out of compassion to the world, for the benefit, weal and happiness of the world at large, . . . for the sake of the complete *nirvāṇa* of all beings.[7]

In short, the Mahāyāna lays greater stress to love and the salvation of every sentient being so that in *nirvāṇa* one awakens to the void in the sense that, free from the constraints of contingent experience, every transient being finds itself in its suchness of "communion" — the state of reconciled and redeemed reality.

In this connection, the doctrine of *parivarta* (turning over of one's ethical merit to the advantage of others) associated with the *bodhisattva*, demands a special mention in our discussion since it shows the inter-connection of reality. The doctrine amounts to vicarious atonement. Early Buddhism emphasized that each life is separate from every other. But Mahāyāna insisted on the interdependence of all life, and this theological stance gave a logical basis to the doctrine of *parivarta*. That is to say, the merit one gains through accomplishing a good deed is shared by all sentient beings. Salvation is not

---

7. *Saddharmapuṇḍarīka Sūtra.*

individualistic but integral and includes the whole of reality because the ontological state is the communion of beings. In consequence, *nirvāṇa* is not non-existence pure and simple but rather the realization of infinite love and infinite wisdom. He in whom the heart of wisdom (*bodhicitta*) awakens, plunges himself into the ever rushing current of *saṁsāra* and sacrifices himself to save his fellow creatures from being eternally drowned in it.[8]

Mahāyāna non-duality thus culminates in the paradox of the identity of *nirvāṇa* and *saṁsāra*, the non-distinction between the unmanifest and manifest.

> This our worldly life is an activity of *nirvāṇa* itself, not the slightest distinction exists between them.[9]

Therefore we can say that in the Mahāyāna traditions *nirvāṇa* is holistic: while it affirms the unreality of phenomena as such it equally affirms their significance. This life is a dream but without meaning.[10] To sum up, the void is the hub and web of a communion of beings, which are ontologically interdependent. As the spectrum of the communion of beings, void is fullness vibrant with life forces, ineffable and incomprehensible, to which one can only *awaken* and in whose "suchness" one IS. In the empirical method, reality is seen as an object, which "objectifies" the subject. Furthermore, the subject objectifies the reality out there, conquers it and controls it. Empirical objectification is a methodology which tries to understand reality from "parts-to-whole." For example, we understand water as H_2+O. But in reality, water, though explained as the sum total of hydrogen and oxygen, is an

---

8. *Vimalakīrti Sūtra.*
9. Nāgārjuna, *Mādhyamika Śāstra.*
10. See Aśvaghoṣa, *Awakening of Faith*, tr. T. Suzuki, Chicago: Open Court: 1900.

entirely different entity — its taste, smell, weight, density and nature are quite different from its components. It means that the sum total of the parts is not the whole. We miss the "whole" (*pūrṇam*) if we understand it through its parts!

Scientists especially of quantum physics, hold that utter objectivity in scientific method is out-dated. They hold to a "physics of non-localization" which says that reality cannot be "localized" in ultimate analysis, for it is always in a "wave" or in a "flux." According to quantum mechanics everything, even space and time, exists in discrete bits, *quanta,* but it exists in "fields" which are holistic entities like a hologram in which every portion is seen in its relationship to the spectrum. That is to say, reality cannot be separated from its texture and its context or "field."

Moreover, the subject is in fact a constituent participant of the "field." There is a continuum between "object" and "subject" in a cosmic web of relations. That is to say culture, history and religion are also important factors in the interpretation of reality. Therefore, the quantum is not existing in a neutral, "no-where" situation but in an inherent "implicate order" or "enfolded order" (David Bohm) which is an "intelligent design" of interconnectivity involving the whole world, of which both "subject" and "object" are the inviolable twin poles of a relationship. Hence reality is ultimately relation![11]

"Quantum consciousness" is now a keenly debated concept in the dialogue between science and religion. For example, Robert Lanza says that according to the quantum view of reality the mind of each human being on earth is instantaneously connected to each other, past, present and

---

11. See Fritjof Capra, *The Tao of Physics,* Shambhala: New Science Library, 1985.

future, as "a part of every mind existing in space and time."[12] Such statements, though they seem to be far-fetched conclusions derived from quantum physics and cannot be proved beyond doubt, call for a paradigm shift from the "part" to the "whole" in the comprehension of reality. Understanding reality in terms of parts is a reductionist view while "quantum consciousness" upholds the view that the "whole is greater than the sum of its parts." Among scientists there is a consensus that science can make only hypotheses, not absolute conclusions; it probes, not proves; it understands, does not conclude. Reality is not an "object" to be controlled and used but in fact a "communion of beings." "Quantum consciousness" has a widespread appeal in the cultural values and trends of modern ecosophy and ecology.

Conclusion

Reality as *pūrṇam* is the web of relations; it is the inherent relationality of quanta. If *pūrṇam* is understood as *relation* then it is not an abstract concept but a mystery to be realized and celebrated in human fellowship as well as ecological communion. Fullness is not a private or spiritualistic notion of salvation or perfection but an event or rather Life itself flowering in a community of beings (eco-community) which is generated through human commitment, compassion and care. In this sense *pūrṇam* is a potential from which everything comes, through which everything is sustained and to which finally everything "returns." Fullness will not be sought, therefore, outside the sphere of life; it is very much the very text and texture of life which is communion and fellowship. Hence simply awaken to *śūnyatā*, the very matrix of Life! Live *pūrṇam*, the flowering of Life, and celebrate the *plerôma*, the *ānanda* (joy) of Life!

---

12. Robert Lanza, "The Wise Science," in *The Humanist*, vol. 52 (1992), No. 6, p. 24.

14

Nietzsche's Encounter with Buddhism

Johann Figl

A CENTRAL purpose of this seminar was the interreligious meeting of three great spiritual traditions of the world, the Buddhist, the Hindu and the Christian. From the point of view of Western philosophy which has been largely under the influence of Christian theology, the Buddhist concept of emptiness encounters the greatest difficulty in understanding. This has to do not only with the ontological structure of European philosophy, which has seen in "non-being" primarily a negative counter-concept, but also with the early reception of Buddhism in the West as a "nihilist" religion, mainly presented as such by Schopenhauer. This idea has also had a strong impact on Nietzsche. In order to overcome this one-sided view of Buddhism and some of its central concepts, it is useful to describe the original perception of this Eastern religion within the modern European history of philosophy.

In this paper I want to focus on some aspects of the understanding of Buddhism by Friedrich Nietzsche, in order to show which were the characteristics that he considered central to this religion. At the same time it will be shown that his understanding of Buddhism had assumed the function of a criticism of Christianity in the context of Nietzsche's general criticism of religion. This has contributed to an understanding of a sharp contrast between Buddhism and Christianity which is still widespread today. An exact historical and philological analysis of such antitheses is required. However, at the same time it will be shown that Nietzsche has created specific preconditions, by his own thought, for a transcultural perspective, which makes possible a new way of an encounter between European and Buddhist ways of thinking. Nietzsche's reflections lead even to a view which negates the contrast between "being" and "nothingness," for he reflects on "nothingness" in highly positive terms (e.g., *"The Eternal Return"* or *"Dionysos"*). Thus he attempts to speak about "fullness" and "nothingness" in a post-religious way. Although his approach was to a great extent influenced by the knowledge of Buddhism of his time, as the following pages will show, yet they are of fundamental importance for the actual interreligious dialogue, since this takes place on the background of a secular culture which has also been influenced by Nietzsche's critique of religion.

From a comparative point of view on cultures and religions I want to examine Nietzsche's appraisal of these foreign cultures. If we aim to understand his knowledge and opinion of Asian religions, our first task will be to ask what in fact he *could* know about these religions. For this purpose it will be useful to give a short sketch of the history of culture and ideas in nineteenth-century Europe that will provide us with background information on Nietzsche's level of knowledge in this field. Therefore this introductory part will deal with the extent and the way in which Asian religions and philosophies were known in Europe at this time.[1]

Towards the end of the eighteenth century and at the beginning of the nineteenth century certain of the Hindu

---

1. The following details are taken from E.J. Sharpe, *Comparative Religion,* one of the best books on the issue.

religious classics were edited and translated: the *Bhagavad-Gītā* (1785, 1st English translation), the *Laws of Manu* (1774); Anquetil Du Perron published a Latin translation of some Upaniṣads; Schlegel's[1] *Über die Sprache und Weisheit der Inder* (Concerning the language and the Wisdom of the Indians (1818). In 1818 the first Chair of Sanskrit in Germany (Bonn) was established, for August W. Schlegel who also composed a Latin translation of the *Bhagavad-Gītā* (1823). In 1822 the Société Asiatique was founded[2] in Paris. Important also for the German-speaking countries was H. Th. Colebrook's *On the Philosophy of the Hindus*, published in the Commentaries of the Société Asiatique (1824 et sequ). German Studies, especially by Jacob Grimm; or more general works, like Georg Friedrich Creuzer's *Symbolism and Mythology of the Ancient Peoples* (1810 ff.).

> But it was the publication in 1816 of Bopp's comparative grammar of the Sanskrit, Greek, Latin, Persian and Germanic languages that ushered in the new age of comparative 'Indo-European' studies and ultimately the still newer 'science of religion,' or comparative religion. Here for the first time was a demonstrable scientific link between the old and respected discipline of Classics and the newer areas of Indology and German studies. . . .[3]

These different approaches were an essential part of Nietzsche's education at Schulpforta. The classical languages, German studies, the linking of the two in Indo-Germanic studies: these naturally led to knowledge about India itself as did Max Müller's essays about the science of religion. But, besides these academic approaches, we have to consider another source of information on India of a more general and philosophical nature linked with the names of two men who

2. Sharpe, 21f.
3. Sharpe, 22.

were of great importance for the young Nietzsche, namely Emerson and Schopenhauer. "The Upanishads provide," Schopenhanar wrote in a celebrated passage of *Parerga und Paralipomena*, . . . "the most rewarding and the most elevating reading the world has to offer. It has been the consolation of my life and will be my consolation when I come to die." Many others have been influenced, directly or indirectly, by Schopenhauer.

This intellectual atmosphere gives the background to Nietzsche's encounters with Asian thought.

Buddhism in Nietzsche's Thought at the Time of the *Birth of Tragedy*

SIMILARITIES AND DIFFERENCES BETWEEN THE TRAGIC AND BUDDHIST WORLD-VIEW

Nietzsche considers the idea of redemption to be the goal of Greek tragedy and he wishes to revive this idea in his own day, considering it to be the answer to the experience of cosmic suffering, which is the basic problem of Buddhism too. Both interpretations of the world conceive of it in a similar way. They both rest upon the conviction of the reality of suffering. In this way, "the illusionary background of tragedy is the same as in Buddhism," as Nietzsche says.

At the same time there is a difference between the two. In tragedy the experience of suffering leads to a "fount of new possibilities of being," which Buddhism cannot reach, because it lacks art, which is the constituent element of tragedy. Art especially saves one from being drawn towards the "Buddhist denial of the will." A tragic world-view without art: this is exactly what Buddhism means in Nietzsche's eyes, as the following phrase emphasizes:

> The Buddhist lack of art: the reason for quietism.

We can better understand Nietzsche's intentions as expressed in this sentence by taking a look at the excerpts he took from works that influenced his view on Buddhism during the time when he worked on *The Birth of Tragedy*, namely C.F. Koeppens' *Die Religion des Buddha* and the Essays of Max Müller. Of the ten commandments of Buddha, as listed by Koeppen, Nietzsche writes down just one: "The seventh commandment of Buddha to his disciples is: to abstain from public performance."

INDIA AS AN ALTERNATIVE TO MONOTHEISM

In his discussion of Schopenhauer and Wagner, Buddhism becomes a main theme for Nietzsche in 1869/1870. The religion of *nirvāṇa* had a great impact on these two men who have an influence on Nietzsche, who does not restrict himself to the idea of Buddhism provided by them but goes to other sources in order to gain an educated view of Buddhism, not only the Essays of Max Müller, who is regarded as one of the founders of comparative religion as an academic discipline. Excerpts of Müller's *Essays*, a book that Nietzsche possessed, are to be found in a notebook from 1870/71. They deal with various religions such as Zoroastrianism, the Vedic religion,[4] the Pre-Hispanic religions of South America.[5] Buddha is mentioned a few times, critically[6] but also affirmatively, as an alternative to the New Testament presumably (5[60]).

I want to emphasize just one aspect : Nietzsche's idea of the relationship between German and Indian character, seen as different from Semitic monotheism.

4. In 5 [53] Nietzsche mentions the *Ṛgveda*.

5. See the entry on a free-thinking Inca 5 [56].

6. See the before mentioned 5 [44] an [58] on art.

Max Müller, in his essay "Semitic Monotheism," argues against Ernest Renan and generally stresses the identity of the idea of bad "primitive" religion, be it Semitic or German and points out the danger both have in common — falling into polytheism. Nietzsche by contrast, after reading Müller's essay, describes Judaeo-Christian monotheism as a yoke foreign to the German character and expresses his confidence that Germany will be able to throw it off, in which case the "Indian air" will remain, being familiar to Germany.

Nietzsche expresses a possible cultural development, which he expects to be realized in the future, a possibility that rests upon the "Indo-Germanic axiom": atheism, as a rejection of the foreign God will arise in Europe, as has been the case in India with its criticism of the gods.

From Max Müller's works, namely in the pages Nietzsche took excerpts from, Nietzsche could get the impression that the Buddhist "theory of redemption" was "pure atheism and nihilism," Buddhism itself being explicitly called a "religion that has no God." In the eyes of the Christian scholar of religions this could only mean that Buddhism was "made up for the madhouse." Some years later, Nietzsche, in his turn, invents the "Madman" to proclaim the death of God, the end of the Christian religion.

These excerpts show that Nietzsche was already considering that the history of India provided an alternative paradigm to European monotheism, namely a critical attitude towards the gods. This can be stated particularly in the case of Buddhism with which Nietzsche was concerned at that time.

To sum up, we can state that from the beginning of 1870, Nietzsche was occupied with alternative religious ideas especially through studying works of comparative religion. In an ambivalent manner, he had the Indian/Buddhist worldview in mind.

Asian Religion and European Atheism (*Daybreak*)

The adoption of the two great Asian religions, Buddhism and Brahmanism, (which was the nineteenth century name for Hinduism) is to be found in many ways, in Nietzsche's writings and notes of the following years. I want to keep track of just one aspect that seems to be symptomatic. Nietzsche is often dealing with Buddhism when he talks about the situation after the end or death of Christianity, or the death of God. Atheism and Buddhism are, so to speak, two modes of the future cultural situation. In a similar way he looks at Brahmanism as a religion superior to Christianity, but one which he nevertheless criticises.

In *Daybreak* (1880) Nietzsche opposes Brahmanism and Christianity,[7] both being recipes for the feeling of power, the first for those who are able to control themselves and therefore already have an experience of being powerful: the second for those who lack this experience. In notes from the same period he states that this feeling of power lies nowadays with science (V,1, 476 [183]) and shows itself in control over nature. He also says (14 [180]), that the *idée fixe* of the twentieth century was Brahmanism, which he characterizes as "Indo-Germanic."

At the same time he reflects upon the possibility of transcending this Brahmanism, which depends on the idea of a scientific community in which the individual is not — like the philosopher — sufficient to himself but merely as a member of the group. Obviously, Nietzsche's views of this Asian religion are coloured by his own opinion of Christianity and individualism so that Brahmanism is taken merely as an argument in this context.

The notes discussed have originated from Nietzsche's reading Jakob Wackernagel's book on the origins of

---

7. *Daybreak,* Nr. 65.

Brahmanism, *Über den Ursprung des Brahmanismus* (1877), which is also the case with the last aphorisms of book one of *Daybreak, in hoc signo vinces*. Nietzsche asserts that Europe has not yet reached the same degree of liberal-mindedness that the old brāhmaṇas achieved and which finally led to "abolition of the gods, a task still to be done in Europe." The next step was found in the teaching of the Buddha, the "teacher of self-redemption," a stage from which Europe was far distant. So the history of Indian culture, leading to the overthrow of the gods, serves as a model for Europe's path towards atheism. Europe's task is to catch up with the Indian, a nation of thinkers who fulfilled this task more than two thousand years before.[8]

This estimation of the two Asiatic religions is thoroughly positive and forward-looking. But it is also hampered by his critical attitude towards theism in these religions. He is almost completely overlooking their original religious concern with transcendence and its meditative character, which he has to refuse in the same way as he does with respect to Christianity. In fact, the character of Buddhism as an a-theistic religion, of which Nietzsche was very conscious, had to be contested in other ways than Christianity, which Nietzsche refutes as belief in God.[9]

Buddhism as a part of a culture after the "Death of God" (From *Joyful Science* to *Antichrist*)

In notes written in the autumn of 1881 we can find the early stages of the texts which proclaim the "Death of God." In the most famous text on this topic in all the works published by Nietzsche (125 of *Joyful Science*), the "madman" proclaims not only that God is dead, but that he will *remain* dead as well. As Nietzsche points out: "Even gods decay." Does Nietzsche

8. See V 1, 83.

9. See *Daybreak*, Nr. 91 und 95.

think that the God of (Christian) monotheism has been overcome in the same way he thinks has happened paradigmatically within Brahmanism and Buddhism? As we know, Nietzsche's madman arrives too early and is not understood by the "too-many" in the marketplace. In Nietzsche's view, European culture has not yet taken notice of this event: that *we* together with the *madman* have killed God.

After belief in God has declined, another task has to be done: the annihilation of God's substitutes, his so-called "shadows," the fight against whom Nietzsche calls for (108 of *Joyful Science*, entitled "New Struggles.") Characteristically this aphorism depends on a Buddhist legend that Nietzsche read in the aforementioned Essay of Max Müller. Nietzsche transforms this legend by treating Buddha analogously with God. He parallels Buddha's death, after which, as the Buddhist legend tells us, his shadow was shown to the people in a cavern, with God's death, after which the existence of caverns, where his shadow was shown to the people is expected for thousands of years. A "godly" Buddha would have the same fate, so that a-theistic Buddhism serves as a model for European culture after the death of God. He does not exclude Christianity as a model for European culture after God's death, in Nietzsche's eyes. He does not exclude belief in God *a priori*. We can conclude this from his well-known saying that only the moralistic God was dead, but that gods "beyond Good and Evil" were still conceiveable. It is of great interest that Nietzsche, speaking about these gods to come, refers to Buddhism as a parallel cultural phenomenon.[10] Nietzsche sees this Asiatic religion and the post-theistic (and also post-atheistic!) time after Christianity as belonging to the same cultural context. A similar paralleling is done by Nietzsche in

---

10. See VIII 1, 112: 2(107).

his famous "Lenzer-Heide-Fragment" about "European Nihilism" (10 June, 1887). There he speaks about the most extreme form of nihilism, when speaking of a European form of Buddhism.

So Nietzsche does not approve of Buddhism in every respect but only partially, with regard to the characteristic properties that set it apart from Christianity. But one can detect an essential relationship between the two, both of them being nihilistic religions, a point that Nietzsche stresses especially in his late unedited notes and in *Antichrist*.

Summary of Nietzsche's Point of View and his Importance for Today

Nietzsche mainly refers to Asian thought, especially Buddhism, when seeking alternatives to Christianity and traditional European culture, be it atheism or after the Death of God, a new way of speaking about the gods. Buddhism serves as a cathartic, purifying means to Nietzsche's end. Thus, Buddhism can be seen as a transitional stage European culture has not yet attained, so that the Buddhist alternative, as proposed by Nietzsche, is of transitional value and does not provide a final solution. It is a purifying means for attaining the stage of a non-theistic interpretation of being that Nietzsche is aiming at. Whilst "historical" Buddhism is thus of functional value in Nietzsche's philosophy, the philosopher himself in fact adopts certain basic convictions of Buddhism in his thought, as Nishitani Keiji has pointed out:

> (. . .), it was not in his nihilistic view of Buddhism but in such ideas as *amor fati* and the Dionysian as the overcoming of nihilism that Nietzsche came closest to Buddhism, and especially to Mahāyāna.[11]

We can name a few more of these basic convictions:

- A new meaning of quietness, distant from the noise of the city, expressed in the metaphor of the stillness of the sea;
- A consciousness of nothingness, similar and different to *śūnyatā* (emptiness);
- An analysis of thoughts reminiscent of attentiveness-meditation;
- A plurality of constituents in the human person and a critical attitude towards the concept of person.

This closeness to Buddhism of which Nietzsche himself was largely unaware, is an important issue on its own and leads away from the question of this closeness to Buddhism in the field of comparative philosophies.

At the end I want to consider the question to what extent Nietzsche's point of view on atheism and his opinion of Buddhism, religion, can be of relevance for us today.

In short, we can say, that Nietzsche, gifted with sensitivity for religious questions, was led to the opinion that the kind of religion that was to play an important role in future times in Europe, would be non-theistic. So he seems to have correctly foreseen an essential property of religiousness in our days: many people, after a sometimes a-theistic period of a critical attitude towards Christianity and religion in their life, turn to Eastern religion, doctrines and wisdom. Nietzsche himself did not follow this path. He finally turned towards philosophical sagacity understood as a counterpart and distancing from

---

11. Nishitani, Keiji, *The Self-Overcoming of Nihilism*, Albany: State University of New York Press, 1990; 180; see also Graham Parkes, "Nature and the human 'redivinised': Mahāyāna Buddhist themes in *Thus spoke Zarathusta*," in *Nietzsche and the Divine*, ed. John Lippitt and Jim Urpeth, Manchester, U.K. 2000, 181-199, esp. 182f.

popular religion. One point of even greater importance is that he "completed" the Christian way of life by reaching its (verbal) extreme opposite proclaiming the death of God and cursing Christianity in *Antichrist*.

Seen against the background of this radical criticism of religion a rash turning towards Eastern religion seems to be an inappropriate answer to the historical situation. At least, it was not Nietzsche's answer.

To a certain extent, Nietzsche's standpoint can be seen as going beyond the alternatives of a theistic, Christian religion and an a-theistic, Buddhist religion. He attains a genuine interpretation of being. Before the "will to power" comes to be the central idea of Nietzsche's philosophy, the experience of the "eternal return" is at the core of his life and thinking. It precedes the experience of the "death of God." Although it presents itself as a new vision of a cyclical structure of reality related to Eastern concepts of recurrence, and although it is of a genuine kind, it does not lead to blunt atheism. Because of this, Nietzsche can be considered as a man of deep religiosity in the eastern view, as Okochi Ryogi, the Japanese philosopher, puts it in the subtitle of his essay "Amor fati and karma."[12]

12. Okochi Ryogi, *Wie man wird, was man ist. Gedanken zu Nietzsche aus östlicher Sicht*. Darmstadt, 1995; p. 65.

References

KGW = *Nietzsche Werke, Kritische Gesamtausgabe*. hrsg. von Giorgio Colli und Mazzino Montinari, Berlin/New York 1967ff., section, vol., page, and number of fragment.

Koeppen, Carl Friedrich, *Die Religion des Buddha und ihre Entstehung*, Berlin, 1857.

Müller, Max, *Essays*: 1. *Beiträge zur vergleichenden Religionswissenschaft;* 2. *Bd. Beiträge zur vergleichenden Mythologie und Ethnologie*, Leipzig 1969.

Sharpe, Eric J., *Comparative Religion, A History*, 2nd edn., London, 1986.

15

Gopinath Kaviraj on Pūrṇa

translated by H.N. Chakravarty

oṁ pūrṇamadaḥ pūrṇamidaṁ pūrṇāt pūrṇamudacyate ।
pūrṇasya pūrṇamādāya pūrṇamevāvaśiṣyate ॥
— *Īśa Upaniṣad*

The above verse tries to describe the real nature of *pūrṇa*. In fact, the true nature of *pūrṇa* is beyond worldly knowledge. Though an effort has been made to present a slight glimpse of it by various means, the human intellect is unable to perceive it.

That which is known as plenitude, *pūrṇa*, never changes. Waxing and waning, increasing and decreasing, issuing from a source or decreasing in the process, all fail to touch it. This perfect fullness remains as an everlasting state of self-luminous existence, always shining everywhere as an undivided singleness of Being. Creation and dissolution, which are based on it, express themselves in the sport of dynamic energy, but the one which is perfectly full, though appearing as possessed of *śakti* on account of the play of *śakti*, remains every shining, transcending *līlā* or sport.

The terms *adaḥ* and *idam* indicate the state both remote and adjacent. Whatever is perceived by the senses is known as "this" (*idam*), while what is beyond the senses is known as "that" (*adaḥ*) Generally, by the gradual development of the power abiding in the senses, the thing that exists beyond the senses becomes the object of the senses. This is the result of action (*kriyā*). In the same way, but in reverse, that which was once perceptible becomes imperceptible and remains a thing beyond the senses. Indeed, it is very difficult to say what is perceptible to the senses and which is non-perceptible to them. Therefore, by the contraction of the dynamic energy and its expansion the perceptible thing expresses itself as a thing beyond the senses, and in the same way the non-perceptible thing shines as an object of the senses. But if we look to the absolute, it is easy to understand that beyond the contraction and expansion of *śakti* Reality (*svarūpa*) remains the same. This *svarūpa* is *pūrṇa*, which is unchangeable.

That which is perceptible is termed *loka* (realm) because it is the sphere that is illuminated; that which is beyond the senses is denoted by the term *aloka*, for it is not illuminated. In this view the entire universe is seen in a two-fold way, *loka* and *aloka*. In our common language we speak of the present world and the other world (*ihaloka* and *paraloka*), but the reality is that they are two aspects of the aforesaid *loka*. When one aspect remains manifest to the sense-organs of a certain person at a certain time, that very aspect is conceived by the person as the present world, while the aspect contrary to it is conceived as the other world.

The one which is undivided and perfectly full, known as Reality, exists without being conditioned by time and space while abiding in numberless objects without undergoing any limitation. This is the Supreme Reality known as *pūrṇa*. Though one, it is infinite, although unrelated to any particular space, it shines everywhere differently, but even then it remains without undergoing any change or fragmentation. It exists as it is. The right understanding of *pūrṇa* should be conceived in that way. When a right understanding of the above truth is acquired, then it is realized that the real truth of *pūrṇa* abides non-differently and equally everywhere. Not only that, it is the same in this world and also in the other world. One can conceive it by the senses, and it is also realized in the region where the senses cannot reach. It is one and inseparable. The philosopher, while viewing the object of the senses, says that everything is "that," that is, the perfect One. It means, further, that whatever is seen by the eyes is *pūrṇa,* whatever is heard by the ears is also *pūrṇa,* Similarly things that are perceived by other sense-organs are also *pūrṇa.* In another way it can be stated that forms, tastes, and sounds are *pūrṇa.* The one *pūrṇa* remains in every object of the sense-organs, manifesting itself. But by contrast some philosophers assert that the truth of *pūrṇa* is beyond the grasp of the sense-organs. It is beyond eyes, ears, and all senses. It is *arūpa, aśabda, asparśa,* so that unless one adopts the process of negation, *neti, neti,* "is not this, not this," it is quite inconceivable.

Looking back to the citation from the Upaniṣad, the phrase *pūrṇamidam* signifies that the one *pūrṇa* shines as "this," that is, as an object of sense perception. Similarly, the phrase *pūrṇamadaḥ* signifies that *pūrṇa* is beyond perception. Both are true. The *pūrṇa* is both perceptible and imperceptible at the same time. It is with a form and without any form at the same time. It is with attributes and without any attribute, near and remote, both immanent and transcendent. The perfect *pūrṇa* is nondual and undivided. It is indeed one, not two. The source and what emerges from it are indeed one and the same. Both are equally *pūrṇa,* as in mathematics, when any number, finite or infinite, is deducted from the infinite, the infinite remains infinite. This analogy is similar to the above concept of *pūrṇa.* The current that flows out of *pūrṇa* and the thing that emerges, are *pūrṇa;* even then *pūrṇa* does not diminish because it does not undergo any change.

A question may be raised here. How is this possible? The reply is that it is the play of the One to become many, just as the single moon is reflected in mirrors as a thousand moons. To become a thousand is nothing but sport. Each of the thousand moons is nothing but that one single moon. The single moon multiplied by a thousand appears as a thousand. When one appears multiplied the infinite one becomes manifest. This is indeed known as the result of *līlā*, play. Just as the one, that is, the original one, is one, in the same way the multiplied one is also one. There is no difference. But this truth is only revealed to one who knows the truth correctly; those who are ignorant fail to understand it. Similarly, whatever may be added to *pūrṇa,* whether it is *a-pūrṇa* or *pūrṇa,* the true nature of *pūrṇa* does not change.

Similarly when a limited number is added to the infinite or even when the infinite number is added, the result is infinite. *Pūrṇa* is *pūrṇa* externally and internally as well. For example, if the *pūrṇa* from outside is taken inside, the *pūrṇa* inside does not become bigger; similarly the *pūrṇa* outside does not become less. The inner *pūrṇa* remains full as before, and the *pūrṇa* outside remains full in the same way. The truth is that *pūrṇa* is not two but one, which remains in both. Though it is beyond time and space, it remains everywhere detached. Similarly, though it is beyond past, present and future, it remains in each moment equally. *Pūrṇa* does not have any sequential development that undergoes development in the future and passes through the present and flows toward the past as a current — this is not *pūrṇa*. Therefore it is beyond evolution.

Patrāvali No. 47, written on 2.1.1945
(Translated from Bengali)

16

The Silence and the Cry

A Meditation on the First and Last Moments of Jesus of Nazareth

John R. Dupuche

Preamble

> India seems, indeed, of all the countries in the world, one — or even the one — best exemplifying an ageless, unbroken tradition of speculations about the Word.[1]

Kashmir Śaivism has a highly developed theology of the word which is set out in four stages. Firstly, there is the word (*vāc*) which is the self-revelation (*vimarśa*) of the light (*prakāśa*) in its act of self-knowledge — for light cannot be obscure to itself. This supreme word underlies and is expressed in the other three stages: "insight" (*paśyantī*) where the eternal and unlimited word is expressed in some inchoate and confined way; the "middle word" (*madhyamā*) where the speaker knows what he wants to say but "cannot find the words to express it," where the words are "on the tip of the tongue;" finally the spoken word (*vaikharī*) expressed in language.

---

1. André Padoux, *Vāc. The Concept of the Word in Selected Hindu Tantras,* tr. Jacques Gontier, Albany: State University of New York Press, 1990. p. 1. (Indian edition: Delhi: Satguru Publications, 1992).

In these pages the four stages will be used as the means to explore more deeply the mystery of the Word made flesh. There is, of course, no attempt to say that the theologies of Kashmir Śaivism and Christianity are equivalent. There is an attempt to show, however, that the rich theology of the Word in Kashmir Śaivism can bring to the surface something of the unfathomable mystery of Christ Jesus.

Introduction

The paradox of fullness and emptiness stands at the centre of the Christian faith. The paschal mystery is essentially the co-incidence of these two extremes and from their paradoxical heart all the other essential Christian teachings spring such as, for example, the Motherhood of the Virgin or the superiority of service. In this meditation I would like to focus on the captivating silence of Jesus when he is born in the stable at Bethlehem and on his last great cry upon the cross outside Jerusalem. Both these contrasting moments illustrate the fullness and emptiness of the Christ event. I then propose to reflect on the groan of distress and the gasp of delight which in their varied ways lead to identity with the ineffable Word. This short paper will suggest that a certain silence and a certain exclamation are in fact more expressive than words and writing because they are at once full and empty.

The Silence

THE SILENCE OF BETHLEHEM

The central figure of the Christmas festival is the new-born baby wrapped in swaddling clothes and lying in a manger,[2] evocatively silent. The infant Jesus does not speak. He will eventually speak since, like any child, he is oriented to language and as he grows he will constrain the unlimited

2. Lk, 2.12.

possibilities of his voice within the accent and language of a culture. He will eventually reveal himself. The significance of his new-born silence can be understood only in the light of his later preaching activity when he tours the villages of Galilee or speaks in the temple of Jerusalem at which the unlettered soldiers exclaim: "There has never been anyone who has spoken like him."[3] Indeed, his teaching inspires the writer of the Fourth Gospel to profess that Jesus is the divine Word made flesh.[4]

Thus, there are four stages of the Word. Firstly, the Word pre-exists from all eternity, as the Prologue states: "In the beginning was the Word."[5] Secondly, the Word is made flesh and lies silent in the deep sleep of the new-born. Thirdly, the child Jesus gradually acquires a language so that fourthly, in his maturity, he announces Good News to the Chosen People.

Corresponding to those four stages of the Word there are four stages of consciousness. The fourth and most public stage, that of conscious speech, is only a partial expression of Jesus' being. "I still have many things to say to you . . ."[6] Consciousness cannot be identified exclusively with its verbalized form. A second, deeper level of consciousness is the dream which according to modern psychology reveals more truly the character of a person. The Bible itself considers the dream to be a place of special divine revelation as when Jacob dreams of the ladder reaching between heaven and earth[7] or when Joseph dreams of the angel announcing that Jesus is

3. Jn, 7.46.
4. Jn, 1.14.
5. Jn, 1.1.
6. Jn, 16.12.
7. Gn, 28.12.

conceived through the Holy Spirit.[8] More significant still is the state of deep sleep where the whole reality of the person is present in its seminal state and where the inactive faculty is not limited to this or that form of consciousness. In the Bible, moments of supreme revelation are experienced in deep sleep. For example, Adam sleeps while Eve, the high point of creation, is formed from his side.[9] After offering sacrifice to God, Abraham sleeps while God makes covenant with him.[10] The disciples of the transfigured Jesus fall asleep while his glory is seen. They sleep yet they see.[11] In these moments of dreamless sleep the greatness of the revelation brushes aside all mental constructs and penetrates most profoundly into the very essence of the person. The first three stages of consciousness are thus "reflection," "dream" and "deep sleep." The fourth and greatest form of consciousness is the divine Word of which the other three are a limited manifestation.

A particular culture is a certain style of humanity. So too a later reflective consciousness is the expression of what is essentially available in one's being. The new-born Jesus instinctually knows his true nature and only later realizes it. In short, the absence of reflective knowledge coincides with the fullness of instinctive knowledge.

The silence of Bethlehem is both empty and full. The silence of the child is the full mass of the incarnate Word waiting to be expressed. All is meant yet nothing is said. The silence intimates the fullness of the divine Word. The silence is full because it contains in essence all that will be said, but it is empty because it contains no ideas, no language, no culture. It

8. Mt, 1.20.

9. Gn, 2.21.

10. Gn, 15.12.

11. Lk, 9.23.

is full because it points to a life that recapitulates all human existence and is empty because it is as yet unlived.

PARTICIPATION IN THE SILENCE

The Festival of Christmas : This paradox of emptiness and fullness is explicitly noted in the sentence from the Prologue of St. John.[12] The sentence begins: "The Word was made flesh" where the term "flesh" refers to human weakness in all its dimensions. The sentence then continues: . . . "and we saw his glory . . . full of grace and truth." Thus the sight of Jesus' weak flesh is also a vision of fullness. By taking part in the festival, the Christian is led away from the words of the adult Jesus back to the silence of the child lying in the crib. The Christian knows the significance of the child and trusting in the child's silence is taken into his own silence, back to the essence of his own person prior to the acts and errors, the words and illusions of later life. It is a return not to the unawareness of infancy but to a sensed rediscovery of one's origin and hope. The moment of emptying is the moment of filling and for that reason the festival of Christmas is often experienced as a time of profound joy.

Meditation : In a society exploding with information, people seek the silence of meditation where they can discover the well-springs of knowledge and indeed attain the state of the Word "through whom all things were made."[13] In meditating together, the participators enter into each other's silence and regain their personal truth. Thus, together they become the Word made flesh. The entry into the pregnant silence of meditation is an entry into the silent, holy night of Bethlehem.

---

12. Jn, 1.14.
13. Jn, 1.2.

THE CRY OF DISTRESS

The Cry from the Cross : The principal teaching of Jesus concerns his own nature; he will be condemned to death on the charge of blasphemy. "He is only a man and he claims to be God."[14] He declares what he has pre-verbally and instinctively always known. He proclaims what he has come to realise and such is his conviction that he cannot be dissuaded from it by the threat of death.

The agony of crucifixion was the most terrible form of death known to the Romans. It was all the more horrible because it did not remove a person's clarity of perception. The victim did not go mad and, indeed, statements made from a cross were admissible as evidence in law. Jesus endures this agony in a way that profoundly affects his executioner, the centurion[15] who has seen many men die. He has endured physical torment and he has known public humiliation, being struck on the face and stripped naked. He has experienced injustice at the hands of the Roman governor, rejection as a blasphemer by the leaders of his own people and dismissal by his disciples as a false Messiah. Finally and above all, he senses that he is discarded by the very One of whom he is the servant. "My God, my God, why have you abandoned me?"[16] At the end of his torment Jesus gives one last great cry, as the first three Gospels relate.[17] The last cry is the exclamation of the

14. Jn, 10.33.
15. Mt, 27.54.
16. Mk, 15.39.
17. "But Jesus, again crying out in a loud voice, yielded up his spirit." Mt 27.50. "But Jesus gave a loud cry and breathed his last." Mk 15.37. "and when Jesus had cried out in a loud voice, he said, 'Father, into your hands I commit my spirit.' With these words he breathed his last." Lk 23.46.

Word being reduced to silence. It is the cry of horror uttered on plumbing the depths, the shriek in the face of annihilation. He experiences the utter void yet, strangely, at the same time he knows the utter fullness.

Such is the interpretation given in the famous hymn[18] where St. Paul speaks of the incarnation as a first emptying (*kenōsis*) and of the crucifixion as the ultimate humiliation. He immediately goes on to make the point: "Therefore, God has raised [Jesus] on high and given him the name that is above every other name." The moment of complete emptying coincides with the moment of utter fullness. The last cry is both empty and full. While the first two Gospels interpret the cry as an expression of dereliction, the Fourth Gospel interprets it as a shout of triumph where Jesus says, *tetelestai*,[19] which means "It is accomplished," or "It is brought to perfection," or "The purpose is achieved." The emptiness of the cross is the moment of salvation when the universe is filled with knowledge and grace.

The silence of Bethlehem and the cry of Golgotha are intimately related. The silence of the manger is the distant prelude to the cry from the cross. As the Angel declares: "To you is born this day in the city of David a Saviour who is Christ the Lord." The child saviour is hushed in readiness

---

18. "His state was divine, yet he did not cling to his equality with God but emptied himself to assume the condition of a slave, and became as men are; and being as all men are, he was humbler yet, even in accepting death, death on a cross. But God raised him high and gave him the name which is above all other names so that all beings in the heavens, on earth and in the underworld, should bend the knee at the name of Jesus and that every tongue should acclaim Jesus Christ as Lord, to the glory of God the Father." Phil 2.6-11.

19. Jn, 19.30.

eventually to give the last, all-revealing cry of the God-man. Jesus' whole life is encapsulated between the silence and the cry.

PARTICIPATION IN THE CRY

Mary : Mary, the mother of Jesus, stands nearest to his cross and is the first to hear his dying cry. We know how much the cry of a person who is unjustly treated profoundly rivets our attention. In situations of extreme horror all words fail and we are reduced to silence. In such cases all speech is impudence. The only admissible response is a compassionate entry into the same agony. She who treasured all the events of Bethlehem and pondered them in her heart[20] is not impervious to the events of Golgotha. She hears the cry of her son and enters into his humiliation so as to share in his victory. She is the first to participate in the emptiness and fullness of Jesus' last public utterance. She can do nothing, say nothing, but experiences everything.

The Cry of the Poor : The cry of the poor is both terrible and amazing, like the cry of the cross. It takes the listener from the trivialities of life to the essential human question: the problem of good and evil which is linked to the paradox of the void and the full. All is taken from the poor so that they lose every support. They are poised over the void and have nothing but the origin of all things. Distanced from everything else, they are closest to God. For that reason God says to Moses: ". . . the cry of the sons of Israel has come to me. . . ."[21]

Consequences flow from that state. The victims acquire real moral power since those who are closest to the Author of life receive his authority. By contrast the oppressors are

---

20. Lk, 2.11, 19.

21. Ex, 3.9.

discredited. "He has put down the mighty from their thrones, and exalted those of low degree; he has filled the hungry with good things, and the rich he has sent empty away."[22] The cry of the poor disempowers the tyrant just as the cross overcomes Satan in his pride.

THE CRY OF BLISS

Whether in a moment of anguish or of delight, the person at prayer may cry out spontaneously. This cry is an unpremeditated exclamation; it is the groan of which St. Paul says: "the Spirit himself expresses our plea in a way that could never be put into words."[23] It is comparable to the cry of pleasure which arises spontaneously in the throat of the beloved in her moment of bliss. It is comparable to the gasp of the audience when the artist unveils his masterpiece. In these various cases the cry, the primordial phoneme *A* which escapes from the throat, reveals the experience of bliss, amazement and transcendence. The cry is at once empty and full. It has no specific, limited meaning because it has unbounded significance. All the analyses of the critics only begin to describe the profound experience which the viewers have undergone.

This has implications in the field of art. A work is great if it arouses again and again the reaction of wonder. It is a masterpiece if down through the changing generations it still provokes the gasp of delight. Thus the spontaneous cry of the audience rather than the verbalisation of the critic is the highest praise. The articulate expresses partially but the inarticulate expresses fully. Emptiness and fullness coincide in the experience of beauty which unlocks the bliss hidden in the heart.

---

22. Lk, 1.52-53.

23. Rm, 8.26.

Conclusion

The cry of the cross is the moment of despair and triumph, of distress and joy, of deepest anguish and highest bliss. The opposites of fullness and emptiness are resolved by entering into the ultimate Mystery, the source of all. By implication the highest state, the Divinity, bears the cross implanted at its centre. The Person of the transcendent God is revealed fully in the ambiguous cry of the cross which the child at Bethlehem was born to utter.

Abbreviations

Ex	Exodus
Gn	Genesis
Jn	Gospel of John
Lk	Gospel of Luke
Mk	Gospel of Mark
Mt	Gospel of Matthew
Phie	Philippians

Speech of His Holiness the Dalai Lama

I AM extremely happy to have this opportunity of attending the Inter-Religious Retreat Seminar attended by distinguished scholars from three great religions, with highly developed philosophical traditions. I also would like to thank Professor Panikkar for giving a very detailed and scholarly account of the proceedings of the Seminar.

However, the subject of your seminar discussions remains very difficult and it has remained a very complex subject for the last two or three thousand years!

There is a Tibetan saying, to the effect: "When a scholar makes a statement then everything becomes true." So, when an experienced and learned scholar basing himself on a different philosophical background makes a presentation, someone from a different tradition who has not only an academic sort of knowledge but also some deeper experience will say: "Oh, that is the ultimate truth;" but when another person from another tradition explains it differently, it seems that that also is true. For that reason, I believe it is very important for a group of people to consult the several truths of several religions.

From my own belief and perspective I do feel that truth has many aspects. When you take a particular object and view it from different angles, from different points, you can have different perspectives on the same object. Similarly when we explain something from a particular angle we can assert that what is found from that perspective is the truth. Furthermore, one can have different levels of experience, different levels of spiritual understanding; and when seen from that particular level there is again another level of truth. At the same time we also have to note that if you try to show that two things are completely the same just because there are similarities, then in that case, from that perspective, we have to say that all objects of knowledge are the same because they all have similarities. However, at the same time, if we try to find a sameness of perspective and attempt to hold that the truth should be the same from every aspect and angle then it is very difficult to find any object, which has the same quality. So I have to adopt the middle way, the middle view. When we talk about similarities or sameness we have to follow the middle way.

Whatever be the case, it is extremely important to discuss such ideas according to the different religious traditions and philosophies. I normally tell people that there are four ways of developing harmony among the different religious traditions.

1. The first method is that scholars from different religious traditions, experienced scholars, should very often come together and discuss the similarities between their different philosophical traditions as well as the differences. In this way we can enrich each other and can understand the deeper dimensions of each other's traditions.

2. The second method is the constant meeting between practitioners from different religious traditions, genuine practitioners who have undergone their unique experience against the background of the

practices of their own tradition. If we could share our unique experience it would again be very enriching.

3. The third suggestion is that the followers of different traditions should go on pilgrimage together to the various sacred sites of their different religious traditions. In this way they will also have an opportunity to come together, know each other and share their experience and if possible pray together. If it is not possible they can engage in silent meditation together.
4. Fourthly, it is also very important for the leaders of different religious traditions very often to come together, as in the case of this meeting. Such gatherings send a very powerful signal to their followers.

So the discussion and seminar that we are having today can, as I said earlier, be categorized as a meeting of scholars, exchanging their knowledge and understanding. I am sure this has also given you an opportunity to share your own religious experiences.

It could also be very useful, I feel, to make a distinction between the philosophical aspect and the religious aspect. Through studying and understanding the philosophy of the different religious traditions, we are able to gain a deeper insight into the reality expounded and taught in our own philosophical tradition. But the purpose of studying and understanding such deeper philosophical realities is to enrich our own life and to be able to express it in the development of loving kindness, compassion and so forth. So this practice of loving kindness and compassion, etc., could be understood as a category within the religious aspect.

When the emphasis is laid more on transforming the mind in a step by step process then I think there is much greater similarity and sameness. But when we examine the philosophical tradition of each religious tradition, there are many differences. The variety of philosophical traditions is not only a fact but is also extremely useful for developing positive human qualities such as loving kindness, compassion, patience, forbearance and so forth. The people who undertake these kinds of religious practice obviously have different mental interests, different mental dispositions. Therefore if we have divergent philosophical traditions we will be able to help people with different mental dispositions. If we are to serve the needs and purposes of the vast masses of humankind who have divergent mental dispositions, interests and so forth then we should have a multiplicity of philosophical traditions and divergent viewpoints.

Take the example of curing one particular illness, which has infected people in different age groups. Even though all these people may be suffering from the same kind of disease, if someone gives only one medicine to all of them just because they are suffering from the same illness then it is unskillful medicine. It will not solve the problem. We need to understand all the backgrounds and find the appropriate medicine.

Similarly, even though our target and purpose is to transform the mind, to change the mind, we need, because of different and divergent mental dispositions and interests, to have divergent and different philosophical traditions. My own viewpoint, with which you may not agree, is that in terms of leading the people to become law abiding in a religious, spiritual sense, all the traditions are same, with the same effect and the same message, namely compassion, tolerance, contentment and discipline. These aspects belong to all the major world religious traditions, I believe. On the other hand, while emphasizing these similarities we must recognize the differences in terms of religious and philosophical stance. There are differences — obviously there are differences — which are necessary because among human beings there are so many different mental dispositions. So therefore, different philosophies are necessary and much more helpful.

It is precisely because of the similarity of religious practice and the similarity of the effects of religious practice, that we have every reason to live harmoniously; we have every reason to respect each other and appreciate each other's richness and qualities. That is the basis of harmony, and the means of developing genuine mutual respect, mutual appreciation and mutual admiration. On the other hand, on the philosophical side, if we try to achieve similarity, we are, I think, undertaking an impossible task. If we try to identify the points of similarity between our philosophical traditions, if we work very hard to try to prove them then, I think, we are trying to do the impossible. In fact I recall the John Main seminar that took place in London. If Christians take a Buddhist concept such as emptiness and try somehow to fit it into their own philosophical tradition it will look very awkward, it will become almost a hotch-potch. To use a Tibetan saying, it will be like trying to fit the horn of a yak on the head of a sheep. The same applies if you try to insert some Christian concepts into Buddhist philosophy, for a rich philosophical tradition is not piece-meal but is a construct built up in a very systematic and orderly way. Take the example of a human body, which is complete in every way. If you try to add another hand, it would look very strange. Of course, if one hand is missing then you can replace it. It is the same with a philosophical system which is a philosophical sort of body. There is no need to add something from another tradition. Of course, we can study and compare it. That is O.K.

In my own case I have rather little knowledge, and the little knowledge I have is only about Buddhism. So I will explain something based on that. Take the Buddhist philosophical schools that accept the selflessness of phenomena, for example the Mind Only school and the Mādhyamika school. Both schools teach the insubstantiality of phenomena, but when it comes to explaining the meaning of the insubstantiality there are divergent views. The purpose of these different philosophical viewpoints is to strengthen and enrich the practice of loving kindness, compassion and other positive qualities. A practitioner, therefore, need follow only that kind of philosophical viewpoint which helps him to enrich and strengthen these positive human qualities. In terms of essential teaching, however, from the viewpoint of the Mādhyamika school the Mind Only school is definitely erroneous and mistaken. The Mind Only school teaches that subject and object are essentially non-separate and asserts that external phenomena are non-existent. Such a philosophical viewpoint, therefore, when viewed by a Mādhyamika scholar like Candrakīrti, is definitely nihilistic. But at the same time we have to realize that the philosophical viewpoint of the Mind Only school is relevant to those who need it to strengthen and enrich these positive human qualities. We can't simply ask the followers of the Mind Only school to start practising the philosophical viewpoint of Mādhyamika for the simple reason that this latter is the more profound philosophical viewpoint. No matter how profound it may be, such a viewpoint is simply not relevant to followers of the Mind Only school. So there are different philosophical viewpoints even in Buddhism. In fact, Buddha himself had taught all these divergent viewpoints keeping in mind the various mental dispositions. So I strongly feel that such divergent viewpoints are extremely useful.

According to the Mādhyamika School the two truths — conventional truth and ultimate truth — are seen as the same entity. Therefore, they talk about the level of appearance and the level of emptiness. The level of appearance on the conventional side and the level of emptiness on the side of ultimate reality are basically the same entity and are also qualities of the same object. So on the level of appearance we need to understand the emergence of different levels or aspects of a particular object which we can explain as dependent origination, inter-dependent, inter-connected nature, and it is because of this inter-connected nature that we can talk about the nature of emptiness. In other words, because of their dependence things do not have inherent or absolute or independent existence.

Emptiness is viewed with great importance in the whole spectrum of Buddhist philosophy. It is repeatedly said that in order to reach liberation and *nirvāṇa* one must realize emptiness. And equally in the study of Tantra the need to realize emptiness is also highly emphasized. So with this emphasis on the importance of emptiness we may think that emptiness is the ultimate truth, the only ultimate reality. However, if we think that because emptiness is the only ultimate truth, emptiness has independent, inherent existence, then you have, in fact, adopted the wrong viewpoint, which is very dangerous and which is very difficult to correct.

This, in short, is my viewpoint and once again I would like to express my deep appreciation for this Inter-religious Retreat Seminar attended by such distinguished scholars and I have no doubt that you have enriched each other by delving into the subtleties of each other's religious and philosophical traditions. In fact, the Central Institute of Higher Tibetan Studies has from time to time organized such gatherings and seminars and it is extremely fitting that you hold this seminar in this Institute. You have very patiently spent your days ensuring the success of the seminar and enriching each other.

So I would like to express my appreciation of that fact and I would also like to thank the participants and the organizers. While I am sure they also had an opportunity to listen to some of the proceedings and derive benefit from them, the organizers may have also been very distracted and may have experienced problems and inconveniences. You have all contributed to making this seminar a success. Therefore, I would like once again to thank all of you.

2. Ven. Samdhong Rinpoche, H.H. Dalai Lama and Bettina Bäumer (on way to the Atisha Hall).

3. 16th December 1999, Lighting of the Lamp by H.H. the Dalai Lama, together with Nirmala Deshpande.

4. Prof. Raimon Panikkar and Prof. Samdhong Rinpoche: Opening address, 11th December.

5. Prof. Raimon Panikkar, concluding speech on 16th December, 1999.

6. Prof. R. Panikkar, Prof. S. Rinpoche and H.H. Dalai Lama in the concluding session.

7. Group photo of Participants (without Tibetan participants).

Panel Discussion

Raimon Panikkar

We have formulated three questions:

The first is a preliminary question, the second is a personal question and the third a philosophical question.

1. The preliminary question concerns the methodology of dialogue. We have been dialoguing for five days. The word "method" means "on the way," but we can't know the way if we have not travelled it before. On the other hand, if we do know the way we don't need any kind of map to tell us the direction. So it is only "in between," in the process of doing, that dialogue belongs. That is why it is so important. Which method should we follow after our experience? This is the first and preliminary question.
2. The second question could be called the personal one. We have prayed together, sung together, meditated, discussed, eaten, enjoyed. Have we really changed, have we modified our views, confirmed our views, strengthened them or in some way enriched them? It is a personal question.
3. The third question is a philosophical question, which I could formulate in two steps:

(a) How do we envisage the relationship between *śūnya*, *pūrṇa* and *plerôma*? Are there bridges, possible ways of establishing a contact and not just mere tolerance and a sort of peaceful co-existence? Is there a mutual connection between different religious traditions, which does not mean mixing them all together and diluting our views, but rather enhancing, enriching and letting our views develop. We have spoken these days about the convergence or divergence of the different views. Perhaps, the best example could be parallelism, parallels, on the basis of which we could perhaps speak to one another.

b) Putting it in a stronger but more precise way, are all philosophies and doctrines necessarily completely immutable so that we can't change anything without betraying our tradition, our *sampradāya, paramparā* or whatever? Are doctrines themselves capable of change, growth and variation so that we can't remain comfortable with our doctrines, thinking that the doctrines in all their limitations are already the answer to world problems?

Three questions: the philosophical question, the personal question and the preliminary question.

What would we like to say regarding the methodology of dialogue?

Alois Haas

I would like to offer a general view of methodology of the inter-religious dialogue but I ask permission first to express my personal point of view on what in these last days was for me quite positive, in regard to this dialogue. A successful dialogue depends on the clear presentation of a question or a problem or subject. When the information is expressed rhetorically in content and when what we hold is perfectly presented then the discussion will be rich. We had some examples of this more often during the last days. It is normal that if the lecture is good then the discussion will be better. The fundamental conversation was between the different views of the world religions about the themes *śūnyatā, pūrṇa* and *plerôma*. In such a perspective this place has been enormously fertile for me. I have learnt that we have different religious and mystical traditions, which must be seen each from their own point of view. We have discussed these special points and they are summarized by the member who said: "My awareness and understanding became much clearer in so far as I received authentically experienced and rhetorically well presented descriptions of different religious perspectives."

Negatively we have said that we have focused too much on *śūnyatā*, the void, but I take sides with Meister Eckhart who said: "The more I am void the fuller I will be of God." That is the dialectic, the dynamic principle. We can speak and we must speak about *śūnyatā* and the void all the time. *Pūrṇa, plerôma*, is always present in the void, I think, because the two are the same. This is not to say that they are the same in all traditions. But we have to perceive the deeper level, the beauty of each philosophical system and associated level of awareness. For example, at the level of transcendental awareness of the Absolute, there can be slight variations in interpretation. The core of the experience is the same but we distill it into different forms of thought or speech. Therefore, when we come for inter-religious dialogue, if we have a reasonably good acquaintance with the other tradition and come with a mind which is open, then we are able to touch the other person. Leaving aside the differences, each particular system has its own beauty. I am able to understand the beauty of another system instead of merely criticizing it. I am in my own tradition; I can become better resourced because ultimately the purpose of all traditions is to go beyond all traditions to the point where all are the same. Furthermore, when we engage in such a dialogue, when we meet people who have real experience, it becomes a very valuable *satsaṅga* and much more happens than merely at the verbal level of communication.

Question: Do you mean to say we understand when we don't speak?

No, not that. I referred to a meeting of people with experience, not merely scholarship, but scholarship together with experience. When that happens this dialogue becomes much more enriched because of the presence of the people who have experience. They talk in a much more intimate way when differences are understood in a context of mutual appreciation.

Bettina Bäumer

The meditation aspect belongs to the methodology itself because if we look at each of the traditions we represent, then the whole quest for knowledge will always be a part of the spiritual quest, as His Holiness said. Only in the modern type of scholarship can we have an academic seminar on *śūnyatā*, which has nothing to do with practice. Our aim, however, is precisely to arrive at this methodology where spirituality is not just for our private satisfaction but is part of the methodology itself. Only in that light can we understand the concepts.

Raimon Panikkar

I think that is a very important point. If I am allowed to play with words, I translate "dialogue" as *dia logon, dia ton logon,* "piercing the word," piercing the pure concept of the word and entering into that experience which Bettina and Swamiji are speaking about. So the methodology of dialogue is to overcome the *logos* by means of the *logos*, *dialogos*, piercing through the *logos*, going beyond to the supra mundane, whatever its name may be.

Nirmala Deshpande

This seminar has been very useful and fruitful on every level, but as a social activist and when working with people I find that there is a lot of *adharma* being done in the name of *dharma*. There are leaders of every religion who talk about religion and do exactly the opposite. We are confronted with this problem while working with people. So can such a dialogue lead to a popular movement inspired by such a group as ourselves belonging to different faiths, leading people in the right direction and showing them how to do it?

Swami Nityananda Giri

The tradition of the Veda itself takes us beyond all concepts, and inasmuch as relationship implies the absolute *astitva*, *śūnyatā* should not be thought of negatively. Without it the whole of reality is non-existent. Therefore it seems that zero with its infinite possibilities is exactly what this word *śūnyatā* represents. In our traditional study of Vedānta we dismiss "this," merely asserting its nihilism or thisness, but when I am open to understanding "this," when the emphasis is on completely emptying the mind of all relativity, when there is question of *nirvikalpa*, when there is no subject-object relationship, when there is *aveda*, when there is no God, no world, no individual, etc., when it is *prapañcopaśama*, *śānta*, *advaya*, experience is ultimately beyond conceptuality. Although there may be certain philosophical nuances to the ultimate experience and although that may satisfy us at a mental level, at a deeper level of being, I understand that their meaning is the same. I am talking about the *paramārtha* level. The experience, when transmitted through concepts, causes the different philosophical systems to arise. This is the very important distinction: between the ultimate *aparokṣa* and *sākṣāt anubhava,* that is the mystical experience, and the philosophical. It is this transcendent element present in all religions that can perhaps be the ultimate meeting point of all religions.

Raimon Panikkar

The beauty of "the beyond" is that it has no boundaries. You can never reach "the beyond" because "the beyond" would cease to be "beyond" if you could reach it. Thus, here we meet a full *plerôma,* a full *śūnyatā,* because it is unreachable and not only unspeakable. In the symbol of the parallels, they would meet at the infinite, not before, and for that we need patience.

The second question is very delicate. His Holiness points out that our responsibility is to work out the foundation on which inter-religious dialogue can proceed. Can we use a very loaded and — in present-day India — delicate word: conversion? This does not really mean conversion to a religion necessarily but the conversion, the kind of change in ourselves, which means growth, that conversion which involves going into the deeper aspect of ourselves and changing our views. And that, I think, is a question which cannot be dealt with only on the political level but also involves highly emotional matters. On the more meditative and deep level we have tried to do something that would be of real value.

Ven. Samdhong Rinpoche

The matter Professor Panikkar has spoken about is not related to the political problems of the present. The other day in Delhi I released a book, which was the compilation of Mahatma

Gandhi's utterances about conversion and also his dialogue with the missionaries. There I mentioned that for me it appears that religious conversion as discussed in these days, particularly among politicians, is not possible. Conversion is not possible. If one is deeply rooted in one's own religion one need not be converted or can't be converted to another religion. This talking about conversion refers to a change of social group that has nothing to do with religion. The fact that a person is born into a Buddhist family doesn't mean that he or she automatically becomes a Buddhist. A person born in a Christian family may not necessarily become a Christian, but in present day society they are considered to be a Buddhist or something else. Religion, the *dharma*, doesn't touch their mind and even after conversion their mental state doesn't change in any way. A person's state of mind after converting into another religion, if you look deeply, shows no change, no conversion, no difference. And even if we talk about the conversion of Ambedkar from Hinduism to Buddhism, I raise the question: was Bhimrao Ambedkar actually a Hindu on the 13th of October and then he became a Buddhist on the 14th of October? If he was a Hindu, what kind of *hindutva* or Hindu attributes did he have at that period? Did he believe in *Īśvara*? Did he believe in the system of *varṇa āśrama* and other things? In my view he had never been a Hindu at any stage but it was considered to be a conversion. This kind of conversion is just a social regrouping about which we need not be worried.

Raimon Panikkar

I was using the word "conversion" in a spiritual context, which means overcoming the mental level and purifying my views. What Samdhong Rinpoche is telling us is a very important matter. But the question remains open: are all philosophies necessarily completely immutable? Perhaps doctrines can be refined, improved, they can discover their own *śūnyatā* and grow. That is why the problems are delicate. If doctrines are only formal systems, two and two are four and we can't assume that two and two are four and a half because I am sympathetic. Two and two are simply four. But are doctrines only formal systems, which cannot grow, change and absorb other ideas? I think that in all traditions there is a process. From Theravāda to Mahāyāna there is a process. All are Buddhists, and yet there is a certain type of growth. I prefer the term "growth." Evolution doesn't mean that others are wrong but it means that doctrines have to become more mature, more flexible. If we grow in that sense could we point to a bridge? What we are talking about is the possibility of understanding my own tradition. Rinpoche is very right in the case of Ambedkar. Through the contact with the other I become a better Buddhist or better whatever. This, I think, is the question, the delicate question that we can't avoid. I am of the opinion that our task as people who both think in intellectual terms and undertake spiritual practice is to be ambitious, to imagine the possibility of change and growth.

May I now request His Holiness to say the last word on this matter.

His Holiness the Dalai Lama

I think that is the practical point. It is, of course, everyone's responsibility. It is a difficult subject but I think it is very important.

Raimon Panikkar

Would you agree that practice nurtures theory and theory nurtures practice? It is a kind of vital circle, a direct relationship between theory and practice.

His Holiness

There are actually two levels, two perspectives. One is related to one's own personal practice, in which your practice and your theory could complement each other and enrich each other. But we are also talking about how your own experience can enrich another's understanding, another's viewpoint.

Raimon Panikkar

Final discussions are always a challenge. The problems are open and I would like to finish with what I began with. We have discussed matters with His Holiness and learned from him, so that we might continue working, living, doing. We may disagree in theory but we agree in the practice of discipline, contentment, compassion, etc. We all agree with each other on that. Let's do that, and I think we may conclude not with human words but perhaps with prayer and finally with the blessing of His Holiness.

Glossary

Sanskrit Words

abhimāna	:	pride, self-deceit
acintya	:	ineffable, unthinkable, inconceivable
adaḥ	:	there; beyond
advaita	:	non-duality
aham	:	"I", the ultimate, divine I-consciousness
ākāśa	:	space, sky, unlimited openness, void space, ether
ālayavijñāna	:	basic consciousness
ānanda	:	joy, bliss, beatitude
anubhava	:	spiritual experience
anuttara	:	the unsurpassable, Ultimate, Absolute
aprapañca	:	unworldly, beyond worldly thought
ātman (*ātmā*)	:	Self
avidyā	:	ignorance
bhakti	:	devotion, surrender, love
bhukti	:	enjoyment
bhuvana	:	world, universe
bindu	:	dot, drop of energy
bodhi	:	awakening, enlightenment
bodhicitta	:	enlightened mind
bodhisattva	:	enlightened being, in Mahāyāna Buddhism
Brahman	:	the Ultimate Reality

brahmajiñāsā	:	desire to know Brahman
caryā	:	practice
cit	:	consciousness, spirit
citta	:	mind, thought
darśana	:	view, vision, philosophy
dhāraṇā	:	grasping firmly, concentration, method of yoga
dharma	:	universal order, religious tradition; the nature of phenomena (in Buddhism)
dhvani	:	resonance, suggestion, allusion, implied meaning
duḥkha	:	suffering
hṛdaya	:	heart
idam	:	this
Īśvara	:	Lord, God
jñāna	:	knowledge, wisdom
kalā	:	digit of the moon, portion; power of limitation
karuṇā	:	compassion
kāya	:	"body," three bodies of the Buddha
kha	:	void, empty space; hole, nave of thc wheel
kriyā	:	action, activity; ritual
laya	:	dissolution, absorption, rest
līlā	:	play, divine play as absolute freedom
liṅga	:	sign, phallic symbol of Śiva
loka	:	world, realm
madhya	:	the centre, middle
Maheśvara	:	great Lord, name of Śiva
mala	:	impurity
maṇḍala	:	sacred diagram
mantra	:	verse of the Veda; sacred syllable or word
mārga	:	path, way, tradition

māyā	:	illusion, power of illusion
mudrā	:	gesture, spiritual attitude
nāḍī	:	vein, subtle channel in the yogic physiology
neti neti	:	"not this, not this," pointing at Brahman as indescribable
nirañjana	:	pure, stainless
nirvāṇa	:	cessation, liberation
nirvikalpa	:	thoughtfree, free from imaginative thought-constructs, a state of pure awareness
paramārtha	:	ultimate truth, level of ultimate Reality
pudgala	:	person, limited self
prajñā	:	wisdom
prakāśa	:	light
praṇava	:	monosyllabic mantra, mostly OṀ
pratītyasamut-pāda	:	interdependent origination of everything, doctrine of the Mādhyamika school of Buddhism
prayojana	:	purpose, intention
pūrṇa/pūrṇatā/pūrṇatva	:	full, complete, perfect, replete; fullness, plenitude, perfection
pūrṇāhantā	:	full or perfect I-consciousness
rūpa	:	form
sādhaka	:	spiritual practitioner
saguṇa	:	with qualities
sahaja		innate, natural; the original state
śakti	:	energy, divine power
śamatha	:	one-pointed concentration
saṁhāra	:	dissolution, reabsorption (of the universe)
sampādana	:	attainment
saṁsāra	:	world of bondage, cycle of transmigration

saṁvṛtti	:	relative truth
śaraṇa	:	refuge; one who has taken refuge; devotee
Śāstra	:	scripture, sacred or authoritative text
śāśvatavāda	:	eternalism, doctrine accepting everything
sat	:	being
satya	:	truth
satyadvaya	:	doctrine of two truths (in Buddhism)
śivatva	:	"Śiva-hood," the divine state of identity with Śiva
sṛṣṭi	:	emanation
śūnya/śūnyatā	:	void, emptiness; zero
svabhāva	:	own nature
svarūpa	:	own nature, essential nature
svatantratā/ svātantrya	:	freedom, absolute autonomy of the Divine
tathatā	:	suchness
tattva	:	element, principle; level of reality (there are 36 in the *Śaivāgamas*)
tṛṣṇā	:	thirst, desire (*tañha* in Pāli)
ucchedavāda	:	doctrine of nihilism, negating everything
upādhi	:	superimposition
vāc	:	the Word
vimarśa	:	self-reflection (of the light, *prakāśa*)
vipaśyanā	:	true insight, insight meditation
vyāvahārika	:	the phenomenal, empirical level
vyoman	:	sky, open space, firmament; emptiness

Greek Words

agapē	love, charity
hybris	pride, self-conceit
kenos	empty
kenosis	self-emptying
logos	the Word
mythos	myth
noūs	spirit, mind
phôs	light
plerôma	fullness, fulfillment, plenitude, perfection
skotia	darkness
symballein	to throw together, hence *symbolon* (symbol)

Contributors

(In the Order of Papers)

His Holiness The Dalai Lama Tenzin Gyatso: spiritual and secular head of the Tibetan people, universally acknowledged leading spiritual figure.

Professor Dr. Raimon Panikkar: Retired Professor of Comparative Religion and Philosophy, University of Santa Barbara; leading thinker of intercultural and interreligious relations (Consultant at UNESCO), author of a number of books.

Ven. Professor Samdhong Rinpoche: at the time of the seminar Director, Central Institute of Higher Tibetan Studies, Sarnath; at present Prime Minister of the Tibetan Government in Exile, Dharmsala (H.P.), great scholar of Madhyamaka philosophy.

Dr. Deba Brata Sen Sharma: Retired Professor of Sanskrit, Kurukshetra University, at present at the Asiatic Society, Kolkata; scholar of Kashmir Śaivism.

Fr. Dr. Paddy Meagher S.J.: Professor of New Testament at Vidyajyoti College of Theology, Delhi; Catholic priest and member of the Society of Jesus.

Ven. Professor Ngawang Samten: at present Director, Central Institute of Higher Tibetan Studies, Sarnath (Varanasi); scholar of Madhyamaka philosophy.

Professor Makhan Lal Kokiloo: Retired Professor of Sanskrit Vidyapith, Srinagar; traditional Pandit of the Kashmir Śaiva tradition and disciple of Swami Lakshman Joo; writes in Sanskrit and Hindi.

PROFESSOR DR. ALOIS M. HAAS: Retired Professor of German Literature at the University of Zürich (Switzerland), leading scholar in the field of German mysticism, especially Meister Eckhart, author of a number of books on mysticism.

LAMA DR. WANGCHUK DORJE NEGI: Reader in Buddhist Philosophy at the Central Institute of Higher Tibetan Studies, Sarnath; belongs to the Vajrayāna school of Tibetan Buddhism.

PROFESSOR DR. BETTINA BÄUMER: at present Fellow, Indian Institute of Advanced Study, Shimla; former Coordinator of the Indira Gandhi National Centre for the Arts, Varanasi, Visiting Professor, University of Vienna; scholar in Kashmir Śaivism, and Indian Art and aesthetics.

REV. DR. JOHN R. DUPUCHE: Catholic priest of the Archdiocese of Melbourne, Australia, Chair of the Catholic Interfaith Committee; scholar of Kashmir Śaivism and Christian mysticism.

PROFESSOR SUNITI KUMAR PATHAK: Retired Professor of Buddhism at Visvabharati University Santiniketan.

DR. RAMA GHOSE: Reader in Indian Philosophy at a Women's College (aff. to Banaras Hindu University) in Varanasi; scholar of Śaiva Siddhānta and Vīraśaivism.

FR. DR. ANTONY KALLIATH: Catholic priest and Professor at Dharmaram College, Bangalore; interested in interreligious dialogue and Indian spirituality.

PROFESSOR DR. JOHANN FIGL: Professor and Head of the Department of Religious Studies, University of Vienna; specialized in Friedrich Nietzsche and in the Buddhist-Christian dialogue.

Pandit Hemendra Nath Chakravarty: Former Chief Pandit at the Indira Gandhi National Centre for the Arts, Varanasi; traditional Sanskrit scholar, specialized in Tantra and Kashmir Śaivism, disciple of M.M. Gopinath Kaviraj.

Swami Nityananda Giri: Head of the Sri Gnanananda Thapovanam Ashram near Tirukoyilur, Tamil Nadu; scholar of Vedanta and interested in Christian mysticism and in Hindu-Christian dialogue.

Sushri Nirmala Deshpande: disciple of Vinoba Bhave, great Gandhian social activist and peace worker.

General Index